Senior Cohousing

A Community Approach to Independent Living
- The Handbook

- Charles Durrett

5-07

Publisher:
Habitat Press
1250 Addison Ave., Suite 113
Berkeley, CA 94702

Distributor:
Ten Speed Press 1⬛
Box 7123
Berkeley, California 94707

Distributed in Australia by Simon & Schuster Australia, in Canada by Ten Speed Press Canada, in New Zealand by Southern Publishers Group, in South Africa by Real Books, in Southeast Asia by Berkeley Books, and in the United Kingdom and Europe by Airlift Book Company.

Library of Congress Cataloging-in-Publication Data
Durrett, Charles
    Senior Cohousing: A Community Approach to Independent Living—1st ed. / Charles Durrett.
    p. cm.
Includes bibliographical references and index
    ISBN 0-945929-30-7
    1. Housing. 2. Elderly housing. 3. Urban design. 4. Sociology.

Printed in Canada

First printing, 2005

1 2 3 4 5 6 7 8 9 10 — 14 13 12 11 10 09 08 07 06 05

Dedicated to Rosemary,
my Mom

ACKNOWLEDGEMENTS

I want to thank all of the extraordinary people who put their heart into this project. To Magnus Soby (a Danish architect) who came from Denmark to the U.S. to help with the last three months of this effort in our office and practically co-authored some of these chapters. I also want to thank Chris Kennedy Pierce, Sheila Madden, Chris Chalmers, Patricia Tirtoprodjo, Carey Clouse, Anna Huss, Kurt McCulloch, Brad Gunkel, Matthew Eghtessadi-Reed, Yvonne Kanis. And to Steven Chantanu for making it especially beautiful.

To the Danes, who start significant movements like cohousing in the first place.

To the seniors who gave so generously of their time, their homes, and their community: Olaf Dejgaard (71, retired architect); Tua Møller (retired statistician for the Ministry of Health); Else Skov (retired secretary); Niels Vonge (retired Four Star general, Danish Army); Arne Ravan (75, retired high school principal); Inga (76, office administrator); Birthe (71, started, owned, operated, and retired from her own chocolate shop); Leif Behrend (69, factory owner); Ole (67, retired); Dan (68, retired seaman); Jørn Ole (68, retired math teacher); Hans and Inga Sørensen (67, retired auto executive, and 56, teacher); Kirsten Mitchel (77, retired radio and TV producer); Karen Permein (80, retired landscape architect); Ib and Grethe Jan-Mittet (75, retired teacher, and 75 1/2, retired teacher); Eigil Nicolaysen (73, retired pharmacist); Anne-Lise Nicolaysen (pharmacist's assistant); and many more.

Danish housing experts, in particular Hans Skifter Andersen, Martin Rubow, and of course, Jan Gudmand-Høyer (who has given his life to building more healthful social arrangements and more beautiful physical arrangements). Max Pedersen (who generously allowed material to be used from his book "Nybyggere - i den tredje alder"), Kate Vial, Henry Nielsen, Erik Skoven, and thanks to the American Scandinavian Foundation for their support.

Thanks to Jessie McCamant Durrett (then ten years old) who practiced being a photographer for weeks before she and I went off to Denmark, and was a patient and grounding influence during the research. And thanks to those who entertained Jessie: Hans, Jette, and Pilar Rasmusen, Sigrid Anne-Sophie Hjort, and to Kirsten and Søren and to all of the bofæller (cohousers) who hosted us.

Thanks to the many Americans interested in Senior Cohousing who have offered suggestions about what they wanted to see in a book and about how to build a community.

Arthur Okner, the Brugels, Jim Leach, Nick Meima, Sue Hellwig, Phyliss Cole, Galen Cranz, and all of those who have attended seminars about senior cohousing at various cohousing conferences, the entire Silver Sage Cohousing group and to all of those seniors around the country who have been saying, "Chuck get that darn book done so we can get going with gusto."

And to my neighbors at the Doyle Street Cohousing community with whom I have lived for twelve years and who indeed made life easier, more convenient, more entertaining, more interesting, and always more fun. Lots of folks helped, lots of folks were essential, but in the end it was my two brothers-in-law Christopher Aldridge (and his lovely wife Rachael Durrett) and Mike van Mantgem (and his lovely wife Diane Durrett) who stepped up to the plate and said, "Chuck, let's do this thing." Chris continuously gave me updated lists of items that were missing, and Mike was the master and masterful editor who plied his considerable wordsmith skills to direct and redirect.

And finally to my lovely, lovely one, Kathryn McCamant, who chose not to write this time, but is always a thoughtful reviewer, and who held it all together through the duration.

CONTENTS

Appendix

FOREWORD

In the first phase of our lives we live with Mom and Dad, or something similar. In the second phase we've moved out, or gone to college or work and haven't yet established a family. We live in apartments, shared houses, or crash pads, with boyfriends or girlfriends, doing whatever is economical and whatever is fun. In the third phase we often have a family and a career, living in a house, loft or whatever makes us comfortable, doing whatever it takes to feel like we have grown up and made it in this world. In the fourth phase the family has shrunk to one or two people and we are retired. Now what do we do? Less of what we used to do? For elderly people who can no longer manage all of their own daily tasks, the options can be lonely, expensive, wasteful, institutional, contrived and completely out of sync because they are created by someone else - someone in the business of caring for us, not with us. Generally speaking it is a setup for unhappiness. No wonder so many people in Denmark are willing to trade in a big house in the suburbs for a small one in cohousing and a network of people that support each other.

My wife and I first encountered cohousing in Denmark in 1980. It was both a revelation and an inspiration. As a young married couple, we had been thinking about where and how we would one day raise our children. What kind of setting would allow us to combine our professional careers with healthy child rearing? So many people seemed to be living in places that did not accommodate our most basic needs – we always had to drive somewhere to do anything sociable. We dreamed of a better solution, an affordable neighborhood where our children would have playmates and we would have friends nearby; a place with people of all ages, young and old, where neighbors knew and helped each other. Enter cohousing, the very answer to our dreams. And 20 years later, we're still living that dream.

Katie and I, through our firm of McCamant & Durrett Architects of Berkeley and Nevada City, California, have dedicated ourselves to translating the Danish idea of cohousing to North America. Thus far we have collaborated on the establishment of almost 40 cohousing communities here, and half a dozen senior housing projects of various kinds.

In many respects, cohousing is not a new concept. In the past, most people lived in villages or tightly-knit urban neighborhoods. Even today, people in less industrialized areas typically live in small communities linked by multiple interdependencies. Members of such a community know each other for many years; they are familiar with each other's families and histories, talents, and weaknesses. This sort of intimacy demands accountability, but in return provides security and a sense of belonging. Cohousing offers a contemporary model for re-creating this sense of place and neighborhood, while responding to today's needs for a less-constraining environment.

What happens when young professionals like ourselves become so-called seasoned veterans? In terms of community, what sort of lifestyle can we expect once we pass our prime and mature into those fabled golden years? The short answer is that it depends on the quality of the choices we make in our youth. The long answer is, of course, much more complicated.

Perhaps this topic can be approached through the notion of intent. I intend to have others around me as I age – family, friends, and neighbors. Family to share a cup of coffee with on a rainy afternoon. Friends who will go to the movies with me (or the beach or the grocery store) on a lark. Neighbors with whom I share a common bond of community, on an everyday basis. This is cohousing.

I remain as committed and driven as always to spreading the good word of cohousing, and I intend to work and enjoy life to the fullest until the very end. But I also intend to age not so much with grace but with clear intent: I know I have a choice when it comes to how I will actually live out my golden years. Will I choose to live with my spouse (or perhaps surviving alone) in suburban isolation, a burden to our daughter, willfully ignoring the inevitable until I "suddenly" find myself a prisoner of my frail circumstances, moved out of a too-big house too late with friends, family, or government caseworkers, well meaning as they may be, calling all the shots? Or will I make a better choice?

And that other choice – that better choice – is what senior cohousing is all about.

W hen Katie and I were in Denmark in 1984-85 researching our first book about cohousing, we interviewed a couple who were planning one of the first senior cohousing communities there.

I met Mr. Kristensen, a 65 year–old retired high school principal, at a planning meeting for his new cohousing community, Abildgården. We discussed not only the communal elements of Abildgården, but also the open floor plan of his own new house in the complex, where the kitchen, dining, and living areas would be separated by level changes and low walls, but not full partitions. The "overlapping" would allow the smaller spaces to appear larger, and at the same time would create opportunities that larger closed off spaces don't. For example, the person in the kitchen would be able to take part in living area activities. The two bedroom unit would be 1,100 square feet. Mr. Kristensen then invited me into his large suburban home (approx. 2,900 square feet) to meet his wife. As I stepped into the foyer, and then to the living room, I was impressed by the nice furniture they had: the turn-of-the-century china cabinet, the stately dining table, the highboy, and the grandfather clock. They would never be able to get all this into their new cohousing unit. "How can you leave all of this?" I gasped, involuntarily. "Sell it, give it to the kids," Mr. Kristensen exclaimed (he'd been asked this question before, I thought).

"We've made up our minds (without regrets) and there's no looking back. We'll sell the house, and the furniture that we've collected over the last forty years, and our parents collected forty years before that."

"We'll keep what's meaningful," Mrs. Kristensen interjected, "but we'll sell the lawnmower, one of our cars, and take a trip around the world. Abildgården will be finished just in time for our return."

"Our life role won't be reduced to being curators/caretakers of things until we can no longer do that," Mr. Kristensen continued. "We're going to be a part of something that's more interesting than this furniture. There, our house will be part of a neighborhood, and 'life's maintenance' will be half the trouble – not by paying someone else to take care of us, but by cooperating with the neighbors. We'll have more time to live. After discussing every detail of the plans, we feel like Abildgarden is ours, we built it, not brick by brick, but discussion by discussion. It will be worth more to us."

Mrs Kristensen continued, "Statistically, one of us will die in the next 10 years. Then, statistically, the other will remain in this big house for another 10 years, increasingly dependent on our children and the government. Then one day, the children will become impatient with having to be with one of us for our birthday, Christmas, Easter, Mothers' Day, whatever, and they'll find a more institutional setting for us where we'll have 'company, support, and attention', but it won't necessarily be what we want. And by that time, we'll be too weak and tired of burdening our children to object to whatever they come up with. And we'll live out our lives there, dependent and unhappy. Instead, we want to stay independent for as long as possible. And we want to be in control of our future and our lifestyle. We believe that by helping to create it now, we'll have the community we need to rely on for support and not institutional care."

The author visiting a Senior Cohousing community in Denmark. The best part was listening to the stories.

INTRODUCTION

Traditional forms of housing no longer address the needs of many older Americans. Dramatic demographic, economic, and technological changes in our society have created a population that lives longer and ages healthier; and is looking for alternatives to their current housing situation as they age. Successful housing solutions for these "young-old" seniors reflect their desire to maintain comfort, control, and independence. Indeed, the booming growth of pre-planned, suburban-style "seniors-only" housing developments is testament to this trend. However, despite slick marketing campaigns to the contrary, these pre-planned "communities" simply do not meet the real long-term needs of today's seniors. This is a speculative, for-profit development scheme like any other of its type. It is not community. It's business.

Individuals often now live many miles and perhaps a world away from their extended families. Traditional forms of social and economic support that people once took for granted – family, community, a sense of belonging – must now be actively sought out. As a result, many seniors are mis-housed, ill-housed, or even unhoused simply because they lack, or feel they lack, appropriate housing options specifically for them.

But they do have an option.

Pioneered in Denmark and successfully adapted in many other countries, the senior cohousing concept re-establishes many of the advantages of traditional villages within the context of twenty-first century life. It is community defined.

This book is designed to provide seniors with the inspiration they need to be proactive in planning for their future living needs; to give them the knowledge and resources to examine whether senior cohousing is right for them; and to show them how to build such a community.

Intergenerational cohousing is a well-established form of housing in Europe and North America. Cohousing specifically designed and built for seniors is already very successful in Europe, and is taking root here. We hope that this book and the many people who are working on it will help put cohousing for seniors on the map in North America.

PART ONE

Introducing Senior Cohousing

Imagine a living arrangement in which multiple, individually owned housing units (usually 20-30) are oriented around a common open area and a common house – a place where community is a way of life. Imagine residents who actively cooperate in planning the project from beginning to end, with one goal in mind – to recreate an old-fashioned neighborhood that supports friendly cooperation and socialization. Imagine senior cohousing.

Night conversation after dinner at Bellingham Cohousing.

CHAPTER ONE

Taking Charge of The Rest of Your Life

"Some years ago I lost my husband and went through a difficult time. But I am glad that I lived here when it happened since it meant that I never felt unsafe. I was not together with other residents all the time but I knew they were there for me if I needed them. And when I came home at night I could feel the warmth approach me as I drove up our driveway."

-- Møllebjerg in Korsør

So many American seniors seem to live in places that do not accommodate their most basic needs. In the typical suburb, where the automobile is a de facto extension of the single-family house, individuals are essentially required to drive to conduct any business or partake of social opportunities. As we get older, as our bodies and minds age, the activities we once took for granted aren't so easy anymore: the house becomes too big to maintain; a visit to the grocery store or doctor's office becomes a major expedition; and the list goes on. Of course many, if not most, seniors recognize the need to effectively take control of their own housing situation as they age. They dream of living in an affordable, safe, readily-accessible neighborhood where people of all ages know and help each other. But then what? What safe, affordable, neighborhood-oriented, readily accessible housing choices actually exist?

Author, Charles Durrett, and his mom, Rosemary, a few years ago.

The modern single-family detached home, which constitutes up to 67 percent of the American housing stock, is designed for the mythical nuclear family consisting of a working father, a stay-at-home mother, and two to four children. Today, less than one-quarter of the American population lives in such households. Almost one-quarter of the population lives alone, and this proportion is increasing as the number of Americans over the age of 60 increases. At the same time, the surge in housing costs and the increasing mobility of the population combine to break down traditional community ties.

Currently, seniors represent a record 12.4 percent of the American population, which, with the swell of post-WWII baby boomers entering the senior ranks, will increase to 20 percent by the year 2030. Clearly, action must be taken, and quickly, to correct these household and community shortcomings. But what can be done, and by whom? How can we better house ourselves as we age?

A Danish Solution, Again

This time last year I was in Denmark studying senior cohousing. Admittedly, I was there for somewhat selfish reasons. The agonies of placing my own mother in an assisted living facility were still fresh. Her story is, unfortunately, typically American: at 72 years old and determinedly living alone, she could no longer competently care for herself. Her children, doing their best, had reached the limits of their competency. Institutionalized assisted care, and eventually nursing care, were her only options. Or were they?

With my mother needing immediate care, she moved into the most-agreeable facility we could find and afford. In the meantime, we continued to search for an institutional care for her that was not an institution. But what we found was a business system of caring for people, not with people: Even the most agreeable senior-living facilities are large and impersonal where even a well-meaning staff of caregivers do not truly care about their clients – institutional, language, and cultural barriers often create a palpable distance between client and staff. Though seemingly competent in their care-giving tasks, many of the staff are young and speak English as their second language. Many seniors, for a wide variety of health and cultural reasons, have great difficulty communicating with them. This, of course, does not endear the staff to the clients; and the staff, in turn, has little patience with this often-cranky elderly population.

Adding insult to injury, institutionalized American seniors also bear a heavy economic burden as they age. Skilled nursing and convalescent care costs much more than in-home care. That nest egg goes all-too quickly. Worse, before the disabled elderly can collect Medicare benefits, they must spend down all of their assets. The result is that the elderly who have the audacity to linger too long have little or no wealth to leave behind.

After twenty years of designing, building, and living the cohousing life in the United States, I was certain there had to be a better way.

In Denmark, people frustrated by the available housing options, developed a housing type that redefined the concept of neighborhood to fit contemporary lifestyles. Tired of the isolation and impracticalities of traditional single-family houses and apartment units, they built housing that combines the autonomy of private dwellings with the advantages of community living. Each household has a private residence, but also shares extensive common facilities

The Senior Predicament

"I'm getting old, and everything around me is getting old too," said Margo Smith, the 70-year-old white-haired organizer of a Grey Panther meeting of six women and two men in Berkeley, California.

"I live in an older house, and just getting a leaky faucet fixed seems to take days of time – if I can find the money and someone to do it. I have to pay, pay, pay to have small things done. I am completely encumbered by my house and I'm not interested, or even willing, to encumber the lives of my children. They have their own families now, not to mention the careers I encouraged them to have."

"My next door neighbors are a young family on one side, and a single guy on the other. When I drive to see others my own age, people get behind me and honk – it might be my neighbors, for all I know. Just because my reactions have gotten slow, which is why I drive slowly, doesn't mean I shouldn't spend time with others I have something in common with. But I do wish I had a community based more on proximity."

Across the Atlantic, 71-year-old Else Skov lives in a large two-bedroom apartment in a senior cohousing community in Denmark. She moved into her home some 15 years ago with her husband, who died two years ago. She is not lonely, largely due to the community's unique layout, which includes a common house where residents can meet with other residents after dinner to exchange stories and jokes, or make plans to go to the opera together.

The difference between the two situations is cohousing. Cohousing offers a new approach to housing and, for many seniors, a new lease on life. Aside from a basic adherence to democratic principles, senior cohousing developments don't tout a specific ideology beyond a desire for a more practical, social home environment. Cohousing is not a commune, nor is it an intentional community; it is simply a neighborhood that works.

Typical senior housing. Expensive, but no one wants to be here.

'Why would I want to live in senior cohousing – wouldn't it be better to live in mixed-age cohousing?' is a relevant question. Neither choice is better; it's a personal decision. But it's amazing how often young people are hanging around in senior cohousing. Kids visiting, grandkids visiting, neighbors visiting. And it's a more fun place to hang around than typical senior or assisted living facilities.

with the larger group, including kitchen and dining area, workshops, laundry facilities, guest rooms, and more. Although individual dwellings are designed for self-sufficiency (each has its own kitchen), the common facilities are an important aspect of community life both for social and practical reasons, in particular the common dinners. I have personally been involved with the design of nearly 40 cohousing communities, and have visited almost 300 distinct cohousing communities in Europe and North America. Their success and growing acceptance attests to the viability of the concept both in theory and in practice.

So I found myself back in Denmark, confident in my understanding of cohousing yet intent to learn all I could from my Danish elders. And what I found was completely unexpected and utterly refreshing. They were actually living the better life.

Imagine...

It's five o'clock in the evening and Karen is still going strong. After she puts away the last of the gardening tools, she picks up a basket of vegetables and freshly-cut flowers. She feels energized to finish the day as strongly as it began. Her long-time neighbor and shade tree mechanic, Andrew, passes by to tell her that he successfully changed the wiper blades on her car. Grateful, Karen offers him a few of the choice flowers in her bunch. She knows his wife will love them. "All in a day's work," he smiles as he accepts.

Instead of rushing home to prepare a nutritious dinner for herself and her ailing husband, Paul, Karen can relax, get cleaned up, spend some quality time with Paul, and then eat with him in the common house. Despite his recent health troubles, Paul wouldn't miss a common dinner – it keeps his mind agile and makes him feel useful and wanted. It invigorates him on a daily basis.

Walking through the common house on the way home, Karen stops to chat with the evening's cooks, two of her neighbors, who are busy preparing broiled chicken in a mushroom sauce for dinner, in the kitchen. The flowers and vegetables she brings to them couldn't be better looking, or better timed. Several other neighbors are setting the table. Outside on the patio, others share a pot of tea in the late afternoon sun. Karen waves hello and continues down the lane to her own house, catching glimpses into the kitchens of the houses she passes – here, a neighbor's grandchild does homework at the kitchen table; next door, George completes his ritual after-work crossword.

As Karen enters her house, relaxed and ready to help her husband with his medications and other needs, she thinks they will have plenty of time to stroll through the birch trees behind the houses before dinner.

Karen and her husband, Paul, live in a housing development they helped design. Neither is an architectn or builder. Karen considers herself to be a semi-retired school teacher, as she volunteers in an afternoon reading program at a nearby elementary school; and Paul is a retired lawyer. Ten years ago, recognizing the fact they were soon going to join the ranks of senior citizens, they joined a group of families who were looking for a realistic housing alternative to the usual offerings of retirement homes, assisted living facilities, and institutional nursing care. At the time, they owned their own home in an affluent suburb, drove everywhere, and knew only a few of their neighbors. But they knew someday their house would become too difficult for them to maintain. They feared that one

or both of them would lose the ability to drive. And if, forbid the thought, one of them unexpectedly passed away, how would the other manage? Would the survivor become a burden to their grown children? One day, Paul noticed a short announcement in the local paper:

"Most housing options available for seniors today isolate them and discourage neighborhood atmosphere. There is an alternative. If you are interested in:

- *living in a large, social community in your own house*
- *participating in the planning of your home*
- *experiencing an alternative to institutionalized health care*

perhaps this is for you.

We, a group of 20 families, all 55-years-of-age and older, are planning a housing development that addresses our needs for both community and private life. If this interests you, call about our next meeting."

In senior cohousing, community is right outside your door.

Dinner in the common house is prepared in turn, usually by one cook and one assistant. However, its significance goes way beyond sharing food and effort. Such dinners are the heart of cohousing, for they are the catalyst for many other social activities.

Karen and Paul attended the meeting. They met other people who expressed similar concerns and fears about aging and their current housing situations. The group's goal was to build a housing development with a lively and positive social environment. They wanted a place where individuals would have a sense of belonging; where they would know people of all ages; where they would grow old and continue to contribute productively.

In the months that followed, the group further defined their goals and began the long and difficult process of turning their dream into reality. Some people dropped out and others joined. Two and a half years later, Karen and Paul moved into their new home – a community of clustered houses that share a large common house. By working together, these people had created the kind of neighborhood they wanted to live in. And in all probability they will live there for the rest of their lives.

Today, Karen and Paul feel secure knowing their neighbors care about them. If Paul becomes truly sick, people will be there to help Karen with groceries or will join her at the theater so she doesn't have to go alone. Common dinners relieve them of preparing a meal every night, and their children and grandchildren can stay in the community's guest rooms while they visit. They are members of a living cohousing community.

Senior Housing as Community

For Karen and Paul, and their neighbors, cohousing provides the community support that they missed in their previous homes. They downsized their liabilities and upsized their quality of life. Cohousing is a grassroots movement that grows directly out of people's dissatisfaction with existing housing choices.

Cohousing draws inspiration from the ideals of cooperative living, in which several unrelated people share a traditional house. But cohousing is different in that each family or household has a separate dwelling and chooses how much they want to participate in community activities. Cohousing also differs from intentional communities and communes, which are often organized around strong ideological beliefs and may depend on a charismatic leader to establish the direction of the community and hold the group together. By contrast, cohousing essentially offers a new approach to housing – it does not impose a new way of life on its residents. Based on democratic principles, cohousing communities espouse no ideology other than the desire for a more practical and social home environment.

Cohousing communities are unique in their extensive use of common facilities, and more importantly, in that they are organized, planned, and managed by the residents themselves. The great variety of cohousing community sizes, ownership structures, and designs illustrate the universality of the concept. And where cohousing has gone, so goes senior cohousing – each community has its own needs, and only the residents themselves know what is truly best for them.

From the moment my wife Katie and I first entered a cohousing community, it was apparent we were in a special place. Always grateful, always welcome, we ate most dinners in the common houses. Our hosts took great pride in what they had created through their cooperative efforts. Yet, they were also aware of their community's shortcomings, freely and profoundly discussing all aspects of building and living in this type of housing – often during a late-night conversation over a bottle of wine.

We find cohousing communities immensely inspiring. Cohousing can be most effectively evaluated on its ability to create a positive and humane environment. This is evident in the feelings of those who live there, the experiences of those who have left, and our own

When the weather is right, cohousers take common dinner outside.

9

I have to say, I've never seen people so consistently upbeat as senior cohousers. They really have a good time. Joy seems to be the operative word.

observations and comparisons among the various cohousing developments and other, typically more traditional, housing schemes.

After all, a home is more than a roof over one's head or a financial investment. It affects the quality of a person's general well-being – one's confidence, relationships, and even one's health. It can provide a sense of security and comfort, or elicit feelings of frustration, loneliness, and fear. A woman who worries about when to shop for groceries and get dinner on the table, while taking care of an ailing spouse, is often unable to concentrate on a job or reserve time to spend with friends or other family members, let alone take time for herself. This aspect

of housing cannot be measured by cost, rates of return, or other traditional real estate assessments. While this book does discuss cohousing financing methods and market values, a more important concern for senior housing should be the people themselves and the quality of their lives.

The men and women living in senior cohousing communities are perhaps the most honest and clear-eyed people I have ever encountered. They completely accept the fact that they are aging. They admit they can't do everything they once did. They know the slope is downhill. That's life. But acknowledging this basic truth does not mean they are fatalistic. Rather, they have taken charge of their remaining years with the expressed

Babyboomers – Danish and American alike – are not content with what institutions have to offer. They are used to taking charge of their own lives.

intent of achieving the highest-quality life possible, for as long as possible. For them, this means choosing to build their own community where they live among people with whom they share a common bond of generation, circumstance, and outlook. And they have a great time doing it.

"Hey, we're getting older, and we're going to make the most of it. We've had a lot of experiences, and now we're going to have some more."

Pleasant Hill Cohousing, Pleasant Hill, California

"Cohousers are simply consciously creating the community that used to occur naturally."

-- Hans S. Anderson, cohousing organizer

Cohousing
An Old Idea –
A Contemporary Approach

In villages people work together to build a schoolhouse, raise a barn, harvest the crops, celebrate the harvest, and more. Similarly, residents in cohousing enjoy the benefits of cooperation, whether by organizing common dinners, social activities, or caring for an elderly resident. Both communities build social relationships by working together to address practical needs. Cohousing offers the social and practical advantages of a closely knit neighborhood consistent with the realities of twenty-first century life.

FrogSong Cohousing, Cotati, California. This mixed-use project won Best in American Living Award 2004.

In non-industrial communities, work is integrated with the rest of life. Small towns are not divided into residential, commercial, and industrial areas; rather, residences are built on top of shops, and cottage industries flourish throughout neighborhoods. Although cohousing developments are primarily residential, daily patterns develop that begin to weave work and home life together again. Most cohousing residents go outside the community for their professional work, but there is also informal trading of skills within the community. One resident, a plumber, tends to a leaky faucet, another helps repair a neighbor's car.

Several residents make wine together. A woman who makes pottery finds her best customers are fellow residents who buy her goods for gifts. These neighbors know each other's skills and feel comfortable asking for assistance, understanding they will be able to reciprocate later.

Technological advances make it increasingly common for people to work part time or full time at home. In most living situations today, working at home can be very isolating (we know a computer programmer who could easily work from home, but chooses to drive to the office for companionship). The cohousing environment allows residents to enjoy the benefits of working at home without feeling isolated. As the trend toward working at home continues to grow, so cohousing responds: a recently-completed cohousing community in Northern California included office space adjacent to its common facilities. In addition to office spaces, this area currently includes a coffee shop, hair salon, and other commercial and retail establishments. With a tip of the hat toward traditional village life, a suite of residential cohousing units are situated above these business spaces.

While incorporating many of the qualities of traditional communities, cohousing is distinctively contemporary in its approach, based on the values of choice and tolerance. Residents choose when and how often to participate in community activities and seek to live with a diverse group of people. Cohousing is a "best of all worlds" solution.

What Is Cohousing?

Cohousing is a living arrangement where multiple houses (usually 20 to 30) are oriented around a common open area and a common building. These communities are custom-designed neighborhoods for residents who do not want to live in typical suburban, urban, or even rural neighborhoods where neighbors don't know each other. For seniors, it is an alternative to assisted living as well. Cohousing residents are proactive in creating viable, friendly, neighborhoods in which residents cooperate and socialize. They sometimes say they aren't doing anything new; but consciously they are creating the kind of neighborhoods that naturally existed in the past.

In addition to its social advantages, cohousing offers numerous environmental benefits. Studies show that residents of cohousing communities use about 25 percent as much energy as Americans in traditional housing, and, most significantly, use 25 percent as much household energy overall as they did in their previous living arrangement and drive about 25 percent less. Cohousing residences are about 60 percent the size of average new American houses, and cohousing communities on average occupy less than 50 percent as much land as the average new subdivision for the same number of households. And through the power of community ownership cohousing residents actually get more and pay less.

While cohousing might be prevalent in Europe, it remains a relatively new concept in the United States. The first American cohousing projects were built in 1991. Currently, there are 100 of these communities in the country, about 20 under construction, with another 150 or so in the planning stage. The trend is catching on.

Portions of this chapter are taken from our previous book, *Cohousing: A Contemporary Approach to Housing Ourselves*, by Kathryn McCamant and Charles Durrett. For a more detailed look at the cohousing big picture, pick up a copy of the book at any public library or quality bookseller. You can also order direct from us online at The Cohousing Company, www. cohousingco.com.

Doyle Street Cohousing residents relax together at the common patio after work.

Participatory site planning to thirty-four units in the Nevada City Cohousing project.

Six Components of Cohousing

Cohousing can be found in many forms – from urban factory loft conversions to suburban cities to small towns. Whatever the form, cohousing projects share six components:

• Participatory Process: Residents organize and participate in the planning and design process for the housing development, and are responsible as a group for final decisions.

• Deliberate Neighborhood Design: The physical design encourages a strong sense of community.

• Extensive Common Facilities: An integral part of the community, common areas are designed for daily use, to supplement private living areas.

• Complete Resident Management: Residents manage the development, making decisions of common concerns at community meetings.

• Non-Hierarchal Structure: There are not really leadership roles, the responsibility for the decisions is shared by the community's adults.

• Separate Income Sources: If the community provides residents with their primary income, this is a significant change to the dynamic between neighbors and defines another level of community beyond the scope of cohousing.

Participatory Process

One of the strengths of cohousing is the active participation of residents, from the earliest planning stages through construction.

The desire to live in a cohousing community provides the driving force to get it built, and in most instances, the residents themselves initiate the project.

The number of residents who participate throughout the planning and development process varies from project to project. Often a core group of six to twelve families establishes a development program, finds the site, hires the architect, and then seeks other interested people. Sometimes a large group initiates the community, and is pared down as the project becomes more defined. Typically, all of the houses are sold or rented before the project is finished. In some cases, the resident group collaborates with non-profit housing associations or a private developer, but even then, the residents play a key role.

The participatory process has both advantages and disadvantages, but no cohousing community has ever been built any other way. Even with the proven success of cohousing, developers hesitate to build it on their own, and couldn't if they wanted to. Experience shows that only people who seek new residential options for themselves will have the motivation to push through the planning and design process without making serious compromises.

One possible obstacle is the opposition of planning commissions and neighborhood associations, usually based on false assumptions about cohousing and clustered housing. This is a common problem for any new development, but people's unfamiliarity with cohousing can make it even more difficult. Neighbors may fear that cohousing will attract "unconventional" people, adversely affect the neighborhood, and reduce property values. Such fears are completely unfounded. Cohousing residents tend to be conscientious, taxpaying citizens, active in school and community activities. Cohousing developments have helped to stabilize neighborhoods and make them more desirable.

In spite of such difficulties, resident groups have pushed their projects through the labyrinth of barriers. When a city council denied approval of one cohousing project, the residents built models, went to meetings, and eventually convinced the council they were respectable citizens with worthy intentions. When banks questioned the feasibility of yet another project, residents risked their own assets to convince the bank to give them the construction loan. When cuts had to be made to build within a construction budget, another group of residents insisted the architect cut the size of amenities of the individual units to preserve the common facilities. Few developers, for-profit or non-profit, would ever take such measures or risks.

Organizing and planning a cohousing community requires time for group meetings, research, and decision making. But anything worthwhile requires time and effort. People organize to build schools, town halls, fire stations and churches, so why not a viable working neighborhood? Residents volunteer their time because of their commitment to the idea and their own desire for a more satisfying residential environment. The most active members are likely to attend one to three meetings a month for one or two years.

Bellingham Cohousing,
Bellingham, Washington.

The process can be long, but those now living in cohousing communities universally agree it was not only well worth the effort, but the best thing they ever did for themselves and their families.

A feeling of community emerges during the period when residents are working together to reach their common goal. Typically, few participants know each other before joining the group. During the planning and development phases they must agree on many issues closely tied to their personal values. Despite the inevitable frustrations and disagreements, the intensity of the planning period forms bonds between residents that greatly contribute to the community after they move in. Having fought and sacrificed together for the place where they will live builds a sense of pride and community that no outside developer can "build into a project."

Deliberate Neighborhood Design

A physical environment that encourages a strong neighborhood atmosphere is the second characteristic of cohousing. People often talk of how enjoyable it would be if they could live someplace where they knew their neighbors and felt secure. Yet, few residential developments include areas where neighbors can meet casually. Cohousing residents set out to build an environment that reflects their desire for community. Beginning with the initial development plan, residents emphasize design aspects that increase the possibilities for social contact. The neighborhood atmosphere can be enhanced by placing parking at the edge of the site, thus allowing the majority of the development to be pedestrian-oriented and safe for seniors and grandchildren alike. Informal gathering places are created with benches and tables. The location of the common house determines how it will be used. If the residents pass by the common house on their way home, they are more likely to drop in. If the common house can be seen from many of the houses, it will be used more often.

Physical design is critically important in facilitating a social atmosphere. While the participatory development process establishes the initial sense of community, it is the physical design that sustains it over time. Whether the design succeeds depends largely on the architect's and organizing group's understanding of how design factors affect community life. Without thoughtful consideration, many opportunities can be easily missed.

For senior cohousing, design must be tailored to seniors, but every possible interior safety feature does not have to be installed at the outset. It is critical that every possible measure should be taken to avoid an institutional look. A flexible building design is also important, so that the units can be modified to suit owners who are aging, and also new owners.

Common Facilities

While each private home is a complete house in and of itself, just like any traditional residential unit, cohousing communities have common areas that supplement the private houses. Private houses in cohousing can be smaller than typical houses because features such as workshops, guest rooms, and laundry are located in the common house. The common house is an extension of each private residence, based on what the group believes will make their lives easier and more economical, not to mention more fun and interesting. And since the residents won't

purchase each common item more than once – one for each household – these per-household costs are dramatically reduced. One lawnmower for 30 households, for example, represents a huge savings over one lawnmower per household.

According to the Census Bureau, the average size of new homes built in the United States at the start of the 21st century was 2,324 square feet. The average private house in a cohousing community is 1, 250 square feet. On the other hand, the average common house for a typical 30-unit cohousing community averages 5,000 square feet, including workshops and other buildings.

The common house, which supplements the individual dwellings and provides a place for community activities, is the heart of a cohousing community. It is a place for common dinners, afternoon tea, games on rainy days, a Friday night bar, crafts workshop, laundry facilities, and numerous other organized and informal

Residents do handywork and hang out in the common house of a senior cohousing community in Denmark.

FrogSong Cohousing, Cotati, California. Designing a place that encourages a sense of community and allows for casual interaction among residents is an important characteristic of cohousing.

activities. The common facilities often extend beyond the common house to include barns and animal sheds, greenhouses, a car repair garage, and in one case, a tennis court and swimming pool.

These facilities provide both practical and social benefits. For instance, the common workshop replaces the need for every family to have the space and tools to fix furniture and repair bicycles and cars. Expensive tools, such as a drill press or table saw, become much more affordable when the cost is shared by several households. Not only do residents gain access to a wider range of tools through a common workshop, but enjoy the company of

others using the shop or just passing by. They may also share and learn new techniques and skills along the way.

The concept of a common space in clustered housing is not in itself unusual. Many condominium developments have a clubhouse or community room. However, a clubhouse significantly differs from a common house both in the way and to the extent the space is used. Typically, a clubhouse is rented out by individual residents for private parties, or used for owner association meetings or exercise classes. More, the clubhouse is usually small in size, which in turn provides just enough room to accommodate small-scale entertainment needs. The exception is "adult" complexes, which may incorporate a bar and a well-equipped gym into its common area. Regardless, there is no place set aside specifically for children; and most of the time the clubhouse is empty and locked – a nice touch on paper but in reality a poorly utilized afterthought. In contrast, a cohousing common house is open all day, and is considered an essential part of daily community life.

As cohousing has evolved, the common house has increased in size and importance. Today, the size of private dwellings is often reduced in order to build more extensive common facilities. These changes were dictated by experience. For instance, many residents of early cohousing developments were reluctant to commit to common dinners, thinking they would be nice once or maybe twice a week, but not on a regular basis. Yet, when the common house is designed well, common dinners have proven overwhelmingly successful, and today most new cohousing groups plan for meals in the common house several times a week, with over half of the residents participating on any given evening. Substantial space is thus allocated in the common house for pleasant dining rooms and spacious kitchens. Children's play areas are often included, so that children can be children, and adults can sit and converse in an adult-oriented environment.

The specific features of the common house depend on the interests and needs of the residents. Their use is likely to change over time in response to new community members and needs.

By allowing residents to become acquainted, discover mutual interests, and share experiences, common facilities and activities contribute greatly to the formation of a tightly knit community. These friendships then carry over into other areas. As one resident said:

> *The common house is an essential element. Through the activities there, life is added to the streets. Without it, the sense of community would be hard to maintain.*

In intergenerational cohousing kids usually are the focus. In senior cohousing seniors are the focus.

The common house is also an asset for the surrounding neighborhood. It is used for meetings, classes, union organizing, and cultural programs. A Danish cohousing group even organized a film club that attracts participants from their entire town. As the community's primary meeting place, the common house has infinite uses both for the residents and their neighbors.

Resident Management

In keeping with the spirit in which cohousing is built, residents – owners and renters alike – are responsible for the community's ongoing management. Major decisions are made at common meetings, usually held once a month. These meetings provide a forum for residents to discuss issues and solve problems.

The community kitchen is designed for efficiency. Although meals for up to fifty people can be prepared here, it still has a comfortable residential feeling.

Responsibilities are typically divided among work groups in which all adults must participate. Duties like cooking common dinners and cleaning the common house are usually rotated. As with any group of people, some residents feel they do more than their fair share while others don't do enough. This cannot be helped. In most cases, community responsibilities become less formally structured as residents become better acquainted.

Under a system of resident management, problems cannot be blamed on outsiders. Residents must assume responsibility themselves. If the buildings are not well maintained, they will have to pay for repairs. If the common activities are disorganized, everyone loses.

Learning how to make decisions as a group is not easy. Most people grow up and work in hierarchical situations. Residents must learn to work together and find the best solution. They may adopt organizational formats developed by other groups, or create new methods for themselves. It is a process of learning by doing. Residents told us that over time they become effective at working together, and effectively applied the lessons they learned at home to their work lives, or to other organizations to which they belonged.

Non-Hierarchical Social Structure

Although residents state opinions about certain issues (for example, people who frequently use the workshop might propose the merits of investing more money on tools), the community shares responsibility. The community doesn't depend on one person for direction. A

"burning soul" may get the community off the ground, another may pull together the financing, and another may arrange the venue for each meeting. This division of labor is based on what each person feels he or she can fairly contribute. No one person, however, dominates the decisions or the community-building process, and no one person should become excessively taxed by the process.

Separate Income

There is no shared community economy. If the community provides residents with their primary income, this changes the dynamics among neighbors and adds another level of community beyond the scope of cohousing.

The economics of most cohousing communities are more or less like a typical condominium project. In a survey, 100 cohousing residents were asked how much money or disposable income they saved each month by living in cohousing. The standard answer was $100 to $200 per month.

A Unique Combination with Diverse Applications

These characteristics have come to define cohousing. None of these elements is unique, but the consistent combination of all six is. Each characteristic builds on the others and contributes to the success of the whole.

This is what matters: caring community life.

"We have a lot of activities together that are not planned. Except for dinner, the unplanned activities are more fun than the planned ones."

-- Cohousing resident

Although these characteristics are consistently present, their applications have been diverse. Each community is different because each was developed by the residents to address and realize their particular needs and desires.

The Architecture of Cohousing

A central path usually connects the individual homes. Often, a common terrace faces the houses and can seat everyone for dinner or other activities. There are gathering nodes along the walkway, such as a picnic table or sand box. Such nodes are associated with every five to nine houses. The houses have front porches at least seven feet deep and nine feet wide, so people will actually use the space.

The kitchen is oriented toward the common side of the house, with the sink facing the community so residents cooking or washing dishes can see people coming and going. Meanwhile, more private areas (such as living rooms and bedrooms) face the rear, or private side, of the house.

Optimally, residents can see the common house from most, if not all, of the houses and can see if others are inside. The common house generally contains a common dining room, a kitchen, a media room, a laundry room, a sitting room, and other activity rooms such as a workshop, craft room, music room, and others depending on the group's desires. In a senior cohousing community, the common house often has large guest rooms to accommodate an extended visit from family, or for professional caregivers if residents need help.

Further Considerations

Building a viable cohousing community requires that the residents remain true to more than the spirit of the ideal. As such, the following issues greatly impact how a cohousing community develops, both in the short and long term.

Community Size

While the average cohousing development accommodates 15 to 30 households, some consist of as few as nine families, or as many as 42 families. We found that housing groups with fewer than nine households who share common areas and facilities tend to function similarly to households in which a number of unrelated people share a house or apartment.

Living in such a small community is more demanding because residents depend more on each other. If one person temporarily needs extra time to concentrate

Strawberry Creek Cohousing won the Best in American Living Award in 1996.

on professional interests, thereby limiting community participation, the others feel the loss. Residents must be good friends and must agree on most issues in order to live interdependently. In addition, residents in small housing groups often have difficulty maintaining the energy to organize common activities over a period of many years. Larger communities can more readily absorb varying degrees of participation and differences of opinion.

The average size of a cohousing community, 40-100 people, allows residents to retain their autonomy and choose when, or when not, to participate in community activities. Many people are seeking a more supportive environment, rather than a new family type. The freedom not to participate sometimes can help to create a living environment that accommodates people's changing needs over the years.

Location

Locations of cohousing developments are limited by two factors, the availability of affordable sites and finding enough people interested in living in cohousing. The majority are situated just outside metropolitan areas where sites are affordable and yet within reasonable distance from work, schools, and other urban attractions. That said, there are no hard and fast rules about location. Some cohousing communities are located in the inner cities. By contrast, at least ten communities have been established in semi-rural settings, some of them using refurbished old farmhouse for the common house. While these developments have a "rural atmosphere," most residents will commute to nearby

Bellingham Cohousing common terrace is a great gathering place . . .

. . . and so are the front porches at Strawberry Creek Cohousing.

cities for work. Bottom line: *cohousing residents decide for themselves what location will work best for their particular desires and needs.*

Design

As already mentioned, most cohousing communities have attached dwellings clustered around pedestrian streets or courtyards, although a few communities consist of detached single-family houses. Some communities mix attached dwellings with detached single-family structures. More recent complexes have dealt with their northern climate by covering a central pedestrian street with glass, thus allowing access between residences and the common house without needing to "go outside."

Cohousing is generally a new construction enterprise because it is difficult to create the desired relationships between spaces in existing buildings. Nevertheless, several communities in Denmark adapted old factory buildings; and another adapted an old school building. In another case, residents renovated nine dilapidated row houses to create a charming community in the inner city.

While all of the newly constructed Danish developments are low-rise in scale, in both Denmark and Sweden high-rises and sections of huge housing projects have been converted to cohousing to overcome impersonal environments that encouraged vandalism and high occupant turnover.

Types of Financing and Ownership

Cohousing developments utilize a variety of financing mechanisms and ownership structures, either by choice or local ordinances: privately-owned condominiums, limited-equity cooperatives, rentals owned by nonprofit organizations, and a combination of private ownership and nonprofit-owned rental units. In each case, residents initiate, plan, and manage the community, whether or not the units are owner-occupied or rented. In Denmark, eighteen of the twenty developments built before 1982 are completely privately financed and owned, similar to American condominiums. Then, for a period, most projects took advantage of new government-sponsored, index-linked loans that structured the developments as limited-equity cooperatives. More recently much government funding of nonprofit schemes has been withdrawn, including financial support for cohousing. Many other cohousing projects have resulted from collaborations between nonprofit organizations and resident groups to build rental units.

FrogSong Cohousing community, Cotati, California.

Other than determining who can afford to live in the development, financing makes little difference in the actual functioning of a cohousing community. Thus, cohousing differs from other housing categories, such as cooperatives and condominiums, which are defined solely by their type of ownership. Cohousing refers to an idea about how people can live together, rather than any particular financing or ownership scheme.

Priorities

The priorities of cohousing groups are as varied as the residents themselves. In addition to seeking a sense of community, some groups emphasize ecological concerns, such as solar and wind energy, recycling, and organic community gardens. In other developments, residents place less priority on community projects and spend more time on individual interests such as local theatre groups, classes, or political organizations. And, of course, others are devoted to seniors.

Why Cohousing Just for Seniors?

Why would someone want to create a cohousing community dedicated to seniors? There is no simple answer, since housing is an individual choice. Mixed-generational cohousing is an option for some seniors, but regular cohousing communities typically focus their energies in places where seniors have already been – building careers, raising families, and the like. As well, concerns of younger cohousers do not usually hinge on health issues. While some seniors will find the youthful vigor of a regular cohousing community to be refreshing, others feel it's a case of "been there, done that."

So what alternatives are there? For too many Americans, who either find themselves widowed and lonely or otherwise unable to effectively care for themselves and their homes as they once did, a planned retirement "community" or assisted-care institution beckons. It's an odd predicament: most seniors have been capable, reliable people throughout their adult lives. They raised families, owned property, worked in various jobs, and/or ran their own businesses. They were active members of a larger community. But those seniors who choose the planned retirement community route too often find themselves just as alone as before, only now locked down behind the walls of a gated compound. As for the seniors in assisted-living care, they become, in effect, patients within an institution, where hired staff dictates the choice of food, the people with whom they can socialize,

Sigrid says that cohousing works for her because at home she has as much privacy as she wants, and right out her front door she has as much community as she wants.

People meeting on their way to and from their destination is what maintains community.

and the types of activities offered. At best, activities might be modified with residents' input, but essentially the residents have given up control of their lives. And there's no going back.

By contrast, in senior cohousing the residents themselves make their own decisions. They are not alone, nor are they lonely. They collectively decide who will cook, what to cook, when to eat, and so on. After dinner, they go to a show or play a card game. They set up quilting racks, make music, and plan the next workday.

Since relationships are paramount in a cohousing community, residents live next door to their friends and, over time, their previous best friends (from life before senior cohousing) move in. These seniors live among people with whom they share a common bond of age,

experience, and community – a community they themselves built to specifically meet their own needs. These relationships provide purpose and direction in their lives and are as meaningful as any they have ever had. This is why cohousing just for seniors.

Having a chat on the balcony.

CHAPTER THREE

"We all helped paint the bike-shed and the large fence by the parking lot. And those who could not manage to paint took care of the food and drinks for the rest of us. Maybe we were not very efficient in a work-related sense but we were very efficient from a social point of view and we had a lot of fun while painting."

-- Rynkebakken in Lejre

Senior Cohousing
A Proven Approach –
A New Application

Usually limited to those 55 years of age or over, senior cohousing takes the concepts of cohousing and modifies them according to the specific needs of seniors. The result is a cozy little village that invites involvement, cooperation, and friendship – a recreation of earlier times when community participation was viewed as an essential part of social, mental, and physical health.

Residents from the first Danish senior cohousing group, Midgården, Copenhagen.

History of Senior Cohousing in Denmark

The Danes first addressed housing for low-income seniors in 1900, when they converted an old monastery into housing for the elderly. There, many people slept in small cubicles in dormitories, a primitive arrangement more suited to monks or schoolboys than the elderly. However, the residents bonded with one another and developed a mutual support system that worked very well. Many of the residents refused to move when later offered better housing.

In 1933, legislation was passed that allowed old workhouses to be converted into senior homes. Unfortunately, these facilities were substandard. After World War II, private nursing homes were built, mainly for the chronically ill, and all seniors were granted a small pension.

Beginning in the late 1950's, programs to help seniors remain in their own homes were established, programs similar to American programs like Meals on Wheels and Nurses on the Go. But these programs didn't solve the problem of loneliness and isolation. As a result, in 1964 a group that called itself "Boligtrivsel i Centrum" (Quality of Living in Focus) was founded to address a broad range of social ecology issues. But its work was slowly recognized and it wasn't until 1983 that this group received many grants.

In the meantime, the Danes reformed their social security system. In 1976, they put nursing homes and senior housing under one agency. What was a good idea in paper went horribly wrong in practice: seniors who moved into state-supported residences lost their pension and were

The people who first envisioned senior cohousing are ordinary citizens who, deeply passionate about their beliefs, simply made their personal dreams a reality for many. Along the way, they learned many invaluable lessons for creating, building, and living in a seniors-only cohousing community. In a nutshell, senior cohousing is similar to the mixed-generational cohousing model, with the following modifications:

- Careful agreements among residents about co-care and its limits

- Design considerations appropriate for seniors

- Size limitations (a maximum of 30 living units, usually 15-25)

- Senior-specific method for creating the community

But before we discuss the specifics of these modifications, a bit of background is in order. After all, we can't know where we're going until we know where we've been.

granted only a small monthly allowance; moreover, they lived with little or no privacy and virtually no independence – they lived in an institution. The Danes described this housing as "the gate to hell," and the elderly clung to their own homes as long as possible. (An unspoken advantage to this avoidance of public housing was that it saved the government money.)

The entire system needed an overhaul, and in 1979 a national Senior Committee was formed to improve the country's overall approach to senior issues. They succeeded in raising awareness about senior issues, and to counteract the view that seniors are merely old frail people who were mostly a burden to the state, this group advocated how seniors are productive, valuable members of society.

Senior Councils sprang up spontaneously in some cities, and they advised local officials about senior matters. The groundswell soon became policy, and in 1997 such councils were mandated by the national government. Additionally, a private national organization with similar objectives, called DaneAge (similar to the American Association of Retired People, AARP), was founded and became a popular force.

In the midst of all of this, starting in 1982 two Danish women, Tove Duvå and Lissy Lund Hansen, campaigned for independent oriented housing for seniors, touting a successful model that was already in place – cohousing. They ran into many roadblocks. A critical issue was that of government-sponsored nonprofit cohousing. Potential residents wanted it because nonprofit status would offer

A Tale of Two Communities

For a variety of reasons Midgården was built in two segments. The first segment was built by, and for, a committed cohousing group. These people had bonded into a group as they struggled together through the various phases of planning, design, and construction. It remains a vibrant success story. The second segment, by contrast, was offered to people through official announcements and newspaper ads – not unlike any other contractor-initiated condominium project. The individuals who answered these ads were less ready for the cooperative aspects of cohousing, and having had no common bonding experience found it more difficult to make the community work as envisioned. (Even today, this second segment has far fewer social activities than the first group.) These side-by-side examples illustrate that resident participation in the planning and development process is essential to the success of a senior cohousing community.

apartments for rent at reasonable prices. Politicians, of course, were wary: How difficult would it be to rent these apartments to newcomers who might – or might not – be interested in a cooperative community?

Finally, the women succeeded in finding a developer, Lejerbo, a nonprofit housing developer, who was willing to attempt the project; and in 1987 the first Danish senior cohousing complex, Midgården came to be. The public response to this new development was overwhelmingly positive. Hundreds attended forums sponsored by "Quality of Living in Focus," and the result was the formation of a new agency, the Organization of Senior Cohousing, whose mission was to educate the public about the matter.

In 1995, yet another significant event in the history of senior cohousing occurred. Henry Nielsen, working with Quality of Living in Focus, developed a comprehensive model for the creation of senior cohousing communities. It was a breakthrough. At last, here was a

Site plan of Skovgårds Have Senior Cohousing by Nielsen & Rubow Architects.

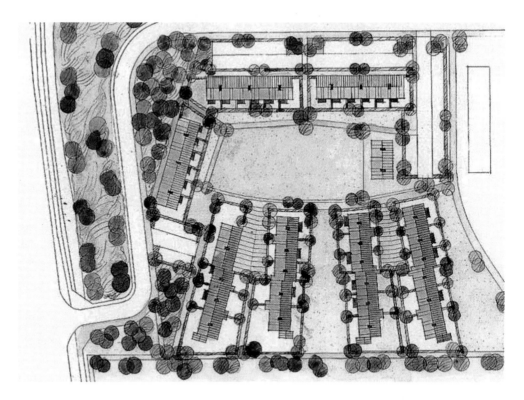

model – a blueprint, if you will – to help groups successfully navigate through an otherwise uncertain, doubtful process. The Nielsen model consists of five critical elements:

- A qualified advisor

- A feasibility and informational phase

- A first study group (Study Group I) – group development

- A second study group (Study Group II) – design

- A third study group (Study Group III) – policy

Nielsen's model neatly incorporates the aforementioned issues of co-care limits, design considerations, community size, and group formation processes.

We will discuss each element of this model in the following sections of this chapter, and have modified them to best address American sensibilities and realities of the American housing development. Once Nielsen's method was in place around the country, the quantity and quality of senior cohousing communities increased significantly. There is a final note in Denmark's support for senior cohousing. In 2001, the three Danish right-wing parties came into power and their platform advocated senior cohousing as a cost-effective method of housing the elderly. They nonetheless withdrew government funding for senior cohousing (many other non-profit programs were also dismantled). Today, implementation of senior cohousing in Denmark is more or less completely privatized.

Henry Nielsen's Model

In 1995 Henry Nielsen recognized that groups wishing to create a senior cohousing community needed a comprehensive model for realizing their goals. This model could be just as effective in the United States as it is in Denmark.

Nielsen's aim was ambitious and multifaceted. He sought a model that would:

- Make senior cohousing an option for everybody (not only the strong-willed)

- Identify and solve key problems that all seniors encounter during the process

- Enhance the social aspects of the process, which, in turn, foster strong and durable communities

- Make it easier and more satisfactory for developers and municipalities

to start or support new senior cohousing projects

- The feasibility phase, and Study Groups I, II, and III

The Nielsen model consists of five successive phases. Each phase and the groups of people involved are outlined later in this chapter. A full explanation of each Nielsen phase appears in the subsequent section. In this book we have chosen to modify the model slightly in order to make it more adaptable to the U.S.

Though Nielsen's model introduces a level of certainty to an uncertain process, it is not meant to be an absolute procedural doctrine. The participatory development processes, by its very nature, requires flexibility and compromise. As such, every situation presents issues differently, determined by the participants,

Bellingham Cohousing, Bellingham, Washington.

Dinner in the common house.

the development strategy, attitudes of local officials, and many other factors.

While Nielsen's Model outlines timelines for the phases and timing of key decisions, it is important early in the planning process for each group to set its own realistic timelines. The group should make every effort to adhere to their timelines, even though it is difficult, if not impossible, to control outside influences. If the decisions required of residents are made as scheduled, the process will keep moving forward and there will be less resident turnover during the development process.

Keeping to a timeline means avoiding backtracking. Once decisions have been made at each phase, the group must move on to the next phase. If everyone understands the issues and the agreed-upon solution at the time, old issues are less likely to resurface.

How new members are recruited and oriented also affects a group's ability

to stay on track. To retain continuity, it is best not to bring in new members in the middle of a phase, such as the preparation of the development program (Study Group II). Ideally, groups should only bring in new members at the beginning of a new phase of the development process. In actual practice, once the initial program has been set, new members are usually accepted at any time until all units are filled. Recruitment campaigns should be organized at key points, such as before site purchase and before taking a construction loan. New members should be oriented as to the history and status of the group, which decisions have already been made, and which are still open for discussions.

Turnover of participants is an inescapable difficulty of the participatory process. Some families are pressured to find other housing before the project is completed; people may move for job opportunities;

and others, for whatever reason, may decide they are not ready for cohousing. In one project with a long planning period, turnover left only four households who had participated from start to completion. However, the number of residents who participate in the entire process does not seem to affect the success of a project once it is completed. The backbone of the project is a combination of the success of the process, and the subculture of the people who intend to live there. And when they leave, they pass the baton on to the new organizer/resident.

The cohousing development process can be trying at times, requiring residents and consultants alike to take on unaccustomed roles. Residents must assume greater responsibility (and risk) in determining their housing needs, and in understanding the planning and development process. Consultants and contractors need non-traditional skills, such as the ability to facilitate decisions, to communicate development concepts to laypersons, and to consult on the consequences of the different choices.

Yet, only through this participatory process have cohousing communities actually been built. The involvement of residents from the earliest planning stages motivates them to take responsibility for the project's success; it allows them to understand the restrictions that must be imposed and the choices that must be made.

If participation is what makes senior cohousing work, then Nielsen's Model provides a senior-specific structure for getting there. The following is a tried-and-true checklist for getting a senior

cohousing project built, modified to address the sensibilities and realities of the American housing market.

Who's Involved:
Roles and Responsibilities

The Nielsen model also identifies the different groups, or parties, who are involved in creating a senior cohousing community and describes the roles that each should play. Before discussing each of the five phases in detail, let's look at the roles and resposibilities of each participating group.

The Senior Residents

The most important task of the senior group is to create their community. Regardless of how much support they get from outside the group, it is the residents themselves who decide what sort of community they want and how to go about making it happen. Creating a vibrant community requires that individuals work to find out the highest common denominator. Because the residents direct

Dinner at Doyle Street Cohousing.

Pleasant Hill Cohousing, Pleasant Hill, California.

the creation of their community, step-by-step, they are responsible for making sure their community actually gets built. This will require the group to listen to the expert advice and interests of the other actors in the planning and building process. This leadership role also requires the group to make a concerted effort to learn all they can about the various aspects of their project, especially the decisions that have already been made, and to orient new members about previous decisions.

The Advisor

Many distinct groups of people are involved in creating each and every senior cohousing community: residents, government officials, contractors, and more. Therefore, to best facilitate the different groups, Nielsen recommends a highly qualified third-party advisor, a

champion who works as a counselor and a coordinator among all the actors, who will follow the project all the way from the initial idea to a well-functioning senior cohousing community.

During the initial discovery meetings, the advisor functions as an educator and facilitator for the residents and prepares them for the process and to some extent their future life in the cohousing community. In the planning and construction phase he or she is more of an advisor, helping the seniors solve questions ranging from budget concerns to how to best organize meetings. In addition, he must ensure that the residents maintain their input at appropriate points in the process.

When the senior cohousing group is ready to bring the local municipality into the process, the advisor will inform and educate the local politicians and officials about the special issues and advantages connected with cohousing. He can also educate the municipality on how they can help find new residents for the cohousing project, should the municipality wish to be involved in that way.

Since the advisor has to balance the wishes of the different actors, he or she sometimes will have to defend the wishes of the seniors, while at other times he might find it most reasonable to explain the side of the local officials. All the while, his goal is the same as the senior group – to see a strong and vibrant senior cohousing community emerge.

Bottom line: *Until the project is well off the ground (under construction) this person's job is very straight-forward. They wake up in the morning and ask themselves, "What do I have to do today to move this project forward?" And the harsh reality is that if he or she isn't constantly moving the project forward, the resident group needs to replace the project manager. A lot of people think that they can do this job, but many can't.*

The Municipality

Be it within a city's limits or in unincorporated land, once a senior cohousing group identifies a potential site for their community, it's time to get local officials involved. The local municipality plays an important role early on in the process in terms of accommodating for zoning regulations, public service availability, financial considerations, and more. It is important to get a slate of key local officials "sold" on the idea of the project early on – both already-committed and potential residents will all feel more secure going forward if they

Hanging out between the houses at Doyle Street Cohousing, Emeryville, California.

know local officials won't hold up, pick apart, drive the costs up, or block their project before it really even starts.

After the project is officially approved and supported, the municipality's role diminishes. Sometimes a small group of officials will follow the project, or even assist in the group's quest for finding potential residents.

The Senior Associations

Every town has associations of one kind or another dedicated to the enhancement of quality of life for seniors. Most towns have many: legal council, resource and referrals, education, medical support, discussion groups, lobbyists and many more. Once they see that you are improving the quality of life for many seniors, that you are modeling cooperation for seniors, and that you will be a great asset to seniors

Common house at FrogSong Cohousing.

city-wide, then they will be key allies in your venture.

The resident group doesn't have to shoulder the full burden of educating and advocating senior cohousing to the municipality and the local community at large. The associations will decide whether, and how, they will support the project. They can recommend the cohousing project to the municipality and help plan and host the initial public meetings and seminars.

The group, however, should keep in contact with the associations as the project progresses – their connections within the community can be invaluable.

The Architect

For a senior cohousing project, an architect does more then just deliver blueprints. Balancing both the technical needs of the developer and the inspiration of the senior

group, he must have the willingness and ability to participate in a collective process where a large group of people have to work together and create the new project. If he or she has never handled such a project, this means a different kind of work than he is probably used to, and it will challenge him immensely as he ensures everyone gets heard, overcomes dead-locked issues, and designs a community that will be both livable and on budget.

The architect's most important job, however, is to teach the senior group about the realities of planning and construction. The seniors have to make very important design and construction decisions – decisions that will directly affect how much they will spend, how long the project will take to build, and how they will live there once it's built – but they often don't have the professional and technical knowledge to make these decisions effectively.

The Developer

The developer's role is large and complex. In some cases, the developer is in reality co-developer with the group, and perhaps even co-developer with the project manager, who might not get paid fully until later. The developer not only manages the development and finance process, but also works with the residents and architect, and takes on risk associated with the housing development itself.

Developers most often work on a risk-for-profit basis. In a conventional residential project, as the budget is being created, 10 to 25 percent of the total selling price is generally targeted for developer and investor profit. In speculative housing, this profit is simply included

I did an all day (8-hour talking head) seminar to 150 Native Americans representing 88 tribes from Alaska to Florida in Washington D.C. a couple of years ago. The topic was getting new housing and schools built on reservation land. Unfortunately the government's default design was tract-like single-family houses on one-acre sites spread equi-distant across the landscape. Everyone complained that this land-use approach was completely compromising relationships between grandmothers and granddaughters who used to be able to walk to each others' house when they lived in a trailer court. Ironically, the concept of cohousing was reintroducing village life to the Native Americans. They were asked in the last hour after an entire day of describing various roles and processes, "What do you think prevented you from making your project happen?" The majority of answers for the spokespersons for each tribe who had not been successful in realizing anything better than the government default solution, was the lack of somebody who only had one thought when they woke up in the morning ,"What do I do to move this project forward?" These were folks who had the land and the money. They just didn't have a good project manager.

You could say the same is true for the rest of us too – we get the default corporate and government solution when we don't figure out and accomplish our own solution. Single-family houses, equidistant across the horizon are not the solution. It plays to an overly isolated, overly consumptive lifestyle. It's the easiest to accomplish (the lowest common denominator) but falls far short of a more supportive hybrid-like system.

Pleasant Hill Cohousing common house.

A simple porch creates a soft edge between the public and the private space.

regular administrator. The maintenance work is ideally shared between the cohousing group and the non-profit administration, where the non-profit entity takes responsibility of bigger projects and the seniors are responsible for basic day-to-day maintenance.

In Detail: Nielsen's Five Phases Explained

Each phase presents its own set of challenges and rewards as a collection of individuals becomes a community. These explanations are borne by more than two decades of creating successful cohousing communities.

Feasibility Phase:
Do We Have a Project?

During feasibility study, the extent to which the following steps are followed (while, of course, retaining space for creativity at the same time) helps determine the success of the project. The core group:

- Compiles 25 names of prospective tenants on a sign up sheet

- Interview all professionals involved with local support for seniors

For those involved in the development, this latter step might seem like busy work, but having done it myself, I'm always surprised at how just a few days of work makes the entire two year project easier. Among the many hundreds of questions to ask local professionals:

- Who sponsors classes?
- Who are recommended teachers?
- How to organize an aging-in-place class locally?

in the price of a given property; and the buyer really has no way of knowing what corners may have been cut in order to ensure the developer's profit.

In a cohousing development, by contrast, since the residents plan their own community they will have far greater access to, and control over, the financial and construction details. The seniors will know what they are getting right from the start.

In the case of non-profit developers, the developer will be the actual owner of the completed project. However, most of the decisions about what to build, and where to build it, is made by the architect in cooperation with the seniors. The non-profit developer is, however, always responsible for the project's construction and the financing; and as such, he has the right and the duty to intervene if he strongly disagrees with decisions made by the group.

After the seniors move in, the non-profit developer role changes to that of a

- What is the venue?
- Which non-profit housing developer should be contacted?
- Are there grants available?
- Which HMO has the best in-house care (for the class)?
- Who helps subsidize/underwrite senior housing?
- Who can help get the word out?
- Can we post in your newsletter?
- Can I come to your next meeting to give a talk?

Questions are answered and of the 25 people who signed up, a core group forms. A building site and financing options are found; agreements are made about the participation of local non-profits or municipalities, or others, if applicable. At this stage, the group will have a general overview of the project in terms of:

- Viability
- Ownership
- Site
- Entitlements
- Zoning
- Funding
- Budgets

The group will also be able to:

- Assess the support of its allies
- Assess the support of the Municipality
- Assess the support of other professionals

Often the most difficult phase – this is when the viability of a project is carefully analyzed. Is there interest in the community for a senior cohousing community? Is there land close enough

to local amenities – preferably within walking distance – and other support services for seniors? What sort of funding is available, be it direct from the potential residents, traditional banks, the government, or investors? If so, what financial tools and safeguards are available to best utilize and protect the assets of the residents? Will the local government be willing to provide land subsidies?

Most seniors want their cohousing community to be rental units, co-op housing, or condominiums. With this in mind, it is critical the group contact funding agencies at an early stage to determine if they will support the project. It's a two-prong dilemma: before ownership type is decided (and the necessary agreements made), potential residents must be able to determine if they can afford to live in the new project.

While issues of financing and affordability are worked out, the placement of

Nevada City Cohousing site plan.

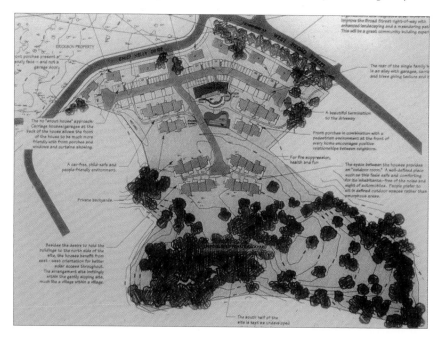

Two Methods

In Denmark, there are two principal methods of building senior cohousing. Both rely on an organization to facilitate this process. One method employs a nonprofit development firm; the other utilizes a for-profit professional design and project management firm. In both methods, the process begins with a group of people who either know each other already (sometimes referred to as the core group), or who sign up on a list of interested parties. The professional facilitators enter into the picture only after a core group has formed.

the new project itself must be determined. Finding a suitable site is important because many seniors understandably don't want to move away from the city or the area in which they already live. It's no use to site a project where residents might not want to live.

Meanwhile, local politicians and officials should be informed about the concept of senior cohousing. There still seems to be misconceptions about cohousing; often people think that "cohousing" is another name for "hippie commune" straight out of the 1970's. It is important that the municipality, already in the agreement phase, get a realistic picture of what senior cohousing actually is.

However, I don't want to over-emphasize the importance of having the bureaucrats on board. Too often they are the last people to "get" it. Luckily in our private enterprise system you can propose anything, and with tenacity and public support, champion it through. It's not unusual to be voted down 2-3 at the first hearing or two, only to win 5-0 by the third hearing. One of the favorite parts of my job, after working with dozens of cohousing communities, is the number of times that dissenting bureaucrats have come up to me after a project was built to say, "I can't believe I didn't support this wonderful village of a neighborhood from the very beginning."

When educating local officials about senior cohousing, it is often beneficial to have the support of local senior associations. When consulted at this first phase of the project, the official support of senior associations can also positively affect how other seniors receive notices and updates regarding the project.

Can one or two people do all of this? You bet. You don't have to be a Tove Duvå or a Lissy Lund Hansen to get a project up and running. You just have to believe that life will be easier, more fun, more interesting, more economical, and of better quality if you live in cooperation with your neighbors; and then decide to make it happen. And unlike Duvå and Hansen, you also don't have to trial-and-error your way through – a seasoned advisor can really help here.

Information Phase:
Spreading the Word

Area seniors learn about the project and get involved:

- Public meeting (one day)
- Information about senior cohousing as a form of housing is shared
- Potential new residents sign up for a follow-up seminar
- Advisor contacts other key parties, i.e. the developer and/or the architect
- Follow-up seminar (one day)
- Thorough information about senior cohousing is given
- Group works on the expectations of the new community
- Sign up for Study Group I

Once the various aspects of the feasibility phase are met, it's time to broaden the scope and bring other interested seniors into the picture. This phase begins with a well-publicized, one-day public meeting where local seniors get an overview of all aspects of senior cohousing. Not only do they learn about cohousing as a concept, but the dynamics of the specific project at hand. Moreover, since this first

Clustering the homes creates a village environment and preserves open space. Bellingham Cohousing, Bellingham, Washington.

meeting is akin to a community outreach event, it can be conducted by someone in the group and one of the professionals involved.

After the first meeting, a follow-up seminar is scheduled for seniors who are still interested. At this seminar, the adviser will detail the next steps for those who haven't been involved to date. An architect should also be present to outline design and construction issues. At this early stage, an architect will not have started the designs; rather he or she is present to demonstrate to potential residents that any architectural questions will be addressed sensitively and thoroughly, and in their due time. The architect can outline the entire design process and when and how people will have input. This half-hour discussion can best assure people that there will be a time when input can be given.

Eventually, potential residents form into smaller groups to discuss how they imagine life in their new community.

These are genuine community-building exercises, and the advisor will assist in making certain that these events maintain their integrity. These meetings are advertised locally in the newspaper, at senior association events, in area senior newsletters, and so forth.

The core of the group will most likely have selected itself at this point, though people are usually still dropping in and out. Taking the input from these meetings – the hopes and dreams of the future residents – the group is finally strong enough for some hard lifting. Welcome to the Study Group I.

Study Group I:
Building the Foundations of Community

The cohousing group defines its needs and goals:

- Discussions and workshops (three months)

Talking to the cook before dinner at Pleasant Hill Cohousing's common house.

- The economic aspects
- Determination of tenure type
- The social structure
- Mutual responsibilities
- Decision making
- Community traditions
- Potential sites identified by professionals
- Ownership types described and probably decided upon
- Who takes care of who
- Conclusions in a report

The purpose of this phase is to create a general agreement about the specifics of daily life in the new community. Just as important, though less tangible, future residents clarify their hopes and dreams while learning how to work cooperatively with each other.

First things first, the financial realities of the project are determined and, hence, the type of ownership is decided. The residents will determine if the community will consist of privately owned condominiums, limited equity cooperatives, rentals owned by the group or by non-profit organizations, or a combination of private ownership and rental units. Regardless, residents take some responsibility for planning and managing the community, whether or not the units are owner-occupied or rented.

Once ownership issues have been decided, the group turns its focus toward the social dimensions of the future community. At first, residents simply discuss aspects of the community they actually want. What traditions would they like to start? How is the decision-making process going to work? How much community life do they want; and to what extent should you feel obliged to participate? How can the common work be divided in a fair way? What co-care limits do they want; and to what extent shall people help each other in case of illness?

Eventually, participants write down the conclusions of their discussions in a report. This report serves a few key purposes. It obligates residents to follow their own commonly decided rules as the project progresses; likewise, it assists potential new residents in learning more about the community. Ultimately it will help them decide if they really want to join the group.

Study Group I typically meets weekly for about three months. Ideally, the project adviser only participates every other week. This hands-off approach forces the group to work together without help from outside.

Study Group II:
The Participatory Development Design Process (3 months)

The senior cohousing group realizes its community:

- Architectural designs are finalized
- Seniors and architect design (program and schematic design) the cohousing community – site plan, common house, living units, etc.
- Start-to-finish design of the project

Residents, now committed to a site for their community, are ready to translate their theoretical plans into a concrete reality. This study group is meant for those who will actually move into the completed community of 15-25 units.

The architect, in cooperation with the group, designs the project. This design phase typically takes about three months.

All of the decisions regarding the site plan, common house, universal features of individual units, and the design of the individual features within the house types are done with the group. Because the seniors themselves play such a crucial leadership role, every aspect of the design process will be appropriate for them to participate in. This process is a balancing act between the desires and needs of the group versus respect for building codes and the project's budget. For example, compromises must be made in regard to budget versus handicapped accessibility; and designs of individual living units should not be so eccentric as to blow the budget or hinder the group's ability to sell the unit if someone leaves during the planning process.

After the design stage, a building contractor must be hired to actually build the project. The cohousing process will

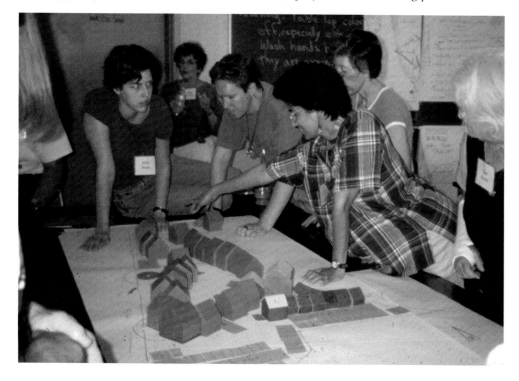

Cohousing is planning your own neighborhood.

It began when Hans and Inge just started having their breakfast at the gathering node outside. Of course, they could have had breakfast at home, in their private backyard, or in the café down the street – instead they chose a more social setting. Susanna offered fresh squeezed orange juice, Jim offered espresso coffee, and Jose from Chile offered homemade croissants. Before you knew it, they were all having breakfast together every Saturday morning. People came and went, always sharing food, plans and stories. "It's fun," said Margarette, who joins them from time to time. In a setting designed to provide as much privacy as you want and as much community as you want.

Having fun in the common house.

likely be a new concept for the construction company, and while this firm must be thoroughly vetted, the contractor must not feel that this project will be any more complicated than any other, or the price will be too high.

Then, once the design plans are finalized and approved, financing is secured, and the contractor hired, it's time to break ground. It's an exciting milestone, to be sure, but perhaps the most critical phase of all is yet to come. Although the design of the project is the main focus of Study Group II, questions and concerns about social life within the community will remain – and therefore we come to Study Group III.

Study Group III:
After Move In Policies
Residents prepare for life in a senior cohousing community. This is done while the architects and project manager are working on construction documents and city approval:

- Discussions and decisions about agreements are made
- Residents, the developer, and the project advisor decide on a process of taking in new residents in the future
- Policies are established: Common meals, pets, who takes care of who
- Methods for turning over vacancies are codified

The plans have been submitted and approved by the city, and the celebration party is a warm memory. It's time to contemplate and make decisions on all of the issues people feel are important prior to moving in: pets, meals, maintenance, and more. The key thing is to not make a mountain out of a mole hill – and try to have fun with it.

Hearthstone Cohousing, Denver, Colorado.

After move in, despite the inevitable adjustments, after experiencing the convenience and pleasantness of common dinners and community life as a whole, residents will soon feel they are home. It will be a place where the landscaping is young, the buildings new, and the shared experiences just beginning; a place where, as the years pass, the residents will wonder why they had lived any other way.

PART TWO

Senior Cohousing
in Denmark
An Inside Look

Enough general discussions. Let's take a closer look at some real places and the people who live in them. The following case studies give a small sampling of the variety of senior cohousing applications. We begin with a close look at one community's planning process, and how they were able to design a community with strong roots in fertile soil.

The entrance to Munksøgård
Senior Cohousing.

CHAPTER FOUR

Roskilde, Denmark

20 Units

Architects:
Mangor & Nagel
(Programming, schematic
design and design
development: Martin Rubow)

Completed: 2000

Munksøgård [munk-so-gore]
Strong Roots in Fertile Soil

I t's early on the evening of the Summer Solstice. The weather is warm and the sun won't go down. The air smells of hay and flowers. In the common garden a lamb from the community's own flock is being roasted. Outside the senior common house, a group of four is preparing a salad for the evening's outdoor potluck party. Some children are working on the traditional witch-puppet while others are playing soccer on the adjacent field. Other people are setting the tables in the garden.

The Munksøgård senior "village".

In July 1995, about a dozen young environmentalists from Copenhagen got together to create a new cohousing project with a senior component. They envisioned a community with significant diversity in the ages and backgrounds of the residents: older and younger, high and low-income, quiet and gregarious, and big families as well as singles. There would be a broad variety of common facilities and activities that would draw people together in their daily lives and establish the sense of community that characterizes a village. In short, it would become a modern version of the traditional village, one that pointed toward the future and could inspire others. Additionally, these people wanted to create a building project to sustain both environmental and social ecologies.

At six-o'clock all of the residents from the four adjacent cohousing groups start pouring in and get seated. This yearly solstice party goes on all night. The bonfire is lit and people gather around it, singing traditional midsummer songs. Munksøgård's trailblazing seniors revel in this lifestyle, one they dreamed about when they joined the project a decade ago. Their separate cohousing community shares a site and some common facilities with four adjacent mixed-generation cohousing communities.

When the environmentalists arranged a public meeting in Copenhagen to present their ideas, 200-300 people showed up. Without a site, developer or

The front of the common house is where people meet.

architect, the project still seemed very vague, and in the following months many people dropped out. The remaining group of about 100 people sat down and wrote a very idealistic proposal. The new project would consist of five different cohousing communities, each laid out as a courtyard complex: one community of 20 units for young first-time settlers under 31 years of age; a second community of 20 units for families and singles; a third community of 20 units for seniors over 50 years of age; a fourth community of 20 co-operative units; and a fifth community of 20 owner-occupied units. The goal was to make the houses as ecologically sustainable as possible without sacrificing basic comfort. Grey water from the kitchens and bathrooms would be cleaned by a biological filter and then discharged into the small river that bounds the site. Composting toilets would be installed so that the project didn't have to be attached to the city sewer system. The goal was to achieve a 20 percent decrease in water consumption and to make the cohousing community essentially non-polluting.

Over a period of about a year, the project was discussed and revised at bi-weekly meetings. After the group had

Cooperation Defines the Good Life

Senior cohousing is simply a neighborhood where you can rightly expect that neighbors will cooperate. The neighbors have the same expectations about how much they will cooperate. Interestingly, in a senior cohousing community, people normally cooperate well beyond any pre-established limits. Residents soon discover that cooperation is not something to be feared: it does not diminish their independence nor does it crimp their lifestyle. In fact, the opposite is true. Time and again I have heard stories of how a "typical" couple reacts to moving in. The wife, leading the charge with a knowing smile, brings her husband into a senior cohousing community kicking and screaming – "forced" cooperation is not for him – and three weeks later he has his feet up on the coffee table, saying what a great idea he had to move in.

Munksøgård site plan with the five cohousing communities encircling the old farm.

Seniors prepare common dinner out in the sun where others can see them and stop by to say hello – and also chop some carrots. Food is one of the major reasons people give for choosing cohousing. Compare this food preparation with how it's done in typical assisted living facilities, where it is unlikely residents can or will get satisfactory meals. Equally important, residents miss out on planning and preparation – a good way to feel involvement and a sense of achievement.

"Cooking is a responsibility I embrace," said Ingrid, "partially because I only have to do it every five weeks and partially because my other neighbors have been doing it for me for the last five weeks. I owe them a good meal, don't you think?"

agreed on their program, they connected with Copenhagen architects Nielsen & Rubow, a firm well experienced with cohousing. The group found a large rural site outside of the university town of Roskilde, near a station on the commuter train line to Copenhagen. Nielsen & Rubow developed an initial feasibility plan in which houses were laid out in a circle around an existing farm on the site with a central courtyard. The farm, Munksøgård, was to serve as a common building for all the residents. A large part of the site was to remain undeveloped, partly as a recreational area and partly as a vegetable garden.

The group then found a non-profit developer, the local Roskilde Cooperative Housing Society. The project was put out to private bid to five contractors. Throughout this process, some ecological features were compromised, either to save money or improve accessibility standards. Among other things, the composting toilets were replaced with low water use toilets with two separate flush choices for economic reasons.

Many design features were discussed by the group. There were compromises and trade-offs. Issues such as health and disease prevention were discussed. The group agreed on a smoking policy, emphasized the importance of quality and diversity in the common meals, and confirmed that car parking would be relegated to the periphery. For economic reasons, they built two-story houses for the seniors. At the meeting where they came to decide who would get which apartment, 18 out of the 20 seniors got the apartment they wanted. The stairs were not considered a problem in Munksøgård. Although cost-cutting required that the originally planned internal staircases be replaced by external ones, the

Munksøgård private house plan.

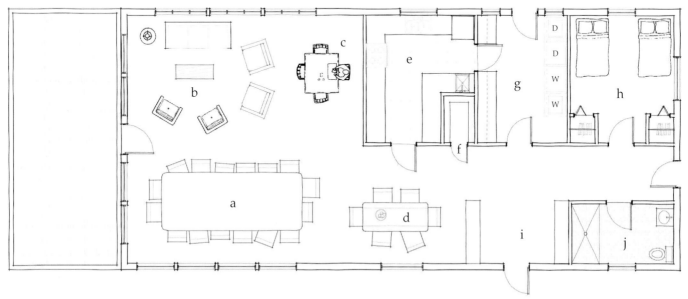

Munksøgård common house plan:
a. dining ; b. sitting ; c. cards ; d. crafts ; e. kitchen ; f. storage ; g. laundry ; h. guest ; i entry ; j. bathroom
The workshop, another reading room, barn, storage, and mechanical room are elsewhere.

When the front of the common house is situated where most people can see it from their houses, then in classic cohousing fashion, activity attracts activity. People see a few people having tea, and before you know it, there's a tea party!

Designing Potential

A great architect does more than create pleasant shapes and colors of buildings. When it comes to elderly cohousing, a great architect is a choreographer of activities and behavior. Not so much a creator, but an enabler. If the seniors wish for a quiet and harmonious lifestyle where both long conversations and vibrant activities are the norm, a great architect will design an interlocking set of common indoor and outdoor spaces to facilitate this way of life. A well-designed community en-courages otherwise incidental and insignificant interactions to become meaningful events that foster deep, life-long relationships. Such is life in Munksøgård.

seniors felt that walking up and down the stairs daily help them to stay fit. The senior group also insisted on wheelchair access to the ground floor units, skid free bathroom floors, and roll-in showers. The three living buildings contain:

(8) 1-bedroom units
(8) 1 1/2-bedroom units
(4) 2-bedroom units

The confidence that the non-profit housing developer had in the senior group was so great that the elderly members weren't required to make a large down-payment before they moved in. The down-payment for others was $3,200 to $4,400/unit – equal to two percent of the purchase price. This is slightly more than the cost of regular housing; however, when access to a variety of common facili-ties and the shared lifestyle opportunities

are factored in, this is not a particularly expensive proposition.

In 2000, after five years of planning and construction, the seniors moved in. As of this writing, none of them have yet moved out, and 80 people are on the waiting list to move in. Despite initial disagreements about sustainability issues, Munksøgård senior cohousing has become a great success. Cars are not permitted beyond the parking lot, but there are plenty of wheelbarrows standing around for people to carry their groceries from their cars to their home.

In addition, the seniors enjoy a variety of common activities, such as playing bridge, singing in a choir, and picnicking. The most important activity that seniors share is their common dinners in the common house, three or four days a week. Cohousing groups often invent

Common dinners open conversations and opportunities.

*"What are you doing this weekend?"
"Maybe work in the garden. Why?"
"Lars and I are going to take the motor boat out on the bay. Why don't you join us?"*

There's a real sense of spontaneity – and enjoying sport events, going to movies and the theater are common activities cohousers like to share.

new common activities. The group at Munksøgård has a "let's see what happens" philosophy as they continue to explore different activities. In reality, it is the continuous activities that occur spontaneously in this community that are the most numerous.

While many senior groups don't want to be disturbed by children, the Munksøgård group wanted to live near a community with children, and the concept has worked. "Everything would be so tidy around here and life would be so boring," one resident said. The seniors still prefer to eat the common meals separate from the other groups most days; but parties for a couple, or even all five of the communities are popular. Despite their proximity, the seniors are adequately self-contained and don't rely much on the neighboring communities. Senior

cohousing has also had a profound influence on the personal interaction that residents share. The senior residents' own children and grandchildren come visiting more often than before, and frequently stay a little longer. Some of their adult children complain that since their parents moved into Munksøgård, the seniors rarely phone them anymore.

Healthcare vs. Co-Care

A common concern for people moving into senior cohousing is what will happen to them when they get older and have problems taking care of themselves. This has caused experts and laypersons alike to argue for written agreements about the expectations of co-care and mutual favors within a given senior cohousing community. The Munksøgård seniors, by contrast, have chosen to have very few written

The residents implement lots of work projects like building a new greenhouse.

... but mostly it's an excuse to have a party and a beer.

co-care agreements; instead, the residents decide these limits for themselves along the way – currently three people with cars have agreed to drive others to the hospital in case of an emergency. Emergencies aside, though co-care often only involves simple shopping errands and minor favors, most of the residents don't like to be too dependent on their neighbors. Said one resident: "I came here for the social contacts. Helping each other was not an important motive for me – it was more knowing that you are there for each other, if needed."

Another resident echoed this sentiment: "We're not going to become an assisted living arrangement," said Olaf Dejgaard. He continued, "It's so easy to do someone's laundry, if needed. We do some shopping, lots of small errands. But all the intimate stuff – dressing, bathing – we leave to professionals. This means that what we will do can remain loosely defined."

In general, Munksøgård seniors rely on the Danish health care system for their healthcare and in-home help. Though the Danish healthcare system is free at point of delivery, in-home care doesn't provide someone to live and laugh with. Moreover, the Danish state-sponsored healthcare is on shaky ground politically and financially, meaning Danish seniors increasingly feel like they have to figure out how to best take care of themselves.

Concluded Dejgaard, "We look after each other. We eat together, talk together, and are interested in each other."

Hedda Lundh, another Munksøgård senior, says: "You get hooked into having all these people living around you. If you're ill, they bring up food, and you're

Sweat Equity as Cost Savings?

The Munksøgård residents made their own clothes-drying shed. In many ways this is a perfect post move-in project. Put the sticks together, brace it up, and put some clear corrugated panels on top of that. It is practical to dry clothes inside when the weather is bad, and very ecological.

Projects completely independent of the regular construction are the best use of time, money, and effort. Obviously, not every group will want a clothes-drying shed. But that's beside the point: what gets built after move-in has everything to do with the personalities involved. This group did quite a few projects like this because they had the inclination, skills, and building know-how. It was also less expensive for them to do the work themselves, as opposed to hiring outside contractors.

"Chip in and do what you can," that's the prevailing attitude at Munksøgård. The seniors here did all the painting themselves. Those who could not paint made lunch or watched the grandchildren of those who were busy with ladders and paintbrushes.

For Munksøgård seniors, community living means turning a mundane domestic chore into something more – a social event.

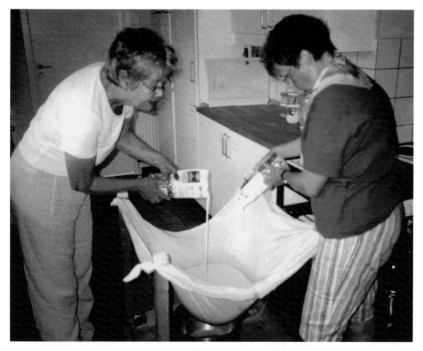

Making cheese. Traditional activities are life affirming and culture sustaining (no pun intended).

Gardens are a major design component in senior cohousing

constantly asked if there's anything they can do for you." The last time Hedda came back from a vacation, someone had turned the heat on in her apartment just before she got home and put a basket of homemade rolls on her kitchen table.

Going Back to Their Roots

The common vegetable garden provides residents with organic produce, and the livestock from their fields even provides some organic meat. Jens Asger Hansen, who is a member of the farming and gardening group, says: "I'm happy to live here and I think it has all happened in a harmonious way. My wife and I are social people who like the fact that the people we most enjoy spending time with live next door. But there is a very precise and defined balance between open doors and private life here."

The average age of these seniors is now 67 years. Olaf feels that this is too high, because there is a considerable amount of common work to be done. The Munksøgård group is now trying to attract more people in their fifties. The seniors do most of the work themselves without hiring outside help; this includes snow clearing, house maintenance, landscaping, tree planting, and work in the vegetable gardens. The senior group even painted the houses themselves. Since moving in they have built a workshop, a storage shed, a greenhouse, a clothes drying shed and a hen house. While the younger seniors painted the houses (with considerable Tom Sawyer-like assistance from neighbors and their own children), the older residents cooked and made coffee for the group.

Common dinners in Munksøgård are intimate, home-like, and very well attended.

The senior section of the community garden is the best kept of the five sections. Despite the high average age of these seniors, the extensive amount of work is not considered much of a problem. There is a general agreement that the older seniors work less than the younger ones, or that they do less physically demanding work. These duties help keep people active and are of great importance to the social life in the community. It is interesting that the buildings in the senior cohousing area are in better condition than the buildings in the mixed-age cohousing. It turns out that five people who take all day to do a task get much more done than fifty who, with young families to raise and careers to pursue, have no time at all.

The Danes, like Americans, value the ideals of individualism and self-sufficiency. These notions are defining aspects of their society. In this regard, Munksøgård is profoundly Danish: the residents aren't so much living in a mutually dependent relationship as they are engaged in a mutually beneficial partnership. But it's more than that. These seniors have created a community. A village where friendships run as deep as family. A world where each individual's social, physical, and emotional well-being is sustained one dinner, one project at a time, every day, in the company of others.

A Summers' Day at Munksøgård

One summer morning, a couple are leaving their flat at 6:30. They go for a walk every day at this time, come rain, shine, snow or darkness, to "keep in shape" as they like to put it. When they get back they let the eight hens and the rooster out into the run that the seniors built recently. A little later the man whose turn it is to see to the hens cleans out their coop and feeds them some corn, scrap vegetables, and water. Now more of the cohousers are up and about, and there is a constant flow of people to the mailboxes that hang at the gable end of the common house, picking up letters and the daily paper. Some of them enter the common house to see what the day's cook is serving for dinner at 6 o'clock. There is a list hanging on the notice board where you can mark down whether you are coming to dinner that evening. Depending on how many people are going to eat, one or two helpers join in with the kitchen tasks. One lady brings her washing to the laundry in the common house. There's a laundry list where you can book one of the two washing machines for two hours at a time, and we've built a drying shed where we can have a chat while we hang up and take down the drying.

At 10 o'clock, one of the cohousers has made a pot of coffee and placed it on the table at the benches by the south wall of the common house. Others gather around, and the talk is lively. The day's plans are being discussed, amongst other things. Just now we're building a greenhouse so that we can grow our own healthy cucumbers and tomatoes. Each of the common activities has a "boss" in charge, and this job is rather complicated. Some of the residents who are involved are getting ready to start working on it. The kitchen garden is almost 13,000 square feet, and it needs a lot of work from the seniors who enjoy that responsibility. We have a four-way rotation of the crops, and in the Spring and Fall more helping hands are needed. The potatoes look good, and the beans are ready to be harvested. Two of us decide to do it today and put them into the freezer. About half of our vegetables come from our own garden.

Nearly everyone has a bicycle. Two of the cohousers get their bikes out of the storage shed that we built ourselves, and cycle about three miles to the nearest shops. They could use their own cars or take the bus, but most of us prefer to get some exercise and go by bicycle.

Other things to do include mowing the lawns, tending the flowerbeds, trimming the hedges or working in one of the five smaller gardens, but today it's hot, and everyone's too busy enjoying the sunshine. Five of the "girls" take advantage of living relatively close to the beach, and set off on their bikes to go for a swim.

Later in the afternoon, someone has made another pot of coffee and found some nice cookies, and some of the cohousers gather together under the sunshades to enjoy them.

Lovely smells waft out through the kitchen windows where dinner is being prepared. Our common dinners are made mostly with beef, lamb, eggs and chicken from our smallholding, and vegetables from our garden. It's a lovely evening, so we decide to have dinner on the common house terrace, overlooking the pond. Everyone lends a hand setting up the chairs and tables, and putting up the sunshades.

After dinner, once the tables have been cleared away, we form two teams and play petanque for an hour or so. A couple of us are pretty good at it, and there's some gentle teasing going on.

As the day draws to a close, I go across to the hen house and close it up for the night. A few of the cohousers go into the common house to share a bottle of red wine; the others head back to their own flats to relax with the late news after a pleasant day.

-- Olaf Dejgaard, 2005

Olaf, 72, is a resident at Munksøgård

A village. Make a cozy little village that invites involvement, cooperation and friendship.

Else Skov in her kitchen in Otium Senior Cohousing

CHAPTER FIVE

Other Danish Senior Cohousing Communities
Otium, Gimle, Mariendalsvej, Korvetten

The organic. The hurried. A cautionary tale. The ideal. Four Danish senior cohousing communities. Four different processes for creating each. Four different outcomes. Since its inception in the mid-1980s the senior cohousing movement has spread rapidly throughout Denmark and is showing no signs of slowing. Demand for this type of housing has been enormous from day one. It is evident that this is exactly the type of housing Danish seniors truly yearn for.

Else Skov in her kitchen.

Remarkably the senior cohousing movement was started by proactive, enterprising seniors themselves and not by the government, investors, or other professionals. In fact these professionals didn't even take these active seniors seriously. Suffice it to say that without initiative and determination of these seniors, senior cohousing itself probably never would have happened.

Today more than 120 Danish senior cohousing communities have been established, and a series of new projects are on their way. Due to its self-grown character, the movement has given birth to a variety of types of senior cohousing communities – some more successful than others. The following four Danish examples show how different the conception, the planning process, and the result of a senior cohousing project can be. Valuable lessons can be learned from the hard-earned experiences of the Danes.

Otium
The Organic

Birkerød, Denmark
16 Units
Architects: Tegnestuen 6B
Built: 1988
Tenure: Cooperative

Else Skov moved into a large one-bedroom apartment in the Otium senior cohousing community fifteen years ago. She lost her husband about two years ago. Else is in great shape for her seventy-one years. She and I walk over to the common house. Along the way she describes the community's layout and its social life: how the peripheral parking gets people out of their cars; and the centrally-located common house helps people to mix. Indeed, people run into each other and chat everywhere we go. Else stops and greets some seven people on the way – a smile, a hello, a plan for later that night, and later that week.

When Else and her husband were in their mid-fifties they started to consider their housing situation. At the time they were living in a big house and they felt like moving into something smaller. They talked about the option of senior cohousing (then newly-invented) but had their doubts. Wasn't it a bit early to consider senior housing at all, more than ten years before they planned to retire? Eventually, they decided to go for it and join the local group that was designing Otium. They never regretted it.

When Else's husband passed away, living in senior cohousing was a great relief for her. During that difficult time she received a lot of support from the other residents, and because she was living in a tight knit community she didn't feel as alone and abandoned as she probably would have if she had been living on her own.

Afterwards, she was happy that she had made the move from the large suburban house to the more moderate unit in Otium before she became a widow. The fact that she had done it when she still had the energy gave her enormous freedom later. As Else says:

> *"What do you need a big house for in your senior years? After all you can't eat brick! Living here makes it possible for me to do everything I want. My living costs here are half of what they were when we had the house. Now I have more money to spend, and I can travel easier. All I need is here. I get much more out of my money. It's such a pleasant way to live."*

Group Formation

In the fall of 1984 a group of middle-aged people in the town of Birkerød got together and started debating the need for better housing arrangements for seniors. They were worried about the prospects of spending their retirement in institutional homes, so they were looking for alternative options. They wanted to grow older wisely.

After a while they found out that they would like to build their own housing community, but they weren't sure about how to do it. Their vision was to create senior housing as a community with lots of common activities, but also with a great deal of respect for each other's privacy. Birkerød had several vibrant intergenerational cohousing communities to lend inspiration, but at the time cohousing solely for seniors had not yet been attempted. The group had its questions and doubts about whether it was possible at all. How would it work? Who would take care of them? Would they know how to deal with serious illness and death? And most important, did they have the energy and resources to carry out such a big project?

Problems and worries aside, the group was very eager to make it happen. The approach they chose was to start an incredibly careful programming and design process. With great energy and lots of ideas and visions they met once a month for the next three years to thoroughly debate all thinkable aspects of their future senior cohousing community. In reality – and without knowing it – they were using a very protracted version of Henry Nielsen's three study group senior cohousing design model, before it was even created. Had they known his

Otium site plan.

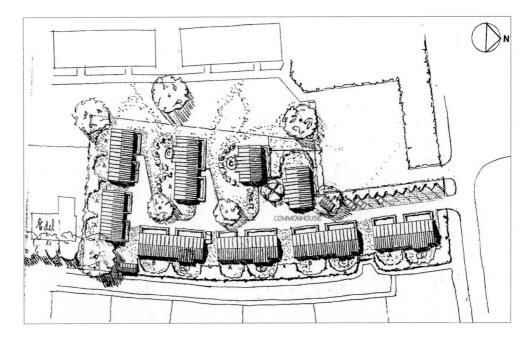

model, their process would of course have gone much faster. Nonetheless they did exactly the right thing by addressing all issues as early as possible, before they turned into conflicts. Luckily the group had good leadership and great discipline. All matters could be discussed freely and consensus was established on all major decisions. Everybody got what he or she wanted from the beginning – and in the end everybody was happy about the result. The many common experiences from the process made the group bond, and a strong community was created long before the project was actually built.

After three and a half years of programming, designing, and construction, the residents finally moved in to their new homes in the spring of 1988. They decided to name it Otium, which is a poetic Danish term for retirement. Their patience was rewarded.

Otium reminded me of living in campus dormitories at college. After dinner people got up and went to pre-planned activities, others joined them, still others dreamed up other activities and went off to do them. Others having been out the night before, hung out at the common house drinking coffee and chatting.

Community Design

In Otium, the private houses are laid out along a pedestrian street to give the project a village-like feel. (Advice from the local police confirmed the seniors' belief that the closer their houses were placed to each other, the less crime there would be.) There are three kinds of one-story private houses at Otium, 748 sf, 840 sf, and 1,078 sf. The houses themselves have zones that are more private than others: The kitchen and front garden face the common area, while the living room faces a private garden behind each house. The private houses are wheelchair accessible and they

Common dinner in Otium.

A Common Economy

The common economy at Otium is a straightforward affair.

1. A guest at Otium pays $6.75 per night to rent the bedroom in the common house.
2. The use of the laundry machine costs $1.50, and each resident pays for laundry every third month. The money goes into a common maintenance account.
3. Community business such as taxes, electricity, heating, water, and new needs are in the common budget that the community agrees on once a year, and are administrated together. An attorney in Copenhagen administers the legalities.

---

are easy to keep and clean – it is simply low-maintenance architecture in action (a programming priority). The size and facilities of the common house compensate for the moderate size of the private houses. The common house has a large living room, kitchen, a laundry room, and a guest room in a separate building.

This Is a Life...

A functional neighborhood, like a functional family, meets, discuss the issues, comes to commonly agreeable solutions, does work together, and plays together. Obviously the issues involved in these two communities are different, but the sensibilities are the same. A dysfunctional neighborhood, like a dysfunctional family, is estranged, non-communicative, and alienated.

In Otium it is absolutely apparent that the residents work with and know each other very well. There is a familiarity, a laugh, a cajole, a whisper, an

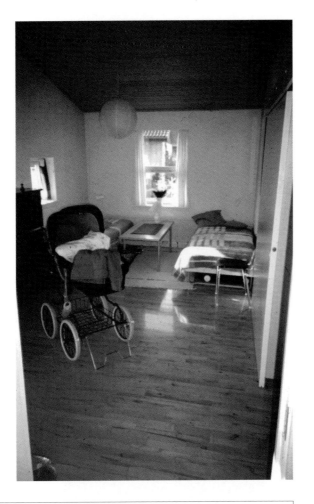

encouragement, which is quite unlike the perfunctory politeness and tense humor of a typical group of suburban neighbors at a yearly block-party.

The residents of Otium seem to be individuals who had real responsibilities before moving in. And once they became members of Otium, they in no way shied away from any responsibilities. However, once in Otium, surrounded by a group of their peers, they offset these responsibilities by having a good time. They spontaneously jumped in the car and drove to the beach, went bird watching, took off to the movies, the theater, and much more. For them, Otium is more than a community, it is an exit strategy where they plan for and get the most out of their last 20 years, without being a burden to their children, without having to completely rely on the government, without compromising their own potential for happiness.

The residents of Otium planned their course of action as carefully and deliberately as most people plan their own financial security, except that they added a plan for their actual lives. By planning with whom they would be around, early on, they knew that they wouldn't have to plan for it later. Which is to say that their happiness is not a function of week-by-week planned functions; instead their happiness is a natural extension of their overall vision.

"This is a life," as the Danes would say, "with goods in it."

The Guest Rooms

Guest rooms in common houses are usually larger than guest rooms in intergenerational cohousing. They are designed to allow for a family to have an extended stay, or even for caregivers to live in. They are more like suites, with their own bathroom and, of course, with full use of the common kitchen, sitting room, laundry, and other amenities they can feel like luxurious accommodations.

Sometimes common houses have several guest units, some for guests and others for caregivers. Caregivers might move in to assist a resident in typical assistant caregiver capacity (with dressing, showers, etc.) for, say, ten hours per week at first. Meanwhile, they might have a full time or part time job elsewhere or they might be a student who needs the part time employment and inexpensive housing.

Sometimes the caregiver is a professional who works at a more typical assisted-care facility nearby. And later, when more folks need care in the community, they might become full time help there. The best part of this scenario is that caregivers grow to be much more than hired help; they become part of the community.

Smaller houses in senior cohousing are designed to improve lifestyle.

Size Matters: Square Footage

Keep it warm, keep it elegant, keep it cozy, and keep it within budget. Smaller houses in senior cohousing optimize affordability in more than just the obvious way. Size also directly affects lifestyle, in that the smaller it is, while still keeping it comfortable, the easier it is to clean. Moreover, smaller size usually means better materials can be used in its construction – and the better the materials, the less to fix later on. Smaller also means more money for the common house which is where community life is enhanced.

Typically 600 - 1,000 square feet, these one-bedroom homes are quite livable, with the kitchen, dining, and living room all in one; and the bedroom, bathroom and 'plus room' (office type space) off to the side. The 3,000 square foot common house supplements every house, so in effect every individual unit is a 3,600 to 4,000 square foot house.

Living in Otium

A number of residents at Otium sat down and talked with me about their community. Included in the conversation were: Else, a 71-year-old retired secretary; Anders, a 75-year-old retired head master; Leif Behrend, a 69-year-old retired factory owner, other cohousing residents who happened to pass by during the discussion, and myself, Charles.

Charles: In Denmark, you are able to retire at the age of 60, and that means that you probably have more than 20 years left of your life. You have to ask yourself the question: "Do you want your golden years to be on your own terms or in the terms of others?"

Anders: Well, you can't just sit and wait for the government to help you.

Else: One of my reasons for joining this new cohousing group about fifteen years ago was that I wanted to create a life in my old age that motivated and inspired me to be active. I wanted to make my own decisions and I wanted an easier life here than I had when I had to take care of a big house and garden and all of that. I didn't want to feel dependent on my children. It would give me peace to show them that I could take care of myself and it would release them from that burden.

Charles: A lot of people say: Why not just build the cohousing community, and then later, find people to live in them?

Leif: Yes, they say that. I'm proud to tell you that we have been involved in the process from the beginning, and because we participated in the planning of our new home, the project became an exact answer to our needs – not another bureaucratic or businessman's estimation of our needs. The trick was to let the professionals do their jobs, but be clear about what we wanted.

Anders: From September '84 to spring '88 we met once a month to discuss the ideas that we had about living together in a community. Most of us knew each other from the beginning, because we came from the same town in Denmark, but during the meetings, we got to know each other better and better. One could say that we actually built the social community even before moving in.

Leif: Those who simply wanted separate houses left and those who wanted to live in a shared house left too. But those of us who decided to go on with the process, came to the conclusion that community was what was important to us. We wished to live in a friendly connection with others but we all had a healthy respect for each other's privacy.

Charles: You could say this is in the middle between a lot of support and no support in your life.

Else: Yes, each resident maintains his/her independence and chooses how much s/he wants to participate. You can see that the houses are situated like that on the site: we have a small garden on the other side of the house where you can choose to be by yourself and where the other residents visit only if they are invited. There are backyards I hardly have been in, in these 15 years in this cohousing community.

Charles: It's obvious that with senior cohousing in Denmark there are not as many cooperative activities as with mixed cohousing, such as in Trudeslund, where they have common dinners seven days a week.

Else: Our cohousing is only for retired people. Only seniors live here. In Trudeslund, most of the residents are young people with jobs and children to take care of. They need a lot of support and they have a lot of support. Their cooperation is used to make everyone's life easier. People there have young children, and have careers where both parents work. Here we have the luxury of spending a couple of hours deciding if we'll have an additional dinner this week or not. In mixed cohousing where people have jobs, kids, and belong to the PTA and 15 other organizations, they just want to figure it out once and not talk about it again for twenty years. In mixed cohousing half of the common activities are planned. In senior cohousing maybe only 20 percent is fixed. Most things that we do together we figure out day to day.

Charles: Many elderly feel that their lives are changing, and the surroundings don't fit their needs anymore. Was the idea of becoming really close neighbors with each other designed to address your real needs?

Another Otium Resident: Yes, it's a good feeling to know that my neighbors in cohousing care about me. It's very important for us to feel safe in our homes and our surroundings.

Anders: And in the cohousing community, there's always someone nearby in the daytime and at night. I lived alone in a house before I moved to Otium. When the children were small it was easy for me to get in touch with the neighbors, because we had the children in common. But in my older years I was all alone in the house and all the other houses on the street, with all the young people and new families, were empty in the daytime. Here there is great importance attached to social contact. The fact that people are always home makes us feel secure and (laugh) we simply can't help meeting each other when we step out of the front door.

Leif: We also feel safe taking a trip, because we know that there will always be someone to keep an eye on our house while we are gone. We haven't had any crime here at all in the 13 years I have lived here.

Charles: Does living in a cohousing community make it a more pleasant, less expensive, or easier way to live?

Anders: I pay 6000kr ($1000) in rent per month, which is a little higher than my rent before cohousing.

Else: Yes, but I think because of the shared facilities there is the feeling of getting more for your money. I spend half as much in costs, outside of rent, as I used to. But I think we all agree on the fact that it isn't because of any economic interest that we live at Otium. And although it's obvious that our costs are lower, we live here for dozens of other more important reasons, such as emotional support, rather than just to save money.

Anders: Frankly, we bring people together like this to live in a cooperative community where our emotional well being is as important as our physical well being and, most importantly, without treating each other in a self-conscious kind of way where people say: "Now, how are we today?"

Leif: Compared to the time when I lived in my own house, I now feel that my responsibilities are reduced. But, even though it is easier to cope with life at Otium, we still have the responsibility to make the community work. Once a month we meet and have a special dinner together and then we have the opportunity to discuss problems and make democratic solutions and agreements.

Anders: In this way, problems don't get out of control. It's very important that some people take leadership roles in the group, because that ensures that everything is taken care of. Besides all the rules we

have worked out together, we don't really have many committees here because we simply expect people to use their common sense.

Else: One could say we have unwritten rules about having the discipline and responsibility and the will and the strength to cooperate with other people in a community.

Charles: It is indeed life-affirming to hear you talk because you sound so vigorous together. You want to take your future into your own hands and make your own decisions. You have dreams that you want to realize and it really sounds as if you take life as a gift, not as a burden . . . sometimes you get the impression that aged people practice the negative in the fact that they are getting old. They lose their strength, feel depressed and lonely, and then they become an economical and social burden to society.

Else: People get in-home nursing care from the government if they want it, but we don't need as much help from outside as we would if we lived alone. It comes naturally for us to take care of each other here. In some settings taking care of each other is a burden. Here it becomes more of a privilege.

Anders: The town has an economic interest in supporting our cohousing community and has profited from the several senior cohousing communities being built here. It seems to help the economy of the town when elderly people move out of their big houses. Back in the 50's Birkerød was a village in the countryside and there was a farm here where the cohousing community is now situated. Then in the 50's and 60's Birkerød suddenly grew very fast, which meant the prices for houses were rising. The people who moved into the houses that we left are people with a good income and that has been great for the local economy.

Yet Another Otium Resident: That's what it all is about. The newcomers have double income – and are therefore double-good taxpayers (laugh).

Leif: We influence the culture in our society; we are the visitors, who have the time. That's good for the town, too.

Residents of Gimle Senior Cohousing.

Gimle
The Hurried

Birkerød, Denmark
12 Units
Architects: Frederiksen & Knudsen
Completed: 1993
Tenure: Cooperative

In ancient Nordic mythology Gimle was a house in heaven. Here warriors rested after their battles in the company of gods. In 1993 when this senior cohousing group settled on a name they chose Gimle.

Gimle was initiated by the local branch of DaneAge (a senior advocacy group similar to AARP) in the Copenhagen suburb of Birkerød. In the early nineties a group in DaneAge Birkerød was debating senior housing issues while another group was looking for a site for a new senior housing project.

The two groups eventually got together and decided to make a senior cohousing community. They quickly finished their version of Study Group I (see Chapter 7), and with help from the municipality they found a site and a developer and finished their feasibility work. A couple of state grants helped fund the project. And they were off to the planning and development phase (their version of Study Group II).

Getting It Off the Ground
In order to get its grants the group had to work very quickly. Luckily their architects were very well versed in senior cohousing design. The potential shortcoming of such a tight schedule was off-set with an exhaustive options package, where the seniors could choose between a variety of interior finishes. The architects then designed Gimle as traditional Danish row-houses along a street resembling a small

village. The down payment per unit was about $33,000 (200,000kr), resulting in a monthly payment of $830 (5,000kr). At the time these houses were relatively affordable. In 1993 the project was finished and the seniors moved in.

Despite having started out as a group, the new residents didn't really feel like they knew each other by move-in. There had been too few discussions about how the social life should be in Gimle. At first they decided to have common dinner once a month – but only in the winter months from October through April. Soon some of the women found that that this was much too seldom, so they started getting together once a week and arranged common dinners and other events. Later, another group started to meet weekly to play bridge, and little by little most people joined in. An aerobics class in town that two women were attending also drew more residents to it, and later they started doing their aerobics in the common house together. In this way the residents of Gimle slowly built a wide range of social activities that, in turn, helped to develop their sense of community.

In 1993, Rita Svendsen, 72, was among the first residents to move into Gimle. She used to run a shop selling home-made chocolates in Birkerød, but retired ten years previously. After her husband died she lived alone for some years but she grew increasingly tired of taking care of a big house on her own. When she first heard of Gimle she contacted DaneAge and got an apartment at Gimle. Rita is visually impaired, and after she was treated for a tumor on the pituitary gland she became very sensitive to fevers.

If her temperature exceeds 101 °F she falls unconscious. The other residents at Gimle are very aware of her condition, and each morning they make sure that she is up and doing well. This gives her an enormous sense of security.

Dan Nielsen, 69, is a retired engineer. He tells how his children visit more often since he moved into Gimle. "It's also a great relief for them to know that we're happy here; that we have someone to talk to." The grandchildren also come more often now. They think Gimle is a fun place.

Overall, Gimle is a fairly well-functioning cohousing community. As a testament to its success, more than 40 people are on Gimle's waiting list. There is no doubt however, that the community would have been fundamentally different (and better) if the residents had been given the time to go through a thorough programming and design process, instead of being forced into taking what was essentially a finished senior cohousing package developed by outsiders.

The semi-private area in front of the house creates a soft edge between the private and the public space.

A private balcony in Gimle.

and goes bowling with some of the other residents, and he is sure that if it had not been for them, he probably never would have started doing it. The residents also arrange common trips to the supermarket since only half of them have cars.

All of these outside activities leave little time for residents to do their required community work – planting, repairs, and the like. Getting all this community work done can, at times, be a problem. To ensure that the maintenance work actually gets done, the residents of Gimle have developed a system of 'time banking' (it was developed after they moved in). All residents have to participate in common work tasks for a certain amount of hours each year. Residents who work more than they are supposed to save up hours in the time bank. For those who work less, they accumulate a deficit. The hours can then be bought or residents can pay them back by working more hours the next year. This system allows people to save up hours for their senior years while they still have the reserves of energy. Or it can simply allow people to pay the community for their absence when they don't have the time to participate in the common work.

Overall, the system of time banking has proved to be a very successful program, so much so that other senior cohousing groups have created interesting variations on it that are wholly germane to the sensibilities of their own community. For example, in another senior cohousing community, residents start out with a requirement of having to perform 20 hours per month of common work (including common dinners). This amount then decreases to zero hours per month

More than most senior cohousing communities, it has become a community for individualists. Nothing seems to appeal to the entire community, but the diversity of the activities means that there is something for everybody: classical concerts, university lectures, trips to art exhibitions, sailing, long distance bike trips, bowling, or just games of petanque on the community street. As Eigil Nicolaysen, 72, puts it: "You hear about what other people are doing and that often gives you the inspiration to try it too." Eigil does yoga

Visionary design doesn't do it alone. Mariendalsvej Senior Cohousing was meant to be the ideal new type of senior housing but it turned out to be a complete failure.

after 20 years of residency. In yet another senior cohousing community, if you perform charity work out in the community-at-large then those hours are counted, or partially counted, towards your cohousing community work responsibility.

These Danish senior cohousing time banking systems work because residents who move in, stay (there is a considerable wait-list to get into each community). Moreover, like any other small village, older seniors are expected to do less: they did their share, and younger residents respect that. New residents therefore come in with the expectation of doing a little more than the older, more tenured residents.

In truth, however, residents work more community hours than required, for as long as they can. They simply enjoy contributing to their community in a meaningful way.

Mariendalsvej
A Cautionary Tale

Copenhagen, Denmark
22 Units
Architect: Box 25 Arkitekter
Completed: 1992
Tenure: Rental
Common House: 4,735 sf (440 m2)

It rarely happens that a cohousing community misfires. Usually disputes within a cohousing community are minor and can be solved without jeopardizing the community itself. It is very rare that a cohousing community fails. Nonetheless, this is what happened in Mariendalsvej.

Inspired by the success at Midgården, the first Danish senior cohousing community, the Danish non-profit organization "Lawyers' and Economists' Pension Fund" initiated the Mariendalsvej cohousing

*Perspective sketch of
Mariendalsvej Senior Cohousing*

project. Their vision was to enhance the life of seniors by creating a rich community life. They would achieve this by creating a housing development that, featuring individual apartments and various daily functions and activities, would make the lives of the residents more convenient, more fun, and more engaged – the very qualities that distinguish senior cohousing from typical institutional senior housing. A rich community life would therefore emerge, and the institutional character of too many senior facilities would be avoided. A noble plan, to be sure.

Best Intentions

A group of consultants and architects were commissioned to develop the project, and the 22 units were to be part

of an informal community that future residents could participate in as much as they desired. The architecture was meant to combine three elements: urban life, community, and sustainability. The senior group was actively involved in the design development process – monthly meetings, field trips, and the construction of multiple models (1:1 mockups of parts of the interiors were even included). The Lawyers' and Economists' Pension Fund supported them financially, in conjunction with the Danish Ministry of Social Affairs and Energy Authority (a department of the Ministry of Economic Affairs). The resident group found a site in the Copenhagen district of Frederiksberg and the Fund then financed both the purchase of the site and the construction of the project.

At Box 25 Architects, the two architects commissioned to do the design came up with a rather non-traditional scheme – a four-story brick clad building with a gigantic curved roof. The building would contain fourteen one-bedroom apartments (840 - 960 sf) and eight two-bedroom apartments (1,020 - 1,100 sf). The extensive common facilities would include a large common room with an open fireplace, and indoor swimming pool, a large room on the top floor, guest rooms, and a garden. This design was approved and construction began.

From the beginning, the bold appearance of the new building in its late nineteenth century surroundings drew a lot of attention to the project. Significant media attention prompted paradigm-changing speculation. Was this the new way of housing seniors; was this an all-new way of looking at seniors and their needs? But despite all of the official governmental support and the best intentions of the participants, one crucial factor was overlooked: the Fund hadn't signed up enough tenants to fill all of the available units. This resident shortcoming was partially because the Fund let the project get too expensive, and partially because they tried to limit purchase to members of the pension fund itself.

The Fateful Sellout

Despite the massive public interest in the project, it proved difficult for the Fund to find tenants within its own membership rolls. Within the Fund itself, general interest among high-income prospects was low – these individuals had very particular demands and expectations and found the apartments to be too small.

Moreover, the Fund found it difficult to convince them about the advantages of cohousing. Despite protests from the existing group, the Fund, running out of options, decided to sell the remaining 18 apartments to anyone – not just those people in the Fund who were interested in senior cohousing. The Fund vigorously marketed to people who first and foremost wanted to buy a house in the area, arguing that the "community" can be built with the new residents, and after move in. For these open-market sales, the concept of cohousing was tacked on as an afterthought. This was a devastating turn of events for the future of the cohousing community.

When Cohousing Isn't Cohousing

The new buyers liked the location, and could afford the increased prices. However, none of the new buyers bought into the cohousing concept. The project was sold out and completed; and among the new residents were five of the original six initiating households. These five households tried their very best to generate interest among the new households in cohousing-style living, starting with common dinners (they'd built state-of-the art common facilities after all). However, no one was interested in the basic cohousing principles of common decision-making, cooperation, compromise, and consensus. Some even openly obstructed it. They refused to see the virtues of living as a member of a diverse community, or the benefit of cooperating with their neighbor on anything, and therefore doomed the cohousing effort. In effect, even before the community had been created it ceased to exist.

As the last remaining resident from the original Mariendalsvej cohousing group, Ole Hersfeldt seriously considers moving out.

Mariendalsvej Today

Today, Mariendalsvej functions like a better-than-average condominium project (they do indeed have nice common facilities), and gather together as a group usually once a year for a holiday party. But the residents otherwise have little or no social interaction with each other. The common rooms are rarely used and the community that seemed so promising a decade ago – this new way of housing seniors – has become noteworthy not for what it is, but for what it failed to become.

Lessons Learned

While the reasons for this particular group's failure to create a viable cohousing community are obvious in hindsight, there are nonetheless some lessons that all prospective cohousing groups need to consider.

Perhaps the most important lessons learned from Mariendalsvej are those having to do with a resident group's formation processes and its leadership roles. Involved professionals likewise must understand the cohousing concept well. Problems in the partnership between the resident group and the professionals become manifest in many interlocking ways:

1. Cost control.

Without a strong core resident group to hold the line in terms of budget, there is real danger that costs will creep up beyond the reach of potential residents who are interested in the cohousing concept (a select pool of potential buyers). For a developer, increased building costs simply mean the final selling price will be proportionally higher. Usually not a problem when a property is sold on the open

The Aftermath

The original resident group of six households were passionate in their wish to create a community together. But as the members of this group grew more and more disillusioned with the direction of their failing community, they gave in and moved out. Four households departed in short order; a fifth hung on for a time but finally called it quits; and as of this writing, one last originating household remains. While they still live there, they don't try to organize anything any longer. They are also considering moving out.

market (a bigger pool of potential buyers). As for Mariendalsvej, the costs problems were made worse because the architect (the lowest bidder) had no cohousing experience, and no sense of cost control. Costs didn't creep up, they escalated. This priced potential cohousing buyers (a small pool) out of the market, which increased the developer's risk beyond what it thought reasonable. In a panic, the developer put the remaining unsold units on the open market, thus dooming the cohousing community.

2. Original intent.

Without the leadership of a strong resident group, the developer may not fully support, or perhaps even understand, the cohousing concept enough to see the project through with its original intent intact – that of creating a cohousing community. In Mariendalsvej, as costs escalated the Fund (the developer) lost track of the project's mission and sold out the cohousing concept in favor of selling units. Instead, the developer should have asked themselves: "How do we serve these future residents who went out and secured the funding grants, who helped get the project approved? How do we fulfill this model of housing that we set out to create?"

3. Feasibility.

Without a strong group process (where a group of people embark on the common task of developing the project, committing themselves, and taking responsibility), the opportunity for group formation and bonding is utterly lost, and the community itself might fail. In the case of Mariendalsvej, the group's lack of

cohesiveness and will allowed a developer to start the project too quickly for its own good. And the developer, failing to appreciate or understand the cohousing concept, failed to perform basic cohousing feasibility studies and market research. The result was that, prior to construction, (since the developer failed to match 22 households with the project's 22 units) it was impossible for them to determine if their market had 22 households that could both afford the units and would buy into the cohousing concept. A strong resident group would naturally address questions like: What "should be" the unit prices for

Mariendalsvej senior cohousing has state of the art common facilities but they are rarely being used.

Private balcony at Mariendalsvej.

residents matches the number of units from inception to move-in. However, in the real world potential residents enter and leave the group at different times for any number of reasons. That's life. But when households leave the group, the group itself is not in peril. A committed core group can (and does) fill vacancies through aggressive recruiting and marketing efforts, typically done at key times during the development process. However, if basic feasibility work hasn't been done appropriately, the task of filling the community will be all-but impossible, as the experience in Mariendalsvej testifies. A cluster of condos is not cohousing, and all of the window dressing in the world will not make up for a cracked foundation.

Otium, Gimle, and Mariendalsvej are three organic models from the infancy of Danish senior cohousing. The faltering attempts of the senior groups made it clear that the random method of making senior cohousing wasn't efficient enough. Obviously there was a need for a non-organic, highly deliberate method. In 1995 Henry Nielsen of 'Quality of Living in Focus' gathered the experiences of ten years of senior cohousing projects in Denmark and created his extensive three study group model of how to make successful senior cohousing. The model has made the process easier and more satisfactory for everybody involved: seniors, officials, developers, and architects. Earlier, potential residents might have had good reason to be reluctant to embark on the process, but with Nielsen's three study group model they could now do it with confidence. Behold Korvetten.

cohousing in its market? What can each household in the resident group afford? A developer might not address these basic questions. A "you can add the community after move-in" philosophy simply does not create cohousing. Prospective buyers cannot be forced to buy into in the cohousing concept itself: An individual or family is either predisposed to cooperating with neighbors or is not – no one is not going to be "talked into it."

4. Recruitment and marketing. In an ideal world, the number of potential

A tight knit resident group is the key to a successful senior cohousing community.

Korvetten
The Streamlined

Munkebo, Denmark
16 Units
Architects: Clausen & Weber
Tenure: Rental
Completed: 1998

Since 1995, many senior cohousing communities have been built with the three-phase study group method. Because it is a process that delivers results, it should come as little surprise that 20 of the last 25 cohousing projects built in Denmark have been senior cohousing. Not that there is that much more demand for senior cohousing over regular cohousing (there are plenty of young families), it's just that the senior groups are more organized. To see the result of the three-phase study group method you have to study the Danish senior cohousing projects built after 1995, and look at the method itself.

Korvetten senior cohousing was initiated in 1996 by the municipality in the city of Munkebo (pop 5,740). In the 1960s, steel workers from all over Denmark moved to the town to work at the expanding local shipyard. Now this generation bulge was slowly reaching the retirement age and the need for more adequate senior housing was imminent. The municipality contacted 'Quality of Living in Focus', and together with Henry Nielsen they arranged a public information meeting to find out if there was any interest in creating senior cohousing in Munkebo. Sixty people showed up, a number that far exceeded the expectations of the facilitators, 47 seniors then attended two seminars following the meeting, and eventually 42 decided to start on Study Group I facilitated by Henry Nielsen. This was considered to be too many individuals for one cohousing community so the

Hanging out in the common yard.

group was divided in two, with the aim of creating two senior cohousing communities.

The city council found two sites and voted unanimously to support the projects. The advantages for the municipality were obvious. The seniors would get great housing, existing rental housing would be made available for others and most likely the seniors would have a better quality of life and need less home care.

The first resident group had 22 members in the ages between 52 and 78. Their Study Group I turned out unexpectedly successful. Somehow the group members built up such great confidence in each other that they could discuss almost everything – even private matters that they wouldn't usually have shared with strangers. Maybe it was the many common experiences from the shipyard (where a lot of the residents had worked), that made them bond so strongly at an early stage in the process. They soon started doing things together

outside the Study Group program like parties, trips, and folk high school stays. They also started common traditions like an annual Summer Solstice Party long before move-in. Some of the more shy residents even felt that the experiences with the group changed their personality in a positive way. It made them more self-confident and extroverted and it significantly enhanced their general social life.

Encouraged by the initial success, the city let the group choose the architect and developer themselves and together they made the mandatory local area development plan for the site – a highly unusual procedure. Three city officials were appointed to help the group and to smooth out the planning submittal process. The developer, without much interference, then let the group design with the architect and the project advisor. Their building site was beautifully situated on the

Kertinge Bay and it was even close to a supermarket, a doctor's office, and public transportation.

The seniors and the architect designed the project as five one-story buildings with private houses and a common house surrounding a large common yard. The residents envisioned that the yard could be used for a variety of common activities: barbeques, parties, games, or just hanging out together on a bench in the shade.

The twelve private houses were designed in three sizes 625 sf, 825 sf, and 900 sf, all with a full or partial view of the bay. All front doors faced the central yard and from the large bay windows in the private kitchens residents can follow what is happening outside. The common house was designed with a kitchen, a large dining-living room, a laundry room, a guest room, and a storage space. Moreover, the building was placed near the parking lot to serve as an entrance to the community. Unfortunately the first proposal went 30 percent over the budget but the developer made a list of potential cost-cuts and then let the residents decide which of them they wanted.

In June 1988 the seniors moved in with an air of optimism. "I'm going to live ten years longer, now that I've moved into senior cohousing!" one man vigorously stated. The residents named their new senior cohousing community Korvetten after an old type of sailing-ship.

In general they had been very satisfied with the community-creating process. All agreed that the three-step Study Group method had been the key to their success. Their experienced project advisor was especially valuable because he actually

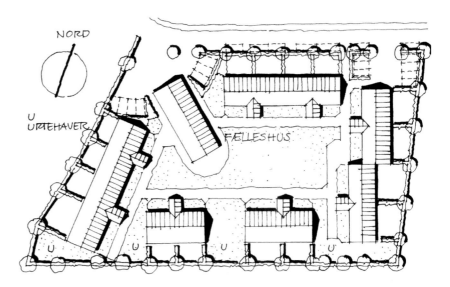

Site plan of Korvetten

knew a good deal of the answers to the seniors' many questions. It was also an advantage that he worked independently of the municipality and the developer.

Today Korvetten is a well functioning senior cohousing community. The fact that the resident group is so tight-knit, means that the residents run the community with practically no interference from the developer and the city. Problems like neighbor complaints are solved within the group, mostly without even voting. The residents themselves also manage the waiting list of future residents.

All involved admit that Korvetten would not have been built, at least not so successfully, without the three-phase study group method and the deliberate community building processes it produces.

PART THREE

Creating a Senior Cohousing Community

ased on decades of Danish experience in creating senior
cohousing, what follows is a system specifically designed
to build a senior cohousing community from the ground
up. Divided into four distinct but interlocking parts – Feasibility,
Study Group I (group formation), Study Group II (participatory
design process), and Study Group III (policy) – this approach is
a proven and practical process that builds not only the physical
neighborhood, but weaves the social fabric of the community itself.

*Nevada City Cohousing resident group in
one of the preliminary meeting.*

Feasibility
Do We Have a Project?

When people first discussed the cohousing concept in the mid-1960s, (the first cohousing project was built in Denmark in 1972) they knew what they were rejecting, namely the isolation of single-family houses and apartments. But they did not know what exactly to replace it with. Through group discussions, they pieced together a realistic alternative. Later groups built on these ideas, each reevaluating priorities and the degree of community desired. Through these discussions, and the lessons learned, cohousing as a notion and an actual living experience evolved.

Bellingham Cohousing resident group.

(the recent experiences of pioneering American senior cohousing communities are discussed in Part Four).

The Core Group

In the United States, a cohousing community typically begins when a small group of people, a single family, a group of friends, or even an individual, decides that cohousing might just be for them. Maybe they know somebody who lives in a cohousing community. Maybe a friend waxed eloquently about it over dinner. Maybe they read a book like this one. Or, as is increasingly the case, experienced developers like The Cohousing Company and Wonderland Hill Development will initiate the process and provide the means for interested households to create a core group.

Whatever the cause or method, and regardless of who or how many people constitutes this core group, these individuals must determine whether or not their dream community has a chance to become reality. As necessary as this feasibility phase is, it is too often under-considered (or unconsidered), leading to the planning of a cohousing project that should not have been planned, or should have been planned differently.

The Core of Feasibility

Feasibility in terms of senior cohousing is simply taking the time to consider the big-picture details. These details create a long list that requires close attention and a sharp pencil. But with the help of someone who knows what they are looking for (an advisor can really help here), it's not a daunting task, and can happen quite quickly.

In the early days, a cohousing community could take as many as five to eight years to go from the first meetings to move-in. However, since cohousing is better known and much more clearly defined, that full-cycle development process can now take as little as two years, or less. Today, groups in the planning process of their community can visit existing cohousing developments. They can take for granted issues such as common dining, smaller individual residences, peripheral parking, community bylaws and covenants, not to mention the community-building process itself.

In the same way the American experience in building mixed-generational cohousing closely corresponds to its Danish precursor, we have found that the Danish experiences for building senior cohousing are directly applicable to developing senior cohousing in the United States. The exceptions are regionally specific issues: site identification, methods for its acquisition, and financing options

A complete and exhaustive overview of a potential project in a given area is the first job. Some of the points to consider are:

- Where are the multi-family zoned sites?
- What uses can be rezoned to multi-family?
- What are the constraints?
- How are comparably sized houses priced?
- Who are the best land brokers in town?
- How can we find sites not on the market; who do we have to contact?
- Where are the services, neighborhoods, public transportation facilities that we want to be near?
- If we build here, here, or here, what will the development costs be?
- What toxins are there, and what will it cost to remove them?
- Who does the best soils work in town?
- What are the costs of earth and infrastructure work for the site?
- What are potential off-site infrastructure costs?
- If we build here, here or here, what are the houses likely to cost?
- If the realtor is not working fast enough, who else will we get to work for us?
- What is the town's experience with planned unit developments? Variances?
- What are people particularly sensitive to these days? Cutting down trees, noise, light, traffic?
- Are there wetlands, artifacts, archeological remnants, natural amenities, bird habitat, etc., that need to protected?
- Budgets, budgets, budgets.

Getting It Built

Building a cohousing community can be a daunting undertaking. The sheer number of details alone can cause some groups to stumble. However, it is not necessary for any group to reinvent this wheel or go it alone, especially at these early discovery phases. The Cohousing Company and others provide a "Getting-It-Built" workshop that is designed to get a group up and running in short order. Though this workshop can even help a core group identify a site, usually we recommend that a core group (no matter how small) identify a site before proceeding into any further development, as a site gives tangible focus and purpose to a group's efforts.

Size Matters

The size and number of households seems to be one of the big challenges facing Americans in terms of their housing sensibilities. The American "bigger is better" mentality isn't necessarily desirable for senior housing developments; and senior cohousing communities in Europe have shown over and again that the optimum size is not too big, and not too small. Create a community that is too big, and an institutional feel and sensibility will result. Create a community that is too small, and the community will become more like a large family and not a neighborhood of actively-engaged households.

In Denmark, a senior cohousing community usually features between 15 to 25 households. And while 20 households is widely considered to be the optimum number, sometimes economics dictate that a community will need as many as 30. Beyond 30 households, it is best to split the development into two or more separate but parallel projects. Regardless of the number of households in a given senior cohousing community, there consistently seems to be about 1.3 people per household, per community.

I dwell on this issue because Americans seem less willing to give adequate consideration to the social side of cohousing developments: Size is subjective, and therefore malleable, right? Not really. At any given scale of community size, the social patterns within each are, in fact, very predictable and almost entirely the point for bothering with it all in the first place.

Muir Commons house blocks layout from design workshop.

Creating a Cohesive Organization

In this challenging feasibility phase, groups often have difficulty maintaining their focus. Identifying (though not yet acquiring) a good building site often serves to rally the group because it lends direction and momentum to what can otherwise be a rather abstract project.

With the site identified (or decided upon), numerous paths lead to focusing the project and creating group cohesion. With the help of its advisor, a group can start the Study Group I process; it can assess and even finish the feasibility of the project prior to starting Study Group I; or it can conduct Study Group I and feasibility assessments at about the same time.

At this point, a group will likely be quite anxious. With so much work already done and perhaps even palpable pressure coming from elsewhere (maybe a group must put down option money for a site soon or lose the option), a group typically wants to get their project built. Right now. As a result, they may want to put off the community-building aspects of the project for later, and as necessary. This is a mistake.

Once a site is identified, for the core group to proceed efficiently it must first take the time to develop an effective working structure, explore shared values, and sharpen its group process skills as it forges a development strategy. What this core group creates now in terms of process and decision-making structure is the foundation of the larger community to come. The more cohesive the core group, the more clearly-defined its goals, the more feasible the project will be.

Development Strategy

Sometimes the development strategy is decided by the initial core group without exploring all possible alternatives. While groups in the fragile early stages need to be careful not to discuss so many possibilities that they never move forward, they do need to consider carefully what is the most appropriate strategy for their particular situation. How many households will their community ideally contain? Will the resident group act as developer? Should they joint venture with an experienced developer? How can the group best accommodate the concerns of local officials?

Questions such as these should be asked early on. If, for instance, local officials and neighborhood organizations are concerned about preserving open space, a design that addresses that concern is more likely to gain support. Conversely, there have been many cases where officials just want to overload requirements in order to address current citizens' feelings about stopping growth. Luckily, cohousing usually presents so many pluses that insightful officials are keen to champion the project. Cohousing addresses so many current issues, including affordable housing, sustainable design, infill housing, strong communities and neighborhoods, support for seniors, and so many more that neighbors and municipalities often support new cohousing projects.

The Quest for a Site

Many groups, no matter how organized, unified, and focused, have been frustrated by the search for a site. It has proven to sometimes be better to get professional help here (it's hard enough for them to do it) – experienced professionals who know what they are doing can work and act more quickly to

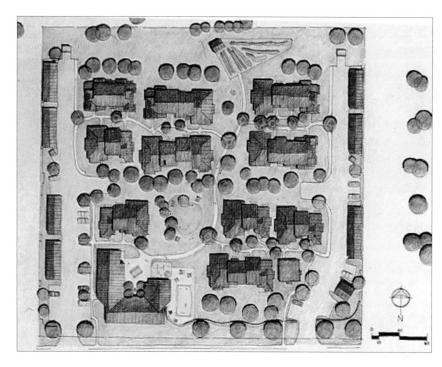

Sonora Cohousing site plan.

the benefit of the core group specifically and the larger group to come.

In urban and suburban areas, sites are often expensive and hard to find, and competition for appropriate sites can be fierce. Core groups consisting of just a few households have to compete with experienced developers; developers who are familiar with the steps involved in securing land and can act quickly to make decisions and put up option money. In rural areas, zoning, septic system requirements, and the cost of off-site improvements can rule out many otherwise ideal sites. All these challenges make finding and securing a site a watershed moment in the cohousing development process. Because a small core group of households may not have enough capital or political muscle to move quickly on a potential site, the actual acquisition of the site may have to wait until the community achieves a critical mass of households (Study Group I).

Why Would Developers Get Interested in Senior Cohousing?

1. Marketing – it seems that most developers are always second guessing "what the market wants." It amazes me how many millions go into trying to answer this question and yet only 70 percent of the answer is right. Why not ask the market directly? Why not build communities where future residents actually tell the developer what they want? Why not build senior cohousing?

2. Buyers – pre-qualified buyers means less risk.

3. Powerful allies – there's nothing like a group of motivated seniors who, interested in developing a new senior cohousing community, help get a project approved (even a project larger than their own). These organized, voting seniors are extremely effective in getting elected officials to listen and act.

4. Gratification – there's nothing more gratifying for a builder than meeting a group of people who want a village, building it for them, and then seeing a life of neighbors between the buildings that simply isn't seen anywhere else.

5. Success breeds success – Cohousing communities anchor the success of a new neighborhood. A recent case and point is Elitch Gardens in Denver, Colorado, where a new 32-unit cohousing community successfully energized the social and marketing efforts of a much larger development of many hundreds of units.

Pleasant Hill Cohousing

In any case, in order for a resident group to move toward site acquisition, they must begin thinking less as consumers and more like developers who are willing to take the initial risks required to get a project off the ground. Before a resident group (regardless of its size) can know what is possible for a site – even how many units can be built at what cost – money must be invested (unsecured and completely at risk) to answer other feasibility questions, such as soils and toxic analysis, design viability, and legal investigations.

Throughout this feasibility process, these resident-developers must constantly assess the obstacles that may threaten the project, and must face difficult questions along the way: Can we obtain planning approvals for the number of units necessary to make the project financially feasible? Will the soil give us the percolation for our septic system? How much will financing cost us?

So what is a core group consisting of just a few households to do? They have a potential site, and have to move fast on it to get an option, but don't have all of the finances necessary to both get the site and conduct all of the feasibility studies. And they certainly don't have luxury of time (at this moment) to go through the entire Study Group I process to build out their household numbers, and thus achieve that critical mass. What to do? In this case, it might be best for the core group to take a step back and partner with a developer.

The Developer

In our experience, when a core group of residents partners with a developer, their project moves faster, more efficiently, and is less costly (especially if the developer knows how to work with a cohousing group). My wife, Katie, and I have actually gone into the development business to facilitate the advancement of new projects (when required) and sometimes in partnership with Wonderland Hill Development out of Boulder, Colorado.

As architects with a great deal of experience in what it takes to design a successful cohousing community, we'd rather just do that – design successful cohousing communities. However, to make that happen we've had to ask ourselves, "What do we have to do to move a cohousing group forward? Conduct seminars?! Write a book?! Learn about development?!" The answers are, yes, yes, and yes.

Working with a Developer

Core resident groups that partner with an experienced development team – project manager, developer, architect, lawyer, and other key consultants – reap huge benefits in terms of actually moving their project forward. The ideal development team has vast experience in residential real estate development and also understands the specific needs of the cohousing process.

This partnership is especially valuable for core groups who wish to create their community in urban and expensive areas where few developable sites remain, and land as well as pre-development costs are exorbitant. In these places, the high costs of development leave little room for mistakes during the complex process of getting a project through the planning approvals, financing, and construction. The developer not only manages this process, working with the architect and other consultants, but can also take on some or all of the risk associated with housing development.

The Role of the Developer

The developer's job can encompass some or all of the following roles:

- Targeting properties and assessing the feasibility of each
- Coordinating pre-development work such as toxic assessment and soils testing on the site, and working with design professionals
- Facilitating the acquisition of planning approvals and permits
- Financing some or all of the pre-development costs
- Securing outside investors to provide required equity
- Arranging for construction financing
- "Signing on the bottom line" to assume the risk for the construction loan
- Hiring contractors and consultants
- Overseeing the construction on a day-to-day basis
- Absorbing some of the risk (i.e. cost) of unsold units
- Occasionally becoming the target of blame for delays and frustrations
- Budgets, budgets, budgets

This position demands experience and expertise. In terms of cohousing, it's important that should the project fall through or units remain unsold, the developer does not solely bear the project's financial risk. The group has to share in this liability, or even take it on. Otherwise the developer has license to make many non-cohousing, unilateral decisions – like selling units to whomever they please, whether or not the buyers are interested in cohousing. Developers who build cohousing must exercise impeccable integrity and understand and share in the cohousing spirit with the resident group.

Developers most often work on a risk-for-profit basis. In a conventional residential project, as the budget is created, 10 to 20 percent of the total selling price is generally targeted for developer and investor profit. In speculative housing, this profit is simply included in the price of the house, and the buyer has no way of knowing what corners may have been cut in order to ensure the developer's profit. Certainly, many developers are conscientious in their building practices, but in speculative housing development, countertops and floor coverings are what sell houses to prospective buyers, rather than less visible features such as quality wall construction and solid foundations.

Pleasant Hill Cohousing under construction.

There are many possible relationships between a developer and a cohousing group, reflecting varying degrees of risk and therefore control assumed by the residents. In the end, whoever has the most money at risk ultimately makes the final decisions. But knowing and separating the two roles makes it a much less stressful experience for all involved. Certainly, it is not always easy for a group to work with a developer, no matter how sympathetic that developer might be to the cohousing concept. Developers are generally no more accustomed to working with groups than groups are accustomed to working with developers.

On one extreme, a cohousing group might see a distinct advantage of building a project without an outside developer, meaning the resident group takes on the full risk of their project themselves. Taking all the risk means they are able to avoid potential conflicts with a developer over design and process because they maintain complete control over the project within the group. Empirically, in the U.S., this scenario has led to projects taking longer and costing more, or sometimes not happening at all. It has also led to wonderful finished projects, but it is no doubt a much more difficult route.

On the other extreme, a cohousing group could essentially concede all risk to the developer. The developer then pushes the project through the inevitable financial and political obstacles. However, this imbalance can lead to developer-imposed changes that threaten to change the character of the given community. As time lines and budgets tighten, a developer who bears all of the risk might not consult with

In a cohousing development, on the other hand, the residents who are planning their community make these professionals feel more accountable, and the quality of the work itself is a higher priority. Residents may initially question the percentage of profit that a developer stands to receive, until they come to understand just what they are getting for their money.

Ultimately, it is at least partially out of the developer's profit that unexpected delays or cost overruns are taken. The developer must be able to predict budgets and time lines with enough accuracy to maintain the prices that buyers are expecting to pay, and still earn a living. Taking all of this into consideration, developers might:

- Finance some early pre-development costs, such as architecture
- Help with project feasibility
- Help coordinate consultants
- Underwrite construction financing

THE DEVELOPMENT PROCESS

	FEASIBILITY STUDY	**DESIGN**	**CONSTRUCTION**
PROFESSIONAL TRACK	FIND A GROUP DO BUDGETS FACILITATED BY ADVISOR/PROJECT MANAGER	PROGRAM AND SCHEMATIC DESIGNS TO SITE COMMON HOUSE AND PRIVITE HOUSE ARCHITECT	ENTITLEMENT, CONSTRUCTION DOCUMENTATION, CONSTRUCTION ARCHITECT AND CONTRACTOR

ONE MONTH

		STUDY GROUP I	**STUDY GROUP II**	**STUDY GROUP III**
GROUP TRACK	DATA BASE OF 25 INTERESTED COMMUNITY MEMBERS ORIENTATION WEEKEND	CONSCIOUSNESS RAISING FACILITATED BY ADVISOR WEEKLY FOR TWO HOURS	DESIGN FACILITATED BY ARCHITECT (3) WEEKEND MEETINGS	POLICY FACILITATED BY GROUP WITH OUTSIDE HELP AS NEEDED MEETINGS ONCE A MONTH FOR 2 HOURS

the resident group on tough decisions. The result might be that the common house is tiny, or the site plan is compromised because the developer didn't have anyone to help argue their case at City Hall, or the houses all have one of everything (washer/dryer, storage shed, guest room), meaning there's actually no reason to have anything in common, or that autos go to each house guaranteeing to short circuit the long term success of the community. In all cases, community is stunted because residents will not be able to cooperate as much.

These above-mentioned extremes are not just theoretical – real cohousing projects have chosen each extreme for their own development process; and all encountered frustrations in their chosen process. In general, a more middle-ground approach where a developer works in true partnership with the resident group makes a great cohousing process and a great place to live, as long as the roles are clear.

It is vital that a developer allow a group access to information that will affect the project. Before taking a developer onto the project, the core group should not hesitate to check the track record and financial background of anyone they are considering. Likewise, a developer should be up front about his or her financial position, since a strong financial

statement is essential to getting a project built. Groups have to be wary of promoters, i.e. folks who may have good intentions, but don't actually have the wherewithal to pull it off.

Beyond providing information, the developer needs to be thoroughly acquainted with the hard realities of budget and time constraints in order to advise the residents about the consequences of their decisions, while still allowing them to weigh the possibilities for themselves. The developer's role is by no means easy, but as cohousing groups across the country are discovering, it's easier than developing it themselves, and always seems to be less costly.

Financing

One of the principal hurdles to determining the feasibility of a cohousing development can be in getting a construction loan. On the whole, banks do not understand the cohousing concept, and what they do not understand they are reluctant to finance. But now that cohousing has a viable track record, this is becoming less of a problem. Committed buyers who have already invested time and money into the project, and a developer with a good track record, are usually readily financed.

Support for Seniors

There's a world of help out there for seniors who are interested in creating their own senior cohousing community. This help comes in the form of organizations ready and willing to give advice or provide practical assistance. Taken in combination, they provide a huge knowledge base for issues of concern to seniors.

The nearest sizeable town to the cohousing community we are currently building, is Grass Valley, California, population 10,922 (US Census 2000). Some 22 percent of the population are over the age of 65, meaning there are around 2,400 seniors in the area. Those seniors have access to a fairly impressive range of services, given the size and relative isolation of the city. What follows is just a partial list:

- Nevada County Department of Community Action
- Nevada County Adult and Family Services Department, a part of the Human Services Agency
- Nevada County Senior Center, which provides a drop-in center as well as a centralized source for information
- SeniorNet, an educational service teaching seniors how to use computers
- High Noon Senior Nutrition Program, for both congregate nutrition and home-delivered meals
- Legal Services of California, providing paralegal assistance for elders
- A4AA Friendly Visitor, matching volunteers to homebound seniors
- RSVP of Nevada County, a program helping retirees and seniors to volunteer their spare time
- Paratransit services, offering door to door transport for local trips
- Senior Outreach, registered nurses assisting seniors in obtaining in-home services to prevent premature or unwanted institutionalization

There are similar associations and organizations available in most towns. All are there to promote the interests of seniors, who can be approached for advice and support with your cohousing project – from putting the word out to recruit potential members, to providing meeting space, to sponsoring Study Groups I and II, to supporting your project during the City planning meetings, to providing services once you live there. This kind of support is worth knowing about in Study Group I, and worth understanding in detail in Study Group III. And at the end of Study Group II, these folks can be great assets in the political process of getting your project approved. The best way to proceed is to go meet with them and see what they do.

In fact, this commitment can be a group's most powerful bargaining tool throughout the financing process. A bank considering making a construction loan wants to ensure that the project will be completed, and that the loan will be repaid in a timely manner. The existence of committed buyers (and, ideally, a waiting list) may ease the concerns of a bank asked to finance an "alternative" housing type. Another advantage of working with a seasoned developer is that they have to explain very little to the banks.

The Non-Profit Approach

Over the years the Danish organization 'Quality of Living in Focus' has established a method for creating a new senior cohousing group that is strikingly efficient. It augments the system created by Henry Nielsen. As soon as 25 names are registered in the national database for senior cohousing in any given city, the organization initiates the process of getting the project organized.

Meanwhile, one or two "project coordinators" from the organization go through the phone book for that city

Strawberry Creek Cohousing, Berkeley, California

(particularly government and non-profit sections which deal with senior concerns), and set up meetings with the directors of three or four different agencies that provide services for seniors.

At the same time, they meet with nonprofit and for-profit housing developers involved with low-income housing. They say, "Look, you're in the business of making affordable housing and you sometimes do senior housing. We have 25 households who need and want affordable housing, and a few who can afford larger houses to help offset the costs of the smaller units. We've been talking to city officials and we think that there is

the potential for real cooperation here. In addition, because this is cohousing, future residents can help bring pre-development funding to the project."

Finally, the project coordinators meet with the local for-profit developers who specialize in building clustered-family housing projects. The project manager also sets the Study Group I process in motion (see Chapter Seven).

Like most Danes, most Americans are not familiar with housing developers. Some current developments are attractive enough, but their basic structure does not support the goals and needs of a senior cohousing community. However,

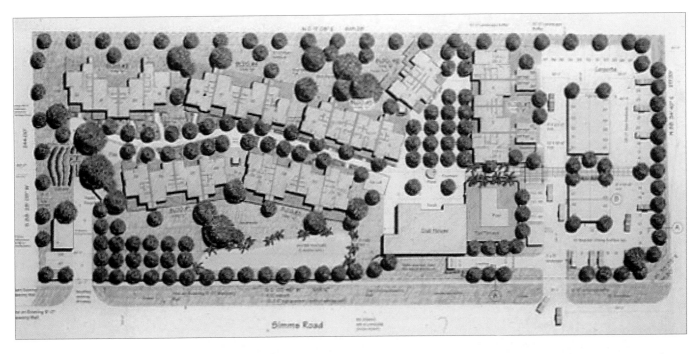

Site plan of Synergy Cohousing,
Delray Beach, Florida

with input from cohousing groups and
dedicated design professionals, there's
no reason why a nonprofit or a for-profit
organization couldn't build some excellent
senior cohousing communities in the
United States. Since 2002 BiC's funding
has been sharply reduced, a number of
private consultants have taken over. Their
intention is just the same. As soon as 25
people in any given area are motivated to
move into senior cohousing, it's their job
to help them achieve that goal. They will:

- Find local resources, and interview
  them to find out how they can help
- Find sites or find a way to find a site
- Carry out site feasibility studies
- Help find a developer
- Help find the group a venue to hold
  Study Group I
- Help find teachers for Study Group I
- Help facilitate Study Group I, if
  necessary
- Help find an experienced architect
  for Study Group II

Final Preparations

Once the core group's project has proven
its feasibility, it's time to build the larger
community itself. A larger group of
prospective cohousing residents will
not only meet and get to know each
other, but they will participate in honest,
straightforward, and realistic discussions
about what senior cohousing is and what
it isn't – and together they will learn
what it means to manage ordinary and
extraordinary tasks as a group, to age in
place, and to build a community of their
own from the ground up.

Group of visitiors at Munksøgård.

CHAPTER SEVEN

Study Group I
Is Cohousing for You?

The cooperative life of senior cohousing offers residents a way to live independently longer; and to have a more practical, more convenient, more healthful, more interesting, and most importantly, a more vibrant life along the way. However, not all individuals are suited for the cohousing life. Other than moving into and living in a cohousing community, how does an individual find out if cohousing is right for them? The answer lies in Study Group I.

When older, it's wonderful to have neighbors who can easily come by.

Looking out for number one, in the context of senior cohousing, means learning how to live daily within the cooperative context of a larger neighborly group. This is not something most Americans have truly experienced before. As such, it is a skill that must be learned.

Study Group I is where prospective residents will 'grow into' cohousing and discover for themselves how suitable cohousing is for them. They do this by sitting down and working through the issues of their project with their prospective neighbors. Along the way participants will learn to relax, talk and walk a bit more deliberately down a different, more purposeful path. And when done, participants will have established the key social foundations and agreements in their community – co-care limits, decision-making procedures, legal agreements, and more – before the process of planning for and building their homes actually begins.

Getting Started:
Initial Informational Meetings

Study Group I usually begins when the core group of initiating households, an advisor, a for-profit developer or non-profit developer (after determining the feasibility of a senior chousing project), places a notice about the proposed project into local media outlets.

At the end of this first meeting, interested people can sign up for a follow-up seminar – Study Group I. Meanwhile, the initiating party will contact other key parties, namely a developer and/or an advisor or architect, and schedule them to present at a later date during the Study Group I process.

The chief expectation seniors should have for Study Group I is to learn whether joining a specific cohousing group is for them. To paraphrase writer Ayn Rand, "In the end, each of us looks out for number one." Stoic and strong words, indeed, though somewhat off the mark. Only by cooperating with others will each of us truly look out for number one, though this takes a little while to learn.

Study Group I

The initial meeting is over and the Study Group I sign up sheet has filled up. It's time to start the actual process of building the community. In this case, community building begins with night classes. Typically held as a series of classes at a community college, adult education school, community center, senior support office conference room or somewhere similarly accessible, Study Group I classes begin by reiterating the senior cohousing highlights addressed in the initial informational meeting:

- The principles of senior cohousing
- What it might be like to live in a senior cohousing community
- The process of getting through a project
- How to work together in a group
- Basic cooperation and participation possibilities for individuals and households – common dinners, committee work, common work days, and so on; and how each facilitates aging in place, independence, and quality of life.

As the classes progress, the aim is to allow potential residents to comfortably explore the issues of senior cohousing prior to actually joining a cohousing group. They are not designed to coax anyone towards senior cohousing. Rather, the intent is to explore the issues of the day, e.g., living in a car-oriented society as it relates to growing older, and to help participants decide whether or not senior cohousing's benefits, and limitations, will provide positive solutions to them personally.

Community Values

There's community values, and then there's community value – the value of community to an individual versus the cost of maintaining that community. At this stage in Study Group I, monetary cost is not at issue. Time is the issue. Specifically, time spent in meetings for the group to come to consensus over any given issue.

Since community consensus is a cornerstone of the cohousing concept, and is usually a new concept to all involved, it is no surprise that the number one concern about cohousing has to do with meeting time. This is perfectly understandable. People, using their own experience, know that achieving consensus is difficult enough in a single household. But a community of twenty households who are just getting to know each other? How is that even possible?

First and foremost, each household or individual must understand that when meetings take too long the value of the community diminishes. Each must learn not to make a mountain out of a mole hill, and to trust others do things without requiring the involvement of the entire group.

In cohousing, community problems large and small are most efficiently solved when the big group brainstorms a solution, refines it, then delegates the implementation to a committee. In this way, the community's values are intact and the value of the community is not diminished.

These classes leave plenty of room for discussing and discovering issues like aging in place and co-care in the context of senior cohousing. In fact, existing senior cohousing communities often ask prospective new members to take Study Group I classes before deciding to move into their community. As the Study Group I classes continue, participants can expect to:

- Have guest speakers
- Discuss and participate in activities for seniors
- Meet people from established elder cohousing communities
- Meet older residents from intergenerational cohousing
- Learn about courses and events for seniors
- Participate in role-playing exercises designed to address specific living situations

Top 10 Reasons People Choose to Live in Senior Cohousing

1. Health
Social connections facilitate physical activities, meaningful purpose, and a general sense of well-being. It is well researched that social connections extend life and give people a reason to stay fit.

2. Safety and security
"Before living in a senior cohousing community, very few of our neighbors were home during the day. And sometimes we felt vulnerable. We no longer feel this way." Enough said.

3. Community
Everyone wants to feel welcome somewhere and have camaraderie and mutual regard, relationships and the rest. Community makes life more interesting and more fun. A sense of belonging, identity and yes, accountability, are all basic ingredients of the good life.

4. "I don't want to be a burden to my children."
The kids live farther away than ever before. Yet these grown children still feel the need to "come home." In senior cohousing, because neighborhood life unfolds just outside the front door, one's children are relieved of having to feel like they have to "do things" for their parents all the time.

5. The food
In senior cohousing, just because someone lives alone doesn't mean they have to cook and eat every meal alone. Common dinners provide variety and companionship. Good food, shared with friends is the spice of life.

6. Impact on the planet
Senior cohousing provides one with a chance to live lightly on the land. Shared resources mean all of the environmental aspirations one might have can finally be achieved.

7. Kindred spirits
Senior cohousing allows people to build a community of actual peers. Even in an intergenerational neighborhood, seniors may find themselves among young people who are not that familiar with events that had a large influence on their lives, for example, the Vietnam War.

8. Life's maintenance
When upkeep on an old house isn't fun any more, when it costs too much, when the quality of hired-out work is suspect, then it's time to think about moving on.

9. An appropriate house
People who desire a smaller house that meets their needs like a glove rather than a grocery bag will find it here. Houses in senior cohousing are more accessible, more energy efficient, and cheaper to live in than traditional housing. In addition, the community's common house allows residents to live big while living small.

10. Financial good sense
Living in senior cohousing is cheaper – a lot cheaper – than the alternatives. Sharing resources and not having to maintain a big house are obvious money savers. Compared to the traditional alternatives, senior cohousing can be about one-half as expensive.

- Learn about conflict resolution and effective communication
- Find out about how senior cohousing projects are financed, and where to go for personal financial advice
- Learn the general issues of setting up a residents' association
- Visit an assisted living complex, although many will have already done so for a variety of reasons. When a group visits together, however, the experience is extremely focused, and even sobering.

Right from the start, potential residents are participating. They are, in effect, building community. In addition to the set agenda, seniors are encouraged to openly discuss and digress into any specific issues most dear to them. Through this process they eventually cover all community tasks, particularly co-care. This process ultimately helps the community to set formal, reasonable limits later on. Unforeseen details can be worked out along the way as they arise, even after move-in.

This is obviously a lot of ground to cover. As such, these classes are typically held twice weekly for three months, with several weekend workshops along the way. As the classes progress, the issues become more complicated. Participants are asked to consider:

- Is senior cohousing really for me?
- What are the likely financial commitments before, during, and after construction?
- What are my real, individual issues with getting older? Within a community?

- What does it mean to age-in-place?
- What sort of agreements about shared responsibilities do I want?
- How will co-care be handled?

Since community building is part of Study Group I, class trips may be organized, such as boat outings, bicycle rides, and country walks. Sometimes groups even have camping trips where their hopes and aspirations are discussed around the campfire. Whatever the activities, members get to know each other and to learn to trust each other. Said one resident afterward:

"Those meetings created an openness between us as we learned each other's strong and weak sides. Without those meetings, I would not have the same relationships I have with the others."

The involvement of residents from the earliest planning stages motivates them to take responsibility for the project's success; it allows them to understand the restrictions that must be imposed and the choices that must be made. "Professionals" would like to think that, if left to them, everything in a given project will work "just fine." Often times when professionals run the show it doesn't go well , as witnessed by the Mariendalsvej project. The strength of the group is the soul of the project.

As it turns out, the self-selecting nature of the Study Group approach itself directly addresses this very real concern, and I might add, quite effectively. Which is to say that these planning phases, especially Study Group I, are designed

Cooperation and Participation

Many things help define the quality of a cohousing community. One of them is cooperative participation. For those individuals who are not inclined to cooperate on a community level, they should consider very carefully whether or not cohousing is right for them. It might not be. Cooperation, of course, takes many forms. In the case of cohousing (beyond the basic willingness to live cooperatively), cooperation typically means:

- Individuals cook a common dinner about once a month
- Individuals belong to one of perhaps a dozen committees
- Individuals participate in common work days (if they are able), about six times a year

But most importantly, whatever the issue of the moment may be, cohousers are willing and able to sit down and talk it through.

At the end of the day, cooperation and participation can be difficult to require, but good recruitment efforts address this difficulty with its built-in self-selection process.

When people go through Study Group I, and particularly Study Group II (where real design decisions are made), they will ask themselves: "Do I like these people?"; "Can I work with these people?"; and "Do I trust these people?" Usually, though not always, people know by the end of Study Group I if cohousing is for them.

Hanging out in front of the common house of Sonora Cohousing.

to help people decide, for themselves, if senior cohousing is right for them, right up front, not after they have moved in. By using a Study Group approach from the start, individuals who have difficulty listening to others quickly exit the group. Those who have a difficult time being diplomatic either mend their ways, or leave. People with inflated egos – those who can't help find the highest common denominator solution to a problem over their own pet solution – bow out. This is the self-selection process in action.

A Resident Group Emerges

After these classes and activities, a dedicated group emerges (ideally about 25 households). These people have decided, at least in principle, that senior cohousing is for them. Moreover, they have found they are comfortable working with others in general and with their group specifically. These individuals, now fully informed and prepared, can then move on to codifying the social and economic structures that form the foundations of their community. The real work is about to begin.

Social Structures

Before we address the "whats" (committees to create, co-care agreements to make, economic structures, etc.), we need to address the "hows" (observations and techniques acquired from over two decades of building cohousing communities), that will keep a resident group on track as the Study Group I process continues. What is started in Study Group I is finished in Study Group III.

Who Cares for Who?

The processes of developing a regular cohousing community and a senior cohousing community are similar in many ways. Both types of communities involve land-acquisition, site planning, design considerations, a strong group process, and the development of community agreements. The senior cohousing process differs in that residents lay out the boundaries and expectations of aging within the community. In open, honest, straightforward, and realistic discussions, residents determine for themselves to what extent other community members will or will not care for each other.

In multigenerational cohousing, once the group forms it usually moves into the actual development phase at a rapid pace. By contrast, participants in a senior cohousing project are, as a rule, more deliberate about each decision and each step – the personal issues at stake are more complex and intimate. Since philosophies and realities of aging are so personal, it takes time for a group to effectively address theses concerns as a community.

That said, in Denmark senior cohousers often do not assign routine tasks to particular individuals, and yet things run smoothly, in a free-flowing fashion. Co-care is the number one concern before move-in, but the problems in reality are seldom anywhere near as great as anticipated.

Three Methods

After watching hundreds of groups in action, there seem to be three main techniques that groups employ (consciously or not), to create their finished cohousing community. And two of them don't work all that well.

The Marathon "Turn over every rock and reinvent"– Deliberate to a fault, this type of group conducts lots and lots of meetings. One group, for example, met every Saturday for eight hours over a period of two years. That's two years before they even broke ground. They eventually got their project built, but they wore each other out. As well, this particular project experienced significant design problems: tired out, they built whatever they had almost agreed on at the time of exhaustion. Moreover, they overspent and had to make cuts at the last minute to stay within budget. Generally speaking, when cohousing groups feel they have lots of time to get things done, they tend to overwork things. Continuity can be lost when a particular problem is discussed over several weeks with different people. Bottom line, this grindingly inefficient group process poses a real threat to the success of a given cohousing project.

The Sprint "Let's take the shortcut" – No time to reflect, the group runs too hot, too fast, and therefore omits the crucial community-building experiences. Intent on rolling through every phase as quickly as possible, whoever is on board does all they can to just hold on. Inevitably, and ironically, it's an inefficient and frustrating process that takes a long time to finish (costs commonly exceed budget), and it quickly burns out the participants. People try to fill in gaps that the group doesn't allow time to be filled in; and over time, small problems become big issues because every missed issue or event simply aggravates the next. Even more importantly, a sense of ownership is missing or stunted and the resulting lack of community is palpable.

The Jog "Pace yourself!" – Going at an even and comfortable pace, this method strikes the balance between the mad dash and the never-ending slog. This group has a master plan (the Study Group Approach), everyone is on board, everyone has input, and therefore everyone has a stake in a positive, meaningful outcome. Because each issue is addressed in its due time with a weight that's appropriate to its merit, the group's plans, as if by magic, continually move forward. Best of all, a community based on trust and cooperation – the very definition of cohousing – is created. A group utilizing the Study Group Approach can expect about 9 to 12 months of planning to reach the construction phase itself. And once construction is finished the residents feel a profound sense of accomplishment – they formed it, they built it, they love it, "now let's live it!"

The Participatory Process

While the creation and development of every cohousing community is different, the participatory process itself is a universal aspect in every community. Regardless of whether the resident group forms with the intention of developing a specific site; or if the group establishes its goals and objectives before a site is found; or if a group of friends starts the process rolling; or if an outside entity ignites interest within a larger community, a cohousing community is literally defined by the active participation of its residents, from the earliest planning stages to move in and beyond.

Of course, some cohousing groups work better together than others. How well a group works together is not so much defined by the individuals of the group itself, but by the skills those people have learned early in the development process. Over the years I have seen some truisms emerge: Groups that institute thorough and deliberate development group processes have fewer, shorter, and less-frustrating meetings. They appear to experience better results through every phase of the building process. They enjoy a life that most closely matches their ideals after they actually move in. Finally, and most importantly, they enjoy the process more.

The cohousing development process shows participants new ways to see the world, and above all, it sharpens their listening skills. In some ways cohousing

The Psychology of Getting Older

Some folks get angrier as they get older. The cause of this anger is as complex as the individual, though the catalyst is often quite common. Boredom. Many seniors, acustomed to working and contributing in a meaningful way, find that retirement is not an escape but a frustration.

Studies show that busy seniors don't get as angry. Building and living in a vibrant cohousing community takes energy. Group members are busy. But the senior cohousing lifestyle returns these efforts many fold through meaningful, dependable, readily-accessible relationships. Study Group I helps seniors to see how, in the context of a senior cohousing community, they can live a truly active life.

is just an excuse to learn how to be more patient, tolerant, educated, and thoughtful. Conversely, when individuals are badly informed, or uninformed, about the particulars of cohousing's tried-and-true group participation process, their project will invariably experience any number of "unforeseen" problems.

Group Process

The single most important attribute in the creation of a cohousing community is a coherent, fair, thoughtful group process. More important than money or land, a capable group process can solve any problem or issue. Not having a good process is like a carpenter trying to build a house without tools – he has the raw materials but can't do much of anything with them.

Study Group I, the process of discussing issues at length before site acquisition and design (a feature unique to senior cohousing), provides the best opportunity for a group to refine its methods of working together. It is a 'boot camp' for group

process, and prepares a resident group for Study Groups II and III, where group decisions are made in rapid fire.

How exactly the members of a given group determine their group process is up to them. Meeting formats and styles vary, but the most successful groups devise a system where everyone has an opportunity for input. Without this feature, a few people can easily dominate the discussions, thus negating the community-building spirit that the participatory group process is designed to create. For some topics small group discussions work well in this respect, as do "round-table" discussions where each person has an opportunity to comment on a topic. The job of facilitating meetings is usually rotated within the coordinating group, or within the entire membership, or is facilitated by an outside advisor. Some communities have found that small groups that meet between common meetings allow for more informal, hence less intimidating, discussions. This "meeting within a meeting" format not only allows people to gain a better understanding of the issues and of other's opinions, but also decreases the need for long discussions during common meetings. The end result is that the big group decisions are made more efficiently.

Decision-making procedures also need to be carefully considered and agreed upon early on in the planning process. Most cohousing groups try to use consensus as much as possible, but fall back on a majority or two thirds vote when time pressures require a prompt decision. Some decisions may also be delegated to committees.

Psychological Preparation – by Olaf Dejgaard, resident of Munksøgård Senior Cohousing

As part of our journey towards living in our own cohousing community, some of us decided that a little psychological preparation might be useful. The change from living alone to becoming one of a group of 24 looked like a real challenge. So we attended a course about psychology in cohousing. I can still remember some of the 'catchphrases':

- Express yourself, don't hide your feelings, make yourself easy to read
- When a conflict seems impossible to solve, imagine that your counterpart may be just 5 percent right, and try to identify the main problems with his/her point of view

In December of 2000, shortly before moving in, we decided to formulate our own course, concentrating particularly on the handling of conflicts. We decided that everybody should attend. We hired a psychologist with experience in conflict studies, and the course ran for five hours on three consecutive Sundays. The main topics were:

Types of conflicts
- Instrumental conflicts about goals, means and methods
- Conflicts about resources
- Conflicts about values
- Personal conflicts

Solutions to conflicts
- Avoidance, fleeing, giving in, sarcasm, making excuses
- Use of aggression, attacking, threatening, use of violence
- Meeting and discussing openly, accepting disagreement, examining the issue, being clear

The language of conflicts
- Being conscious of the words you use, using relaxing instead of escalating language
- Using 'I' language instead of 'you' language
- Listening right to the end instead of interrupting
- Using open questions instead of leading ones
- Focusing on the problem rather than on the person

Escalation of conflicts (Disagreement)
- "The other person's fault"
- Other problems come up
- Dialogue is abandoned
- Personal hatred, not just disagreement
- Other people become involved
- The protagonists end up having to avoid one another, "this town isn't big enough for the two of us"

Perhaps the most important part of the course was the many different points of view and opinions which were presented, and which gave us a richer picture of those we were going to live with.

Having lived in Munksøgård for four years now, I think we have succeeded in developing a viable, and a valuable decision making culture. We have avoided making decisions that would be detrimental to any one member of the community. We have taken the time needed, sometimes letting a problem lie until a better proposal came up. We discuss proposals and work toward the solution until there is almost no resistance. For example, when we built a 55 square meter shelter we had around 40 sketches of position, size and shape before everyone was happy. The color of our houses was discussed for months (I didn't get what I wanted), but all the possibilities were examined, the majority got the color they wanted, and in some strange way my mind was at ease.

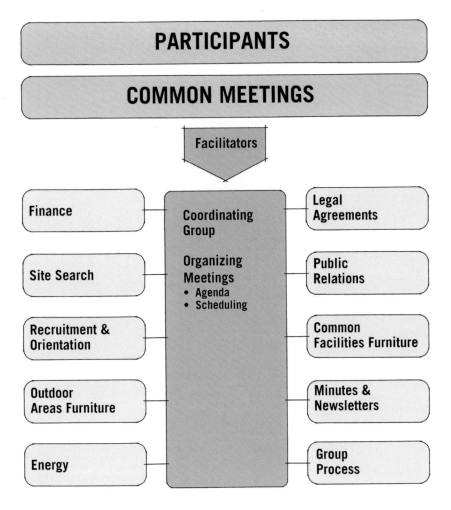

PARTICIPANTS

COMMON MEETINGS

Facilitators

Finance

Site Search

Recruitment & Orientation

Outdoor Areas Furniture

Energy

Coordinating Group

Organizing Meetings
• Agenda
• Scheduling

Legal Agreements

Public Relations

Common Facilities Furniture

Minutes & Newsletters

Group Process

Committees ebb and flow as required. If something needs to be done, a few people get together and do it and call themselves a committee. When no longer needed, they dissolve. Some form of this is engaged to eternity. This structure for forming committees is introduced in Study Group I and refined in Study Group III.

and work methods must be established early on. The most common method is for people to join a committee, as their services are required. These committees come and go as they are needed – up and running when there's something to do, gone when there's not. The committees may work with consultants on complex issues such as financing or technical considerations, and then present options and recommendations at common meetings where decisions are made. Typical committees include:

- Coordinating Committee (keeps things on track)
- Financing Committee (show me the money)
- Energy Committee (investigates energy options - solar, etc.)
- Public Relations Committee (Hi. How are you?)
- Membership Committee (recruits and orients new members)
- Common House Furnishings Committee (Beautiful. Now we just have to get it here)
- Landscape Committee (examines needs and desires for outdoor areas)
- Facilitation and Process Committee (Thank you. Next.)

Ultimately, a group's goal should be to create a fair and democratic policy – there is no better way to create trust. And with relationships based on trust, people can achieve and accomplish much more as a group than with any other process.

A participatory process need not entail endless meetings and discussions. However, anyone who has ever built anything of significant scale, whether it's a school or a church or a community, knows that it requires working with others. As with any other effective business venture, efficient organizational structures

This participatory group process isn't always easy. No matter how well intentioned or planned, conflicts invariably arise. Impassioned people form passionate opinions. The challenge is for strong-willed people to give the more timid a voice; and the more timid to make their opinions heard. Those individuals who are hesitant to provoke others, and those who are prone to steamroller over others, are both deferring and delaying the real problem at hand – communication.

Accommodating Conflict

Building a senior cohousing community is about open communication and if a given individual or group is unable to discuss sensitive, delicate topics together it's better to discover the extent of those limitations early on in the process. But how do groups discover those limitations?

A qualified advisor knows the issues, is unafraid to raise them, and all the while remains sensitive to the needs of the individuals within the group. With hindsight, the most common criticism people have of their own group process is not having an experienced enough advisor during each phase of the process. It's also worth noting that the more provocative the advisor, the more productive the experience.

Seniors (like everyone else) should be formally introduced to the art of speaking with others in a way that best assures appreciation for what they have to say. Everyone has heard of the "crotchety old man" – someone with a bad attitude who doesn't endear himself to his neighbors. Sure, an impatient, unyielding know-it-all could be just as lovable as anyone. But first the layers of angst and anger need to be peeled away. Only then will that person be ready to receive the love and appreciation they deserve. I have seen many angry seniors (the "I'm never going to get that novel written; I didn't spend enough time with my kids when I had the chance," sort of anger), in the course of planning a cohousing community, become lovable again.

The Small Town Effect

The impact a community can have on an individual is positive, powerful and well documented. Here's what one senior cohousing resident had to say about her community:

> "I wake up in the morning and look forward to a visit from at least one friendly neighbor. There's an element of surprise and interaction. Here, I feel a strong sense of belonging ... of caring and being cared about."

The secret is simple. People thrive in a community that interacts and cares. The town of Rosetta, Pennsylvania, has been the subject of numerous studies to discover why such a high percentage of its residents live to be well over 90 – an age significantly above average. Surveys show the people here smoke at an average rate; they eat red meat, and drink wine. Such studies repeatedly show that the number one reason for their longevity is the town's heightened sense of community.

People who enter into a senior cohousing community plan to bond with their neighbors in a caring fashion. However, what compels a person to care about others is a more difficult question. When people create a project together, or make dinner for each other, or spend time with each other year after year, they begin to really care about each other. In a small village like Rosetta, when residents do things for the community and help others, they earn respect. And just like neighbors in a small village, cohousers earn a sense of mutual regard. While proximity helps to make this sort of co-care feasible, the "glue" is caring: There is no overestimating what people will do for each other when they care a great deal about one another.

If you've ever lived in a small town, you know that the community takes care of you. My grandmother, Dorothy Durrett, lived in a such a town (Downieville, California, population 325) for her final years. About fifteen of her neighbors and friends kept an eye on her, brought her food, her medicines, movies, stories, and gossip. That's what happens in a community. Another good friend of mine, Geoff Quinn, died recently aged 77 in Goodyears Bar, a town in northern California with a population of about 90. Again, about ten people came by on a regular basis to stoke the fire, give massages, change his bed, take him to his chemotherapy sessions, and a hundred other things he needed help with. All of that supplemented the help he received from other institutions such as the local health clinic, and HMO outpatient services.

When 77 year old Margaret in our Doyle Street cohousing community was diagnosed with breast cancer, it was an honor to drop in on her on my way to or from work, and take her a coffee, read the paper to her for a few minutes, tell her stories about our projects under construction around the country. Through her last six months we had three or four projects under construction, and Margaret loved hearing about them and comparing their experiences with ours at Doyle Street.

As for senior cohousing communities in general, there are, practically speaking, 30 to 50 people nearby if a person becomes ill. These people are the 30 or so residents of the cohousing community, plus the family, friends, medical organizations, nursing establishment, and so on. In other words, 30 people above the norm – a small town worth of people – who live right next door. Five minutes here and five minutes there, all just a part of the ebb and flow of daily life, can mean the world to someone who is ill.

Care for the Elderly in Asia

Kala is a woman who I had the good fortune to sit by on a recent flight I took to Chicago. As I spoke with her and her mother, I was amazed at the difference between the way that people care for their elders in India vs. here in the U.S.

Throughout Asia, (India, China, the Philippines, Taiwan, Indonesia, etc.) there is another system of care. For the most part, the extended family, and in particular the children, take care of the elderly. If the children have moved away, to the U.S. for example, they can afford to hire help back in the Far East to take care of Mom. Labor is still relatively cheap in Asia, and there is extensive professional training in care for the elderly. In addition, in these Far East cultures a great emphasis is placed on inter-generational socializing. Kala said:

> "I made my children from age two spend a minimum of one hour conversing with their grandparents at each visit. They had no choice in the matter. I wanted them to get into the habit of sitting down with them and talking, and it worked. Now my 30 year-old daughter, who is a busy physician, comes over and talks with my mother once every weekend, for at least one hour."

Professional care supplemented with consistent and profound family interaction provides a complete care package. Americans and Europeans may have more than covered the professional side, but the family side is too often lacking. Senior cohousing as a lifestyle is designed specifically to make up for this western culture's social deficiency. After all, not all of us have a Hindu mother to guide us and make certain we will be properly cared for in our old age.

For the sake of building a viable community that enhances the quality of life for everyone involved, individuals need to be able to listen, reason, and find common cooperative ground. Said one Danish senior cohousing resident:

> "Some people in our group were very good at processing information and at the same time keeping the stress level low. Others were not. But because people are here for new life experiences, even at 70, they are motivated to learn to communicate in an open, honest, diplomatic manner."

Very talented effective communication teachers can be found everywhere in the U.S., and they can really help a group to learn how to communicate effectively.

Outlining the Boundaries of Community

As a group develops, it is important that members be honest about the issues before them. Developing a senior cohousing community is the perfect venue to explore the issues regarding the fourth quarter of one's life. A lot of ball games are won in that fourth quarter.

Participants in these discussions confront the realities of living and aging (mostly individually and how a group fits into that), and plan for their future together by examining the issues important to them. The conclusions drawn from these discussions will help the group to set some basic community boundaries. Then, once everyone in the group is in agreement about their community's boundaries, the group is ready to consult with an architect and initiate the design phase (Study Group II).

The following section highlights some of the bigger issues that every senior cohousing group will eventually consider as they build their community.

Aging in Place: the What and the How

This seemingly straightforward issue is, in fact, a far-reaching topic. On the surface, aging in place is merely about living in one location, as well as possible, for as long as possible. This definition answers the question, What is aging in place? But what about the real question: *How does one age in place?*

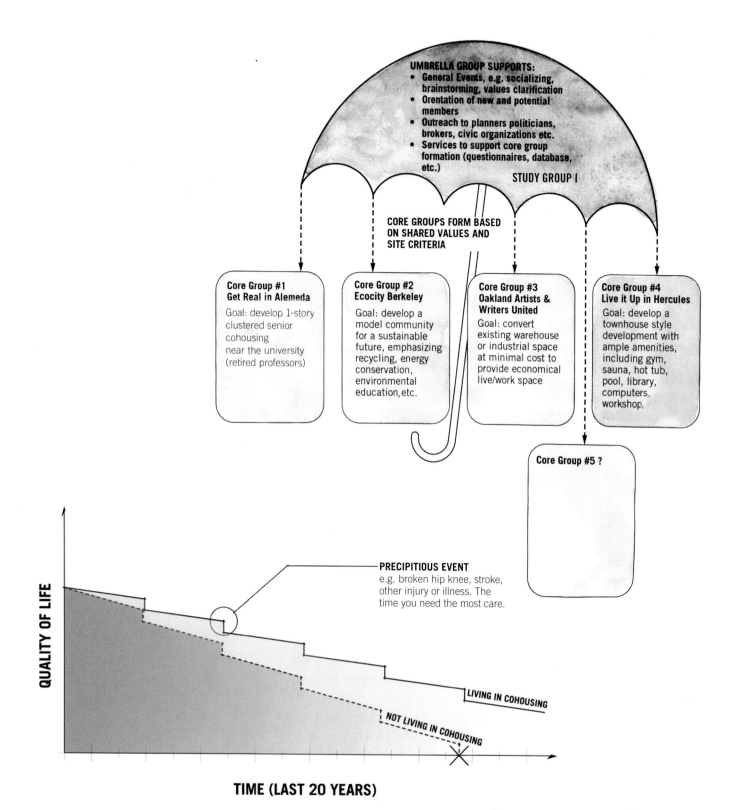

UMBRELLA GROUP SUPPORTS:
- **General Events, e.g. socializing, brainstorming, values clarification**
- **Orentation of new and potential members**
- **Outreach to planners politicians, brokers, civic organizations etc.**
- **Services to support core group formation (questionnaires, database, etc.)**

STUDY GROUP I

CORE GROUPS FORM BASED ON SHARED VALUES AND SITE CRITERIA

Core Group #1
Get Real in Alemeda

Goal: develop 1-story clustered senior cohousing near the university (retired professors)

Core Group #2
Ecocity Berkeley

Goal: develop a model community for a sustainable future, emphasizing recycling, energy conservation, environmental education, etc.

Core Group #3
Oakland Artists & Writers United

Goal: convert existing warehouse or industrial space at minimal cost to provide economical live/work space

Core Group #4
Live it Up in Hercules

Goal: develop a townhouse style development with ample amenities, including gym, sauna, hot tub, pool, library, computers, workshop

Core Group #5 ?

QUALITY OF LIFE

PRECIPITIOUS EVENT
e.g. broken hip knee, stroke, other injury or illness. The time you need the most care.

LIVING IN COHOUSING

NOT LIVING IN COHOUSING

TIME (LAST 20 YEARS)

Caregivers in the Common House

As members of a senior cohousing group age, accommodations should be made to allow for caregivers to reside on-site for extended periods of time. The best place for this on-site residence is the common house itself. Therefore, it is extremely important that the common house operate comfortably as both a common space and a private space. This dual-purpose requirement, however, seems to present a huge challenge for most architects. It turns out that the more experience an architect has, the more likely it is that he or she will be able to accommodate this seemingly challenging request. A small handful of architects in Denmark do half of the senior cohousing projects there.

Suites in the common house are a convenient, temporary place to stay for guests, visiting family, and live-in caregivers. Residents agree upon how many suites they want to build during Study Group II. Sometimes with only 20 households there will be as many as four suites. These common house suites are a key component for making the co-care environment work. On occasion, there is both a male and a female caregiver who move into the common house suites. One caregiver helps the women; the other helps the men.

In the case of Bjorn, our 22-year-old nursing student, he gets reasonably inexpensive accommodations because he cares for Mrs. Jensen six hours a week and Mrs. Olsen four hours a week, and also assists others in the community by doing things like delivering breakfast or lunch. This arrangement allows for Bjorn to live in his own space, and not in the houses of the seniors under his care, a distinct benefit for all involved.

Moreover, if Mrs. Jenson has a son, who himself has a wife and young child, the entire family can visit. Mrs. Jenson's son can then care for his own mother while his wife cares for their child, all without the entire extended family living under a single roof. And because the suites are in the common house, both Bjorn and the Jenson family will have use of a 4,000 square foot facility and won't get in each others' way.

This is where senior cohousing really comes together: the highest of possibilities, rather than the lowest common denominator, expresses the society's potential.

As one ages, how does one effectively meet a host of changing logistic, social, and emotional needs? How, in terms of senior cohousing, can a group of potential neighbors effectively address such deeply personal issues? First and foremost, the group must take a step back and decide what aging in place means to them, what they themselves want to experience, and then plan for it.

The First Meetings

When a resident group first addresses aging in place issues, the new opportunities that come with growing older might (at first) be best explored on a more philosophical, somewhat removed level. Limitations should also be considered in this manner. To help these initial meetings remain as objective as possible, group members should bring their favorite facts, figures, and statistics about getting older.

Then, after a few meetings, very often something interesting happens – meetings that begin as objective, informational sessions about "the issues" gradually turn into meaningful, profoundly personal discussions about growing older. Even spiritual questions come into play.

Aging in place issues should be discussed in a group of about 10 to 12 individuals, for about ninety minutes at a time. This allows enough time for each individual to get to the deep and meaningful place where, by discussing issues together, potential neighbors can best address individual and collective life issues, needs, and circumstances. Each person will probably get to a place they had not imagined before, and consider possibilities they hadn't even previously contemplated.

Someone in the group can really get the ball rolling by just asking, "What does aging in place mean to you?" People will usually answer with their worst-case physical scenarios. A common refrain is, "When one of my neighbors hurt herself, she had to move in with a kid or have someone move in with her. In either case it seemed like a decrease in her quality of life."

This indeed is a real concern, though in this context it is only a small component of a bigger picture. At this stage a group should try to avoid the obvious pitfalls of discussing every similarly grim scenario, and in lurid detail, as this type of discourse too often digresses into discussions of how housing can best accommodate physical disabilities. In truth, people go into accessibility design issues far too quickly (accessibility design issues are covered in Study Group II). Though sometimes it feels like the answer to aging in place questions, physical handicap accessibility is not the only issue, nor is it the cure-all solution. Case in point, the amount of money spent retrofitting houses for elders, only for them to move into assisted care soon after, is mind-boggling.

Let the call for handicap accessibility be raised (as it will), but then let it go for the time being. These worst-case physical scenarios set aside, a group can then focus its attention on how senior cohousing addresses the emotional, social, and logistical issues of aging in place. These sorts of responses start to bubble up:

- "We'll get to know each other better."
- "I'll have neighbors I can depend on."
- "If I can depend on my neighbors, then I can leave Henry for a week and go down the coast with my girlfriends."
- "I don't have to be home to feed the dog if I want to go away for a day or two."
- "I'll have people living next door who I can go to the movies with, have a glass of wine with, travel with, go to the opera with, talk

---

Why Children Spend Less Time Caring for Aging Parents

Facts:

1. Raising a family in an increasingly complicated world is more and more time consuming.
2. There are fewer children to care for their parents.
3. Children live farther away. With a global economy, children are able to move where the opportunities are.
4. Most women work outside of the home and are less available than in previous generations (when they provided most of the care).
5. Children are less inclined to care for their parents. Most young adults don't have jobs, they have careers. They don't just go to work and come home: they work, schlep their own young kids around in the family car for records of miles; they have to attend the right parties and classes; you name it. And they certainly won't be guilt-tripped any more.

Some have argued that our young adult population is more narcissistic, more selfish. The days of hanging out on the front porch with an older person, the days of just being there hour after hour, breaking bread together, listening to stories, are over. We have to recognize this reality. Most older folks, of course, don't blame their children. They see their children as a product of their culture, something no one can ignore or fight, not at least without extraordinary vigor. After all, these grown kids are pursuing careers they themselves encouraged them to pursue.

While researching this book, one of the most common reasons people gave me for wanting to move into senior cohousing can be summed up with, "I don't want to be a burden to my children." A noble desire.

Co-care Planning on the Fly

Nyland Cohousing (a mixed generational cohousing community in Denver, CO) recently had several of its members diagnosed with cancer. The first sick individual received total care from the community. But when others became ill the community became overloaded.

The group responded in a way that both benefited those who were sick and those who were healthy. They contacted a local assisted living facility and obtained a list of real-world co-care tasks. They then went down the list and agreed to what they would do and what they wouldn't do. Once agreed, the group lived according to its new rules, thereby relieving each individual from being responsible beyond his or her comfort zone and level of competence. Professionals were called in accordingly, and thus ensured that each resident received both equal care by the group and quality professional care, as needed.

Dementia

Dementia is an increasingly common condition in our aging population. A cohousing group generally won't make a decision as to when someone has become incapable of living independently. More often, a couple of community members contact the person's children, or if they can't find the kids, the Department of Social Services when they think he or she needs outside help or advice. These outside entities are the ones who decide the course of action. Usually, the combination of a spouse, in-house care, and cohousing community mean that the person can remain at home longer than would otherwise be the case in traditional housing.

Trudeslund Co-op Store

The Trudeslund mixed-age community in Denmark invented another way to lower costs and increase convenience for their residents. They established a dry-goods co-operative store on site for the community, knowing that would be a particular boon for seniors. Items there are purchased at wholesale prices, there are no hours, there is no shopkeeper everything is on the honor system. Each community member has a key and can access items from toothpaste to breakfast cereal at any time of the day or night. The only requirement is that each records his/her purchases, and at the end of the month the accountant bills the household accordingly.

There is, of course, a bit of slippage in such a process, particularly if children are sent to pick up goods and then forget to record them. However, this shortfall is minor because residents want the project to succeed and do not cheat deliberately. The community typically makes up the difference out of the maintenance budget, and simply absorbs the petty sums involved. The economic benefits and convenience of the store and this cooperation (they buy the delivered products at two thirds of retail) far outweigh the minor losses.

with, be with, and all the other things that I didn't get to do when I had kids."

- "I won't have to worry about who lives next door. I'll know them, and I won't need to be afraid."
- "I'm so tired of the high turnover in the neighborhood where I live now. I can imagine it will be much more stable in cohousing since we've all put so much into it and planned it to be just what we want."

When real feelings get expressed, participants will see just how their own quality of life will be enhanced by living in a senior cohousing community. Not only do their own aspirations become tangible, but new possibilities that they hadn't otherwise considered become manifest. It can be a huge revelation. For the first time participants will see their future next-door neighbors as their community's greatest amenity.

Age of Residents

Broadly speaking, senior cohousing groups typically look for people over 50 who enjoy good health. Sometimes a group will set an upper limit of 65 or 69 at move-in. But the range can be 50 to 75, with even some exceptions to that – one community I visited had a 74-year-old former movie star resident with a 36-year-old live-in boyfriend.

Since physical health and chronological age often does not correlate, groups can knowingly respond. Case in point, one recent senior cohousing project had an age breakdown of just over one half aged between 50 and 60 years, a quarter aged between 60 and 70 years, and just under a quarter more than 70 years of age.

All the groups I interviewed agreed that it is best to stagger the ages of residents, erring toward younger people in the early days of the community when there is a lot of work to do. They also stated that all subsequent "move-ins" should be younger (never older than 69), again to keep the ages as staggered as possible. The most consistent age range was between 55 to 69.

After considerable discussion on the topic, and in order to come to a true consensus on the matter without acrimony, some groups cast secret ballots about what age ranges they think should be admitted to their community in future recruitment efforts.

Religion and Spirituality

Usually during the Study Group I meetings, there will be some discussion about religion and spirituality. This is useful, inevitable, and meaningful. Future residents will have to eventually address the issue of mortality, both as individuals and as a community.

In 13 months of interviewing people who live in multi-generational cohousing, no one ever cried describing their experiences in building and living there. By contrast, within two days of interviewing residents of senior cohousing communities, three people cried – all of them when discussing their experiences working through the issues of mortality during their Study Group I. This discussion for them was both individual catharsis and recognition of this common ground among their future neighbors.

It's possible to see this topic as a negative one, and traditional active-adult community marketeers ardently avoid the topic. Remember, these development firms are in business to construct units and to sell property, not to build community. But since community-building is the centerpiece of senior cohousing, discussions of this nature are not only entirely appropriate, but if done right can really bring people together.

As previously mentioned, some of the established senior cohousing communities in Denmark require that new applicants be no older than their early 60's and leave it at that. As simple and as reasonable as that seems, we all know that life is much more complex. Rather than a long dissertation on the subject of ideal senior cohousing co-care agreements for acute disability, let's hear what three Danish senior cohousing residents have to say:

Said one, "We had a couple of elderly ladies living here without any family or friends to take care for them when they got very ill. So a couple of us took care of them in the last part of their lives. We didn't do a lot. We were just there for them. The people from the city took care of all the nursing, and you could say

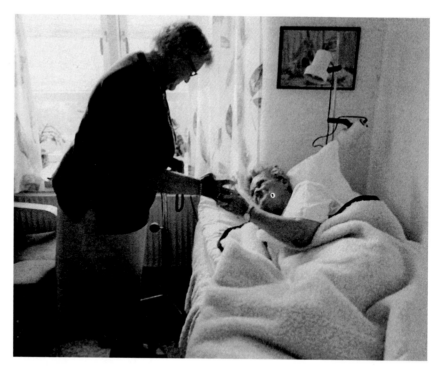

Visiting a neighbor in senior cohousing.

that we took care of the social aspect. We visited them, talked to them. Things like that."

Another reports, "We even visited one of the ladies at night, because she kept getting out of bed. But in the end we could not take care of her anymore. Sometimes she didn't even know where she was. We couldn't handle that. We had to let her kids know it was probably time: She needed more care than we could give her. She had to move to a retirement home and we went to visit her there. In the end she was hardly ever present. We just sat and held her hand."

A third commented, "We have agreed to ring each other's doorbell if the curtains are not drawn back by 10 A.M. Most of us singles keep a key at our neighbor's house. This way others can always get in, in an emergency. We also keep a phone

When Smaller Is Bigger
According to E magazine, the average house built in the U.S. last year was 2,300 square feet. By comparison, the average private house in cohousing is 1,200 square feet. However, the common house for a typical twenty-unit cohousing community could be 4,000 square feet, including workshops and other outbuildings. This means, effectively, that the average cohousing unit is equivalent in size to a 5,200 square foot house – big enough.

Comparative Expenditures: Senior Cohousing vs. The World

People who choose to live in a senior cohousing community can save substantial amounts of money. The following two examples, taken from the United States, show how much can be saved when buying into both low-end and high-end cohousing. Finally, this example considers the cost of senior cohousing versus assisted living. The numbers are rough, and simply illustrate the differences among these three options.

Senior Cohousing vs. Single Family Housing: Low-Market

There are savings in the low-market case as well. Consider the following low-market twenty-unit cohousing community:

- 1,100 square-foot private house x $125 per square foot (sales price) = $137,500.
- 4,500 square-foot common house x $100 per square foot (additional construction cost) = $450,000
- $450,000 divided by 20 units = $22,500 for each unit's share of the common house
- $22,500 + $137,500 = a total cost of $160,000

By comparison, a 2,300 square-foot single-family house, in a conventional subdivision, selling for $100 per square foot costs the purchaser $230,000. In senior cohousing, each individual house saves $70,000. It is important to remember that a 1,100 square foot cohousing house with a 4,500 square foot common house is like having a 5,600 square foot house.

Senior Cohousing vs. Single Family Housing: High-Market

There are savings in a high-market environment. Consider the following high-market twenty-unit cohousing community:

- 1,100 square-foot private house x $300 per square foot (sales price) = $330,000.
- 4,500 square-foot common house x $100 per square foot (additional construction cost) = $450,000.
- $450,000 divided by 20 units = $22,500 for each unit's share of the common house
- $22,500 + $330,000 = a total cost of $352,500

This compares favorably to a high-end house in a conventional subdivision, in which a 2,300 square-foot house selling for $300 per square foot costs the purchaser $690,000. Each individual house saves $337,500. This is just one way to look at it.

Senior Cohousing vs. Assisted Living

The comparative costs aren't even close. Senior cohousing offers better economy and quality of life than single-family houses and assisted living.

- The average cost per month for a mortgage and utilities in senior cohousing = $1,500
- plus $300 per month for food ($450 in a single family house)
- plus $400 per month for a visiting caregiver, once a week
- $1,500 + $300 + $400 = a total of $2,200 per month.

Compare this with the average cost per month for assisted living, which is about $4,000 (includes meals and care). See Appendix: The Senior Dilemma for more cost comparisons and detail.

The economics of aging are filled with trepidation and false economies. One woman at a workshop said that she couldn't order a copy of this book because she had so many expenses in her life, which she then proceeded to reel off. While listening, I couldn't help but think that more than half of her costs would be halved if she lived in cohousing. I ended up giving her a copy.

list handy with the telephone numbers of those closest to each of us so that we will not have to look for them if somebody suddenly falls ill. It gives us a sense of security in our everyday lives that we would not have had if we had lived more traditionally."

As the Danes illustrate, in senior cohousing people will only give the type and amount of care that they feel like giving. However, residents will probably want to do a lot more than they ever otherwise would have imagined.

Some residents of senior cohousing say that those individuals who expect to be taken care of should find another form of accommodation. But many residents do enjoy the feeling that simple co-care tasks bring. Some even say it helps keep them young.

In regard to early co-care discussions, existing senior cohousing groups found that they worried much more about these issues than was necessary. Their concerns rarely came true. That said, one of the key reasons these established and successful groups did not experience their worst co-care fears was because they had worked through the issue so thoroughly prior to move-in. The individuals in the group all know the agreed-to limits have contingency plans, and simply live accordingly.

What about Professional Caregivers?
Normally when people plan for the care of frail seniors, they fully expect to hire professional caregivers for the more difficult nursing tasks. But cohousing offers an option that is far and away superior to traditional in-house nursing care. It's an

The mundane becomes cheaper and more fun in senior cohousing.

option that is quite literally built right in.

In Denmark, senior cohousing groups plan for professional care by adding suites to the common house during the community's design and planning phases (Study Group II). These suites are meant to serve as apartments for on-site caregivers.

Let's take another hypothetical example to illustrate how this design feature might work in practice. Bjorn, a 22-year-old nursing student, likes hanging out with older people and has a job in the nursing home down the street. He gets free accommodation in a senior cohousing community because he takes care of Mrs. Jensen for six hours each week. Then, it turns out, Mrs. Olsen also needs help for four hours a week. Pretty soon he has quit his job at the nursing home and is only taking care of people in the cohousing community, bringing frail seniors breakfast and lunch.

There is a plus here for everyone. Bjorn becomes part of the cohousing family, rather than being simply a caregiver

Dinner in the common house.

Consensus

Fundamental to all cohousing, everyone who wishes to participate in a decision can participate. In other words, everyone has a say in the business at hand, if they so desire. Thus, a clear decision-making process, based on consensus, is the first step in ensuring the complete involvement of all. When everyone is involved, people get to know each other quite well and this fosters community.

Key items for the group to agree on include:

- Identifying and selecting consultants – architects, financial consultant, attorney, development consultant, etc.

- Identifying potential sites

- Formulating a development strategy: addressing the concerns of local officials and neighbors, resident's role, developer's role

- Considering financing options

- Drawing up of legal agreements for partnership or joint venture arrangement; form the LLC or cooperative.

living alone in an expensive apartment. He gets to know these people while they are still in good stead. He grows to care about them as people first and then, when they become more dependent on his care, he is more accountable to them as people, and not just as clients. Moreover, when he is taking care of Mrs. Olsen he is actually accountable to the whole community, which means that the quality of his care dramatically improves.

A suite that houses someone like Bjorn can also be used for other purposes. Family members, for example, can stay in these common house guest suites for weeks at a time, or longer if necessary. Regardless of how co-care is defined by any given group, with the commitment to care as the "glue," senior cohousing offers reasonable solutions to some of the most difficult problems associated with aging.

Cooperation Brings Down the Cost of Professional Care

Residents of senior cohousing plan to be neighborly, and plan to take care of each other within limits. Later, when the helpers themselves need assistance, someone will help them – after all, they are members of the community.

A live-in caregiver may also occupy a house in the senior cohousing development itself, thus becoming even more of an integral part of the community. In this manner, this professional caregiver will be able to provide truly personal care to a sick or disabled individuals, over and above that of a visiting caregiver or hospital staffer, even one who lives temporarily, albeit for an extended period of time, in a common house suite. All of this is much more affordable than a traditional means of care.

But what does affordable mean? Just how affordable is senior cohousing? Let's find out.

Economic Structures

Senior cohousing makes sense for a variety of economic reasons. Residents purchase smaller, custom-tailored, low energy-use, well designed houses. The unit size alone means a low relative cost, both to build and also to furnish and maintain. Seniors typically pare down their possessions to join the community, and many welcome the task because they can share common items. As well, fewer personal items and fewer rooms mean less to take care of individually. Seniors offset the smaller unit size with a large common house and its extensive array of common amenities. Moreover, by cooperating on upkeep and by pooling their resources, cohousers reduce some of their cost of living expenses, including those involved in hiring and housing outside caregivers.

In the Study Group I phase none of the economic discussions have to be specific – no one asks how much money someone else has. But mortgage brokers are welcome to come to designated Study Group I meetings to help people discover exactly how much house they can afford. As a level of trust develops within the group, economic issues will come into sharper focus.

To open these economic discussions, a group doesn't need to know how big the houses will be, how many units the community will contain, nor what neighborhood it's going to be in. Instead, a group should work backwards: After all, the size

New residents to Bellingham Cohousing.

of each individual house, and the location of the neighborhood, is a function of how much the group can afford in combination with other financial goals. Each individual should therefore be extremely deliberate during this process and monitor his or her own ability to afford a house within the community. It just comes down to how much house a household can afford. At this stage, that's all anyone needs to know.

At these initial stages, the group should contact outside financial experts, including mortgage brokers and financial advisors who specialize in the finances of senior citizens, including those on fixed incomes. Some people may also choose to include their own adult children in these discussions, as negotiations between seniors and financial professionals have to be seen as fair, honest and open. This engaged third party (the adult children) helps to ensure fairness for all involved. The last thing a financial pro wants is to be accused of fraud or elder abuse.

A New Old-Fashioned Neighborhood

Living in cohousing is different from living in an isolated single family house or an apartment. However, the economics involved in creating a cohousing community are not much different from those of current subdivisions, or Planned Unit Developments (PUD's).

Most people who move into cohousing today move out of a single family house, a condominium, or an apartment. Today's developers of subdivisions and senior-specific planned "communities" often overlook the quality of the actual community they create, with their sprawling complexes organized around cars and driveways. Cohousing makes new old neighborhoods, with the idea of building a close-knit community. And they do it by using the same financial and real estate tools that developers use to make sprawl.

Pooling Equity: The LLC

The difference between cohousing and a typical development is that cohousing communities either develop the project themselves or co-develop it with an industry professional. Prospective members usually pool their equity and form a Limited Liability Corporation, or LLC. The LLC assumes the role of developer, negotiates with the lender, buys the land, and hires the architect. When the project is completed, each individual resident then "buys" their house from the LLC, and assumes responsibility for their own mortgage. The benefits of the LLC system are enormous:

• By cooperating to build a large number of units (comparable to a suburban subdivision), cohousing residents take advantage of economies of scale that are usually available only to large developers. Also, by participating in the process from start to finish, residents avoid paying realtor fees, excessive developer fees motivated by risk, as well as extra expenses for things they don't need or want.

• The addition of the common house usually means that residents do not need their own private units to be as large as the industry-standard "McMansion." Instead, by pooling resources, they get the amenities afforded by a larger house at a much lower per-household cost.

Garden work in Strawberry Creek Cohousing.

• By initiating the project as future home-buyers, cohousing residents can guarantee that each unit will be sold (to themselves) at the end of construction. Risk is reduced, and loans are easier to secure.

• Because cohousing residents plan their neighborhood from the start, rather than buying individual units piecemeal from a developer, they get a better quality product. Developers are typically uninterested in future equity, and as a result generally pay less attention to quality construction. With resident involvement, a developer will be held accountable for work quality. Moreover, a well-planned neighborhood results in a predictable increase in property values, a consideration that appeals to most lenders and buyers.

Cooperative Ownership

Most cohousing groups, at some point in their discussions, bring up the possibility of organizing their community as a cooperative. In this ownership structure, the entire community is owned by all of the residents as a non-profit corporation, and each household buys a share in the corporation equivalent to the price of their home. Philosophically, a cooperative seems to be an ideal structure for a cohousing community. As one resident put it, "In a sense, I own everybody's unit. I'm responsible for everyone's unit working. It has a different feeling."

Although cooperatives are a proven form of home ownership, American banks are generally wary of financing them. Even the National Cooperative Bank (NCB), which was created to support

cooperatives, will not provide complete construction financing and offers only a limited range of loans. As a result, most cohousing projects have been set up as condominiums, a structure that banks and city officials already understand.

Cooperatives: Limited-Equity vs. Market-Rate

For those groups determined to form their community as a cooperative, they should know that in the U.S. cooperatives come in two basic flavors. One provides limited-equity returns; the other provides market-rate returns.

In a limited-equity cooperative, owners agree to limit the return on their investment, generally in line with the consumer price index. When they sell their share, the price they ask may be increased only up to a limited amount over what they originally paid. Typically, a limited-equity co-op is formed with

Katie McCamant with the Pleasant Hill resident group and the consensed site plan.

Passive cooling design precluded the need for air conditioning in this cohousing project.

special government funding designed to make the project more affordable to residents whose income is required to fall within certain government guidelines.

A market-rate, or stock, cooperative provides that a home's price be based on the market value of housing, equivalent to other housing options. This preserves the investment value of the home, allowing the owner's equity to be treated as the available asset it is, just as it would be with non-cooperative ownership schemes.

Legal Agreements

Bylaws for a building association or a development partnership are drawn up with the assistance of an attorney, and generally include provisions for:

- The group's general intentions
- Membership requirements
- Decision-making procedures
- Financial liability (individual and joint)
- Who can legally represent the association
- Members leaving the group
- Settling financial accounts when someone withdraws
- Amendment procedures

If a group joint ventures with a developer, the development agreement will reflect the nature of that relationship. Once construction is completed and the construction loan is transferred to individual mortgages, a permanent homeowners' or residents' association and its bylaws replaces all previous legal arrangements. Organizations like The Cohousing Company have sample contracts. Our company can be found online at: www. cohousingco.com.

Before a group can proceed very far into the Study Group II planning process, it must give serious consideration to its legal organization and shared liabilities. Luckily, there are lots of professionals involved with cohousing who have turned this daunting task into standard fair.

Legal agreements serve several purposes besides settling questions of liability. Requiring members to sign an agreement, even in the initial stages, clarifies who is able or willing to commit to the project, thus sorting out those who are serious from those who are still curious observers. Becoming a legal entity also inspires confidence among members and consultants alike.

There are generally three stages at which legal agreements need to be drawn up, reflecting the needs of each development phase. These agreements are:

1. An initial pre-site acquisition agreement (Partnership)
2. A "building association" or development partnership (LLC)
3. A definition of the final ownership structure and management association (HOA DOCS)

The initial agreement, drawn up before the group is ready to purchase a site, generally outlines the group's purpose, decision-making procedures, membership recruitment methods and limitations, and fees to cover operating expenses and consulting services.

When the group is ready to purchase property and/or hire consultants (architect, lawyer, etc.) for extended services, a more extensive legal agreement is necessary. At this point the group typically incorporates

Planning a new project.

as a building association, which functions through the construction phases. It is at this stage that members are generally required to invest a minimum amount toward the down payment on their house.

Final Meetings

If the group hasn't already done so, it needs to clarify social expectations for the community. Just as importantly, at this juncture the group needs to specify its needs in terms of financial commitments, per household. At this stage, there ought to be a sense of trust built up among its participants such that participants feel confident about investing in the group together. Only then is the group capable of purchasing a site.

The subtility of the care is what gets the care done. "Let me give you a trim; I'll be over in an hour."

Issues not actually included in the written development program, such as organizational structure, decision-making procedures, development strategies, financing options, and legal agreements need to be addressed prior to purchase of the site. Ideally, these issues and the development program will have been thoroughly considered before a site is acquired. Then the group can quickly finish the program (which is not complete until there is a site) and proceed with the architectural design in a cost-effective manner. The completed development program is written down in a report. This report clearly defines the values and visions of the new community and helps future residents to learn about the senior cohousing before they decide to move in.

In Denmark and the Netherlands, the final meetings of Study Group I classes visit an up-and-running senior cohousing community. In the United States, a visit to an intergenerational cohousing community could be arranged. The Cohousing Associaton has a running list of all cohousing groups in the United States and up-to-date contact information.

A visit to an existing cohousing community provides a perfect segue into Study Group II, where the physical community itself will be designed from the ground up.

Estimate of U.S. Caregiving for Elders vs. Senior Cohousing "Care"

(while recovering from a precipitating event such as a broken hip, sprained knee, broken ankle, stroke, heart attack or similar)

Percentage of help with spouse, children, relatives, HMO

1.	Spouse	45%
2.	Children & relatives	15%
3.	The neighbors	5%
4.	Hired help (in house)	20%
5.	Friends	5%
6.	HMO (outcare, if insured)	10%
		100%

These figures assume $70,000/year combined income just before retirement. (If more income is available, assume a higher percentage of hired help.)

Percentage of help without spouse with kids

1.	Spouse	0%
2.	Children & relatives	30%
3.	The neighbors	15%
4.	Hired help (in house)	20%
5.	Friends	5%
6.	HMO (outcare, if insured)	20%
7.	Meals On Wheels and other non-profits	10%
		90%*

Percentage of helpers: without spouse, and without children:

1.	Spouse	0%
2.	Children & relatives	5%
3.	The neighbors	5%
4.	Hired help (in house)	37.5%
5.	Friends (they are getting older as well)	5%
6.	HMO (outcare, if insured)	25%
7.	Meals On Wheels and other nonprofits	7.5%
		85%

This assumes a single income of $40,000/year. The more the income, the more the cost of hired help goes up. You are lucky , if you qualify for informal institutional, in-home care by various non-profit organizations such as:

- meals on wheels
- senior in-home care volunteers   10%
- government care
- district nurse

Percentage of help without spouse, children, and HMO coverage:

1.	Spouse	0%
2.	Children	0%
3.	The neighbors (bring mail, newspaper, fix TV)	20%
4.	Hired help	30%
5.	Friends	20%
6.	NO HMO (40 million Americans)	0%
7.	Meals On Wheels and other non-profits	10%
		70%

At this point you might as well go to a government subsidized assisted-care facility if you can find it. Medium quality assisted-living starts at about $3000/month, or $5000/month in expensive urban areas such as the San Francisco Bay area, Boston and Boulder, Colorado. Quality of life drops precipituously. About 23% of American adults are involved in the care of someone over 50 years old (National Center for Caregiving). That can be fine when it's not overwhelming. They live close by and they have plenty of other options for support and care such as friends and community.

Care in Danish Senior Cohousing

The Danes have always been at least 20 years ahead of North Americans, perhaps more, when it comes to community housing. And our culture is headed in their direction, in the sense that in both places there are fewer children, more-distracted children, and more need for alternatives that enhance quality of life for the elderly.

Percentage of help in Senior Cohousing in Denmark (with spouse and children):

1.	Spouse	30%
2.	Children	10%
3.	Neighbors	40%

- bring in the paper and mail
- get you to common house for dinner
- make you laugh (but not too much, because it makes the knee hurt.)
- bring you tea
- get you out into the sunshine
- read you books
- massage your leg (this may seem overly optimistic, but I've seen it happen)
- bring you coffee

4.	Hired help, friends	10%
5.	Public medicine	10%
		100%

*90% is a 10% shortfall in care

** These rough percentages are based on our own interviews. This document will be considerably more complete at the next edition.

Participatory site design. Nevada City Cohousing resident group in action.

CHAPTER EIGHT

"When done right, the group design process never delays a project. In fact, it makes it go faster."

Study Group II
The Participatory Design Process

Acohousing community's environment either promotes or discourages interaction among residents, resulting in either a lively or lifeless place. The best cohousing design begins with a process that will sustain residents long after the honeymoon has worn off and ends with blueprints for the physical community that emphasize a neighborly approach to living, while protecting individual privacy.

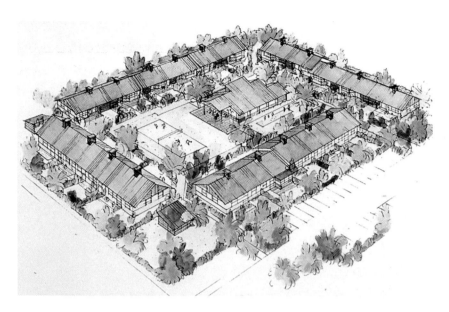

Ledøje-Smørum Senior Cohousing by Nielsen & Rubow Architects.

Efficiency Means Progress

The biggest threat to the viability of cohousing is an ill-planned and inefficient design process. A disorganized design process threatens a cohousing project because it puts developers and other professionals in the position of wanting to do the job without input from the resident group mostly because they think that they can be more effective. And without resident group's input and ownership, the very foundations of the community will be compromised.

People do not generally think about the impact of design on community life, but the social consequences of good (or bad) design in senior cohousing are dramatic. Designed to ensure individual privacy, conventional senior-specific condominium and single-family housing developments rarely incorporate design factors that encourage neighbors to meet, much less to interact, in an organic, meaningful way. As a result, residents of many senior "communities" barely know each other, despite their close proximity. Sure, small gardens and comfortable, shared outdoor sitting areas make it easier for people to meet and talk, but the mere presence of these features alone does not necessarily mean residents will actually interact. Amenities are not community.

By contrast, in a senior cohousing community the participatory development process forges relationships among residents. Community is created prior to construction, and the environment they create together maintains these ties. Designed from the ground up, the participatory development process gives residents a rock-solid foundation for daily interaction, and the pathway seating they share gives them the perch from which to survey the health and well-being of their community.

A Well-Trod Path

Resident participation in the development process is cohousing's greatest asset and its most limiting factor. It can be a huge task for a group of people, inexperienced in both collective decision-making and the building industry, to take on a project of this scale and complexity. Most future residents have little knowledge of design and construction issues for housing development. They encounter problems in maintaining an efficient timeline, avoiding the domination of a few strong personalities, integrating new members without backtracking, and more. Fortunately, in addressing these issues today we can benefit from decades of senior cohousing experience in Denmark.

The participatory design process has played an integral part in the evolution of cohousing. As cohousing became more clearly defined, the participatory process itself became more clearly defined. And so the evolution of the participatory process continues with senior cohousing. In senior cohousing, the group process and the design process are more coordinated than in the development of non-senior cohousing. As such, the greatest challenge in senior cohousing is to get enough input to get the design right and "owned" by the residents, but not so much input as to delay the process; thus making it too expensive and burning out the prospective residents and professionals involved in the project.

Building a viable community of this scale is a huge undertaking, to be sure. But when a resident group follows the well-worn path blazed by their Danish predecessors and commits to taking small, deliberate, well-planned, and incremental steps, what can otherwise be an overwhelming project instead becomes a very manageable and immensely rewarding experience.

Study Group II

After the members of a new senior cohousing group have completed Study Group I and a site has been identified, the group and their architect create a cohesive program (design criteria). This program is broken into three parts: the site program, the common house program, and the private house program.

The process for going through these programs includes the following steps:

- Site program and schematic site plan workshop
- Common house program and schematic common house plan workshop
- Private house program and schematic unit plans workshop
- Design closure workshop
- Submission to the city for approval

Design Program

A strong sense of community is the cornerstone of every senior cohousing project. This sense of community is physically created through a deliberate process that translates a group's goals into design criteria (design criteria are requirements that provide the basis for the architectural designs), also called the design

Community and Privacy

If I seem to focus more on encouraging the social side of senior cohousing versus the protection of privacy, it is because American architects and developers are as socially conditioned as anyone else to put privacy above all other social concerns. Groups that create a senior cohousing community must, in effect, break the old habits of all involved.

It's worth noting that of the hundreds of cohousing residents we've interviewed, not one complained about the lack of privacy in their community yet many readily pointed out design features that discouraged sociability. The point is that community design should encourage social interaction and at the same time allow residents to choose whether to be with others or to be alone, and to what extent. When you walk into cohousing, you should always feel like you have the choice between as much privacy as you want, or as much community as you want. In typical suburban neighborhoods you feel as if you have as much privacy as you want and as much privacy as you want. One the the reasons cohousing works in America is because Americans like a choice.

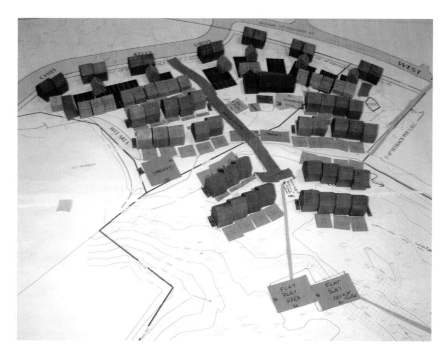

Site plan generated from participatory design for Nevada City Cohousing.

135

Intimate spaces between buildings that contribute a warm atmosphere.

program. The building program outlines the functions and characteristics desired by a resident group, and thus clarifies the criteria on which design alternatives will be judged. An architect can facilitate a group's discussions by laying out the range of possibilities, outlining important considerations, and providing inspiration and resource materials. Field trips and analysis of favorite places help to broaden the group's understanding of design alternatives.

Building on earlier decisions about goals and priorities, participants identify exactly what functions the private dwelling, the common facilities, and the outdoor areas, should accommodate. Is a work space needed in some dwellings? Are some households adamant about having their own washing machine? What are the eating, food preparation, and entertainment needs of the private dwellings? Of the common house?

Creating a Design Program

To assure the success of the social aspects of the community, and to best assure a deliberate and cost-effective design process, the group must create a cohesive design program (criteria) that defines the

Creating a hierarchy of spaces from the most private part of the dwelling to the most common, allows residents to choose how private or public they want to be at any given time, and makes transition between spaces more relaxed.

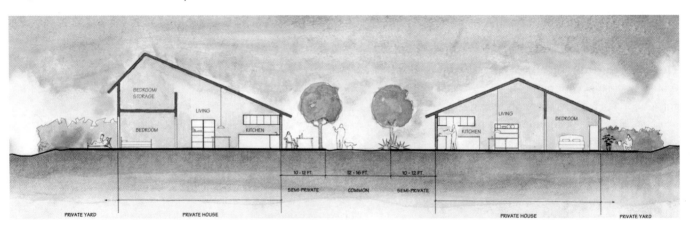

group's goals, priorities, activities, and design requirements for the project on-site. A quality design program ensures that the actual design and construction phases of the project are efficiently executed. Efficiency in this case means that everyone involved, from the group to the architect to the builders, will spend less time and money to complete each task. In addition, a cohesive design program, just as much as the community's social agreements, greatly helps to recruit and integrate new members into an existing group. For senior cohousing, the foundations for a group's ability to make decisions, and therefore proceed efficiently with a design program, are contained within Study Group I (see Chapter 7).

The actual creation of the design program should be considered a learning period for all participants, including the architect. Later on, the design program is the tool used to evaluate the actual designs. In other words, residents can refer to the design program to answer the question, "Did the consultants actually design what we wanted them to design?"

Finally, having all of the development plans in a single, cohesive document allows members of the resident group to relax: they won't need to tell the consultants the same thing over and over again throughout the process. Instead, they can just say, "Now, what does it say in the program?" Moreover, a solid design program prevents wasteful backtracking – new members to the group (after the design program is finished) will be able to see how thorough the group has been and won't be tempted to backtrack. "Did you consider how big the front porches should be?" Larry, the new participant

Fill in the Blank

Questionnaires are often useless: real information only comes from personal facilitation. To illustrate the point, in 2005 I attended a seminar on the housing preferences of seniors aged 55 to 75 in Orlando, Florida. One question in a survey carried out by staff and students of Harvard University asked senior respondents if they preferred a bedroom on the first floor. Fifty percent said "yes". An interesting result because approximately 97 percent of the units built for seniors in this country last year have a bedroom on the ground floor. In other words, despite what this survey says, when it comes to actually buying a home the vast majority of American seniors apparently wants a bedroom on the ground floor. I should mention that every one of the 40 line items in this Harvard survey produced drastically different data than what was found while working with seniors in focus groups or other interactive settings.

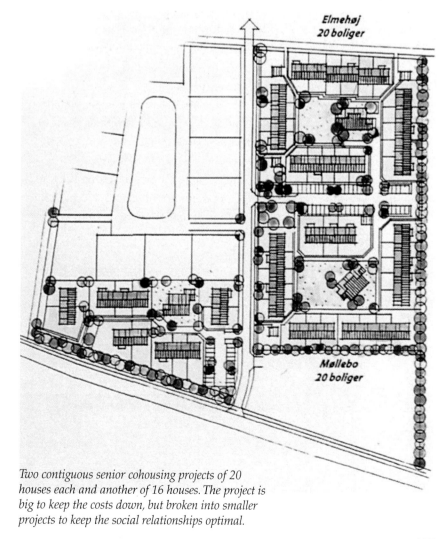

Two contiguous senior cohousing projects of 20 houses each and another of 16 houses. The project is big to keep the costs down, but broken into smaller projects to keep the social relationships optimal.

Maximizing Potential

Organized and executed by the group, a thorough design program enables group members to:

- Share their knowledge in a complementary fashion
- Make firm personal commitments: recruitment, payment of initial fees, etc.
- Lobby the municipality to get the project approved, if necessary
- Help keep costs down with careful planning
- Maintain a non-institutional feel to the project
- Push the percentage of common areas up and the individual house sizes down. This ensures that the project stays affordable and that the community operates at its fullest potential.

A low window provides good light for the kitchen counter but more importantly facilitates ongoing social contact.

asked, as if he just found the cure to polio. "Yes, look at the program," Sandra replied. "And stop wasting my time," she thought.

Goals and Priorities

In preparing the design program, the group will clarify and expand upon their previously-stated goals and priorities to answer questions like: Which shared facilities are most necessary, and which are less important? In order to keep costs down, which amenities can be done without? The development program requires tradeoffs – few people can afford everything on their wish list. This can actually be done efficiently and accurately in a well-facilitated and organized weekend effort.

Of course, clarifying earlier goals and limiting development priorities is easier said than done. While cost limitations force these issues to the forefront and truly assist a group into making the tough development priority choices (especially in terms of quality and quantity), keeping costs in line with the budget isn't necessarily as easy as keeping a clear priority list – there is always the temptation to increase unit size just a few square feet more or to add just one more common

amenity. This feature creep can be accomplished either by increasing the budget or by using low-end building materials and cut-rate services. While these bigger-budget or cost-cutting schemes may seem like good ideas in the design phase, in practice poor construction materials and below-market labor isn't worth the added or expanded feature and the headaches that come along with the installation. The adage "you get what you pay for" applies here and those added features won't seem so necessary when residents discover that they can't actually afford them.

Rather than incur excessive debt or suffer through inferior materials and services, it's better for a group to keep amenities and construction costs within their original parameters of quality; to keep unit sizes from creeping up until it blows the budget, and to establish clear development priorities and stay true to them.

Order of Design

The architectural design starts with the design of the site. After the site is designed, the design continues on to the common house, and then to the private residences. The site plan is addressed first because its configuration leads directly into the city planning approval process and key questions about feasibility – cost, the number and type of houses, the number of parking places, and so on.

Once the site is planned, design of the common house is taken up. The common house design precedes the individual private houses because once group members know the amenities featured in the common house, they will be able to see how the common house will supplement and become an extension

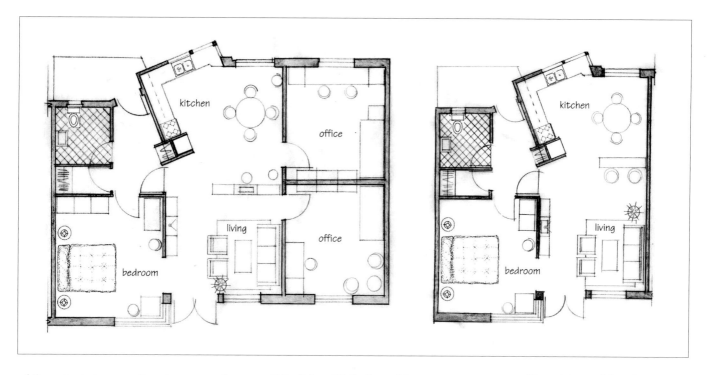

The quintessential senior cohousing house units. The kitchens are like lighthouses in their prominence.

of the private houses. People are much more comfortable with smaller private houses when they see that the common house will contain guest rooms or suites, laundry facilities, entertainment rooms, a sewing room, and other amenities, as well as a gourmet kitchen and large dining/living space for that twice a year party or family gathering (as well as dinner several times a week). Once the common house is designed, the private house discussions typically go quite smoothly and rapidly.

In most cases, residents understandably want to be involved in the initial design of their project. As such, various participatory methods specific to cohousing have been developed to help promote resident involvement: models, field trips, discussions, furniture paper cut-outs to develop floor plans, and more. Questionnaires can also be used, though more often than not the results are of dubious value.

Working Relationships

As mentioned earlier, cohousing's participatory process is its greatest asset and its most limiting factor. The residents, new to the collective decision-making process and the construction industry, must trust the professionals to be frank, honest, and open during each phase, and as interested and dedicated in creating a quality cohousing development as they are.

The architect earns this trust through demonstrating his or her competency in facilitating the development process itself. The architect must obviously be fair and efficient, and possess a good understanding of the cohousing concept itself. More than that, a good architect will educate the group about the social and ecological consequences of various design decisions. This honesty also means that the architect must sometimes challenge a group's decisions or priorities, because only through

Distance Between the Houses

In order to establish the "right" distance between the houses of a given cohousing community, we ask the group to form two lines 110 feet apart from each other (a common distance across a street between front doors of suburban houses). We have the group pretend it's Monday morning and that they are all leaving their house at the same time as their across-the-street-neighbor. As well, we ask everyone in the group to pretend that they care about their neighbor across the street (we have them imagine that a resident's daughter is sick and that each wants to ask how she is doing without yelling at the top of their lungs). The group members in each line then walk toward their neighbor in the opposite line until one grows uncomfortable. When one person in the pair stops, the other stops. In a recent project, the end distances between "neighbors" ranged between 26 and 40 feet; and those were the distances between the front doors that we designed for their community.

this dialogue will a resident group clarify its objectives and priorities. When it comes to real people's lives, only honest, face-to-face discussions and challenges will produce a design that everyone will actually want to live with.

Experience also teaches that the success of a senior cohousing project does not solely depend on the quality of the relationship between the resident group and the distinct design professionals – the residents themselves must have developed an effective working relationship among themselves. If not, any design professional will have great difficulty working with the group.

Preliminary elevation design sketch for Munksøgård senior cohousing by Martin Rubow.

Once that trust is earned, both among the individuals within the resident group and between distinct groups, it is maintained only when all parties learn when and how to challenge each other, always seeking the highest common denominator.

The most effective participatory design processes recognize both the value of resident input and where it should be limited. How much influence residents want over the design, and where they should step back, is the art of the process. The group should, of course, be involved in the establishment of design criteria. Many past participants, however, recommend leaving most technical and aesthetic decisions to the architect, since it is almost impossible for most groups to agree among themselves on these issues.

Looking at the Options

There are many special design considerations that separate senior cohousing from regular cohousing, and also from other types of senior living. Senior cohousing is different from other types of senior housing in that prospective residents directly discuss the issues of accessibility and mobility and how to incorporate these needs in the design. These decisions

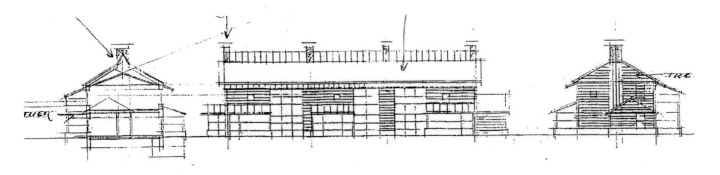

ultimately affect their quality of life, both at move-in and beyond.

Before such discussions happen, group members generally visit other senior housing projects to see how the "experts" have responded to these issues. What seniors say in response to these visits often boil down to the notion, "I want my cohousing community to be accessible without looking or feeling accessible." This sensibility is something that American architects often overlook (unless prodded by the actual residents) and is another reason why a senior cohousing group must be proactive in the design efforts of their community. This is also an opportunity for the group to establish where this issue fits in with their priorities. Senior cohousing communities in Denmark typically decide the price they can afford and their accessibility goals while the architects optimize the solution. (See Appendix: Access Friendly Design.)

Some of the most important means of sustaining individual health are visitors, people, social interaction, obvious regard and care, a sense of identity, and a sense of belonging. In other words, "community." The bottom line is that accessibility features can foster a sense of community, encourage independence, and not look "accessible."

Building Upon a Strong Foundation

Study Group II should prove to be an exciting experience where friendships are formed, tested, and made stronger. The foundations of the group process that were laid in Study Group I are utilized and built upon. It is now time to consider the landscape, common facility, and home designs that will house and nurture the community.

Site Design

There is a distinct sense of neighborhood that all senior cohousing communities share – it is the payoff for the time they spent putting it together. Outsiders quickly recognize and appreciate each cohousing development as a community with the strong neighborly bond that's usually missing from a typical seniors-only development. It is no accident. A senior cohousing development requires a special set of design considerations that, in turn, support this special kind of neighborly community.

The Site Program Defined

At The Cohousing Company, we dedicate four days with the group to come up with a schematic site design. We:

• Establish a common language (using slides of completed projects to educate and inspire). This helps the group to visualize their concepts and to broaden and communicate their ideas.

• Agree on goals for the site plan (e.g. community friendly, easy to know your neighbor, living lightly on the land, good solar orientation, etc.).

• Brainstorm/discuss and decide on the activities between the houses that facilitate community and individual goals (sitting and talking, gardening, washing the car, playing games, hanging out the clothes, drinking a pot of tea, laughing, etc.).

• Establish which activities require their own place (e.g. parking lot, gathering nodes, common terrace, clothes line, swimming pool, bocce ball court, private front porch, private front yard, private backyard, etc.)

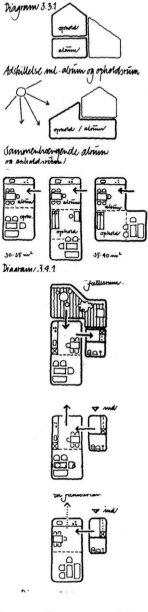

Diagrams illustrating spatial relationships among the dwellings in a cohousing community.

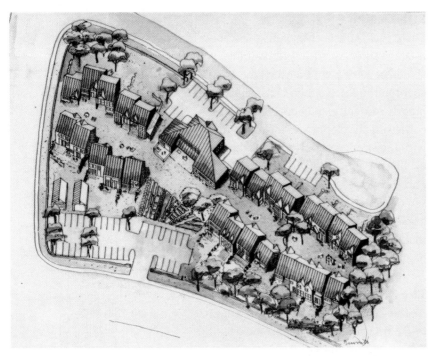

Muir Commons site plan, Davis, California.

• Establish where activities occur that don't need their own place (e.g. car washing at the car park, basketball court at the overflow car park, etc.).

• Create clear design criteria for each place (e.g. a garden with 18 fruit trees and 12 raised beds; a watering feature; compost; greenhouse; tool shed; south facing; picnic table; etc.). More specific decisions, like type of fruit trees, are usually established later by a gardening committee.

• Establish the character of each space, where each space is in relation to other places, and the details of each place.

• Establish acceptable distances between houses (front door to front door).

• Use house blocks on a scaled survey of the site to establish house locations, parking location, garden location, picnic area, bocce ball location, etc., based on the above criteria. This is often done in two different groups in order to explore different alternatives.

• Evaluate the block designs until they merge into a solution that fulfills the program requirements and therefore represents a first pass at a viable schematic design. Presuming that the education process along the way is smooth and thorough, this phase is not only a fun and valuable basis for community building, but also results in the best and most thoughtful plan possible.

We've used this method for every cohousing project we've built since our first project in Davis, California, in 1990, and it really works.

Number of Households

The size of a senior cohousing development is generally discussed in terms of number of households. Senior cohousing, dealing with a smaller number of units than found in mixed generational cohousing developments, usually features 15 to 25 households. In fact, 20 households are widely considered to be the best number in Denmark, and 24 in the Netherlands. In both cases, there consistently seems to be about 1.3 people per household in each community. (See Chapter 6 for a full discussion on number of households per project and its impact on community.)

Circulation

Pedestrian circulation can serve as an organizing element for the layout of buildings. Like the main street in a small town, circulation can be organized along a spine, as with a pedestrian lane; or, as in some older cities, it might be focused on a plaza-like courtyard. A resident living in the Munksøgård senior cohousing community explains:

> "What I like most about the design of this place is that when I walk out of my front door someone will say, "Hello Anna. Come for a stroll with me." It's easy to bump into people and usually that's enough for me. Usually I like the casual contacts more than I like the formal activities, except common dinners. I love common dinners."

Circulation to the individual houses from the parking areas and the main pedestrian entrances into the development should be centralized along a limited number of paths in order to increase the chances for neighbors to pass one another and to help maintain privacy on the back sides of the houses. Site plans organized around a central street or courtyard work particularly well at promoting such encounters. When houses are scattered around the site, connected by a multitude of small pathways, no one route gets enough use to ensure the likelihood that people will actually meet other people. With centralized circulation, life unfolds between the houses.

The Site Plan

Mixed generational cohousing and senior cohousing have been built in many forms – attached row houses, dwellings clustered around courtyards, rehabilitated factories and rehabilitated schools.

The majority of cohousing takes the form of one-, two-, and three-story attached houses, often referred to as

clustered or medium density, low-rise housing. This building type has many advantages over both detached single-family houses and high-rise apartments. It uses land, energy, and materials more economically than detached houses and the relatively high density of clustered housing also supports more efficient forms of mass transit. (While high-rise apartments use less land, living four or more stories above the ground creates feelings of anonymity in many people.) In rural and semi-rural areas, clustered housing can help preserve open space, an increasingly sensitive issue in high-growth areas where demand for housing often conflicts with agricultural needs. This practice can be beneficial in general but is particularly compatible with cohousing.

Everyone in a well-designed community benefits from easy access to outdoor spaces that, in turn, accommodate people with differing abilities. All residents are therefore able to take part in outdoor activities such as gardening, or simply sitting around and chatting. To sustain healthy lives, the design of outdoor accessibility is just as important as indoor accessibility design.

Clustered housing can provide many of the amenities of single-family houses, such as direct access to a private garden and an individual entrance for each dwelling. Moreover, grouping the houses together can create larger, more usable open spaces for such things as community gardens and sitting areas. Modern building techniques can prevent sound transmission between shared walls, a concern people often mention in regard to attached dwellings. The ability to provide

The central path in elder cohousing is where people meet; where life between buildings eminates.

Close Proximity Fosters Community

Americans always look at a cohousing site plan and say, "Wow, that feels like a village." In practice they do operate as a village, and a visit to any well-designed cohousing community will prove this out. In the case of senior cohousing, the seniors themselves often argue most forcefully for a tight village-like street/courtyard design. An intelligently-crafted site design creates proximities that foster community.

both privacy and community is what makes clustered housing such a popular aspect of any cohousing community.

In cohousing, the treatment of spaces between buildings contributes to the quality of life as much as the buildings themselves. These outdoor spaces can be used for sitting, pedestrian traffic, spontaneous encounters, gardening, and socializing. The site plan, because it defines how the site is used (where buildings sit, how they relate to each other) largely determines how well these activities are accommodated.

Some site plans are formal in their organization, while in others the dwellings are situated very informally. With sensitive handling of the relationships among all spaces, all of these site plans work equally well. Which one the group chooses usually depends upon their goals, the site itself, and the surrounding context.

A senior cohousing community site plan.

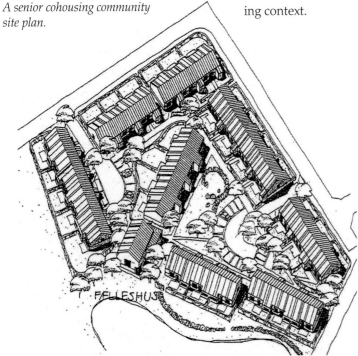

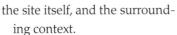

A Living Place Without Cars

Car access and parking have a major impact on every site plan and are often the first aspects considered in an architectural design. Almost without exception, all cohousing developments are pedestrian-oriented with the parking relegated to the periphery of the site. Many years of experience teaches that no matter what the housing type, whenever residents participate in the design of their own communities they restrict the cars to the edge of the site. Car-free pedestrian lanes and courts are essential to creating places where everyone can move about relaxed and worry-free. Clustering the parking also frees up the orientation of the houses, allowing them to optimally relate to people, the sun, and the terrain.

Residents or their caregivers may want to drive to an individual house to deliver groceries, drop someone off, or move furniture, but cars should not be parked just outside the front door all of the time. One resident exclaimed while gesturing down the pedestrian lane:

> *"There is no reason for automobiles to occupy the most valuable areas of our site, and lots of good reasons why they should not."*

People who live in cohousing communities have clearly stated that they would rather walk in snow and rain than compromise their immediate living environment with cars. Given the often harsh winters of the American West, Midwest, and East Coast (and Northern Europe), this is no small choice.

The primary reasons residents give for preferring a car-free site are community, safety, and ecological considerations.

"When cars don't dominate the space between the houses then there is a life between the buildings," said one cohousing resident." The cars live in the parking lot and we live here in between, as well as in the houses."

However, even the personal encounters that occur while going to and from the parking area serve important social functions. People meet in the parking lot going to and from errands, plan outings, and maintain friendships through casual chats on the way home. "Hey, I'm headed to the store, do you need anything?" is a common refrain. Along those lines, the common house should ideally be placed between the parking area and the houses so residents need to walk by the common house to and from their car and their own home. It's all about community on a human scale.

"But wait!" outsiders stammer. "Shouldn't these older folks live close to where their car is parked because of mobility issues?" My response: Seniors should not design-in or -out any feature that they themselves don't feel is important. It's their community, and it's their choice.

Whether a group chooses to place their parking area in a single central location or disperse them depends on the site, the community size, and the preferences of the residents. Usually one or two centrally located lots are adequate. Using pervious structurally supported lawn or gravel surface and interspersing trees can make parking areas attractive. Wouldn't the social life of any neighborhood be enhanced if cars were parked at the end of the street?

The amount of parking per resident depends on many factors beyond the residents' ability or inability to drive – the site's size and location and availability of mass transit, are also key determiners. Cohousing in general reduces the need for separate cars since the concept itself promotes the possibility of sharing. A couple who needs a second car can easily arrange to share one with another household. In fact, senior cohousing developments often average less than one car per dwelling. American condominium planning codes typically require parking for more than one car per dwelling, but officials usually

General Site Design Criteria
- Number of units
- Site amenities to preserve (views, trees, etc.)
- Location of common facilities, residential buildings, open space
- Building type and form (two stories, clusters, detached, etc.)
- Building materials (general)
- Energy considerations (electric, gas, solar, wind, conservation, etc.)
- Accessibility considerations

Outdoor Areas:
- Parking (location, how much covered/uncovered)
- Car access on site (traffic-free, access to houses when necessary)
- Open space
- Shared amenities (sitting areas, gardens, etc.)
- Transition between private residences and common areas
- Private outdoor functions (sitting areas, gardens, etc.)
- Fences, hedges, plantings
- Personalization

About 15 years ago, working on a cohousing group in Sacramento, California, Susan, one of the group members, called me up and said, "Chuck, it looks like we're not going to go for that 1.25 acre site. We think 25 units on a site that small won't work." Most of the future residents were moving from modest but single-family homes. I said, "Wait before you finalize your decision. Bring the entire group to the San Francisco Bay Area and I'll show you how it can work."

I knew that at that time there was almost no quality multi-family clustered housing in Sacramento, at least nothing that anyone who could afford to buy, or even rent, a detached house would want. They were sure that clustered housing that dense would look cheap, that you'd be able to hear your neighbors breathing next door, and that it would degrade their self image.

Two weeks later most of the group showed up in several cars. In the morning we visited some poorly designed clustered housing developments. I noticed, and later at the end of the day pointed out to them, how they would walk up to windows, brim their eyes and peer in. They stepped onto people's front stoops, and basically felt they had free reign. These are good, upstanding citizens, who would never intentionally disrespect a neighbor.

During the afternoon we visited four well-designed clustered housing developments, but this time I noticed how, from the very first step onto each property, the group appeared to stop and think, "Oh, someone lives here, I have to be on my best behavior." The difference between the housing developments we visited during the morning and those we visited during the afternoon, was in the transitions and other architectural signals that proclaimed, "Somebody lives here, is taking care of this place, is accountable for it, and you should feel accountable for your behavior too."

We headed back to our studio and dissected the differences between good and bad design. Since they hadn't previously seen good multi-family housing design, they hadn't realized how positive that density can be. Several days later they made an offer on the property, which was ultimately accepted. Two years later they moved into a wonderful cohousing community.

allow a parking reduction if an actual car count for future residents can be provided, and when residents show how parking can be expanded at a later date, if needed.

It is absolutely clear that placing cars close to the houses short-circuits sustained relationships. People-hours at the common house and people-contact between the buildings drop many, many fold when parking areas are placed adjacent to the houses. As a direct result, community, physical, and emotional health deteriorates. Special circumstances, however, can be accommodated. Inevitably, just by virtue of how a site plan works out, some parking spaces end up relatively close to residences. These residences are usually chosen by folks who have mobility concerns.

Location of the Common House

The location of the common house greatly affects the frequency of its use. For the common house to be an integral part of community life, residents must pass it in the course of their daily activities. Three sometimes conflicting requirements for the location of the common house are:

1. That residents pass the common house on their way home
2. That the common house is visible from each house, or from just outside of it
3. That the common house be equidistant from all dwellings (This is the least important of the three requirements)

The first of these considerations is the most important. Passing the common house on their way home, residents can see if anything is going on. You stop in to check for Hannah – you've been wanting to chat with her, see what's for dinner, or look at the bulletin board. Because the common house is along the path home, visiting it becomes part of your daily routine.

Likewise, if residents can see the common house and the terrace from their own homes, they are more likely to join in when there is an activity. Finally, no dwelling should be so far from the common house as to make someone feel isolated, although some residents prefer to be farther from the central action than others.

Transitional Spaces

The attention paid to the transitions between the private, common, and public realms affects the residents' ease in moving from one to the other, and also defines the relationship between the community and the surrounding neighborhood. There should be a hierarchy of spaces, from the sanctity of the private bedroom to the openness of the common plaza. Each transition – from the private dwelling, to the community plaza, to the public realm – helps support community life and the relationships among people. If these transitional spaces are not well organized and perfectly designed, there will be missing links and fewer opportunities to continue the relationships that keep a group of houses a community. The omission of any of them makes the appropriate use of spaces ambiguous, inhibiting people's activities. These links and thresholds should be indicated physically, although the demarcation can be as subtle as a change in ground cover.

In cohousing, there is less need for territorial definitions, and the relationships between private homes and community areas can be more relaxed (but still clear)

The Backyard Shed

The two most unfortunate mistakes in designing transition areas are providing only a hard edge between the individual residences and the community realm, and placing storage buildings in front of dwellings. We have seen that a soft transition between the private interior and the common areas encourages informal movement from one to the other, with more time spent outside. Storage sheds are often used for extra household wares, since cohousing dwellings often lack garages. When these sheds are placed in front of the house, they block views of passers-by or activities in the common areas. They impede the "conversation" between houses, just as holding your hand in front of your face would impede a conversation with another person. Once built, it is difficult and expensive to correct such mistakes. Storage sheds are often better placed out back. Like fences, residents can build them after moving in, when they have an understanding of how the areas between buildings are actually used. Basement storage areas eliminate this problem altogether, but they are not always economically feasible.

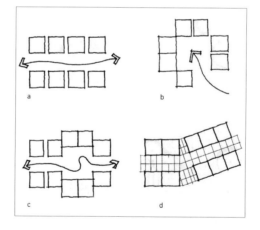

Different types of site plans: a: pedestrian street; b: courtyard; c: combination of street and courtyard; d: one building (glass-covered street)

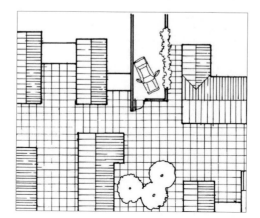

Automobiles are as much a part of our culture as they are a practical necessity. A community car wash area has both practical and social benefits.

Body Language

With all the discussion about design to encourage casual socializing, someone who hasn't lived in a cohousing community might wonder whether a resident can take out the garbage without getting sidetracked. Cohousers told us they quickly learn to use and read body language in a variety of situations. "It's easy enough just to say 'howdy' and walk on. People know that everyone has their own lives – it's natural and accepted," explained a resident. Body language readily signals approachability. One resident told us that some people may not be approachable for months because of how things are going on in their lives; but soon enough they will open up again.

"People in cohousing tend to be very honest with each other," said a cohousing resident of sixteen years. "In my old house, when a neighbor used to ask to borrow a tool, I felt obliged to loan it, even if I felt uncomfortable doing so. In what might be a rare contact, I didn't want to come off as unneighborly. Here if someone wants to talk, or have coffee, or borrow a tool, and I don't feel like it, I don't hesitate to say no. They know me, and there is less likelihood that they will be put off by my honesty. In fact, it's a sign of respect and intimacy to be able to say no."

than in other housing types. A resident's front door faces a common area shared by friends, rather than a public street crammed with cars.

This traditional area can support the spontaneous social atmosphere and community life that residents value. Generally, the kitchen-dining area is the room most people "live" in, and the area of the house that people don't mind being seen in. Locating this room at the front of the house increases opportunities to observe the common area while tending to domestic activities. A door and window connecting the private kitchen to the common area allows a resident to call out to a passing neighbor. Visual access to the common areas, whether indoors or outdoors, allows people to see activities

This gathering node in Strawberry Creek Cohousing supports spontaneous social atmosphere and community life.

they may want to join. As one resident said, "I can't decide to join the neighbors sharing a pot of tea if I don't know they're there." Casual surveillance is also a highly effective form of building security, with neighbors "watching out for each other" and taking notice of suspicious strangers.

Direct access between the dwellings and a semi-private garden patio increase the use of outdoor space. When it is easy to just "pop out," people flow between indoors and outdoors many times during the day. This threshold to common areas is a particularly important element of cohousing. In order to make it as easy as possible to pass from indoors to outdoors, the design should avoid corridors, extra doors, and level changes. If a vestibule is desired for winter entry, a secondary entrance can provide direct access from the living area to the outdoors.

A "soft edge" – that is, a semi-private area or garden patio between the front of the private dwelling and the common area – further increases opportunities for casual socializing. Like a front porch where people sit for hours on summer evenings, this semi-private area provides an easy-accessible and comfortable place to be outside and "watch the world go by." Here residents may set out tables and chairs or plant a small garden. Set apart from footpaths by plantings, low fences, or changes in paving, this area need not be large; a space only eight feet deep will suffice. In fact, a front yard more than 15 feet deep will actually deter the flow of activity between the house and common areas.

A study by Danish urban designer Jan Gehl compared outdoor activities in two Danish clustered housing developments

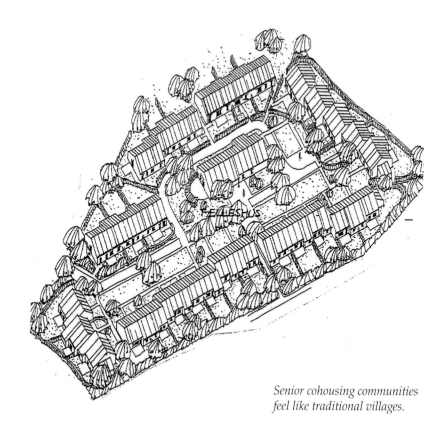

Senior cohousing communities feel like traditional villages.

(not cohousing). He found that when a soft edge was provided, residents used the area in front of the houses 68 percent of the time they spent outdoors, compared to 32 percent in the more private backyards. When there was a hard edge and no semi-private area, residents spent only 12 percent of their outdoor time in front. Even more importantly, the total number of hours spent outdoors increased four-fold when there was a soft edge.

Our findings show that people's preference for sitting or working in front of their houses is even more pronounced in cohousing: Approximately 80 percent of the time people spend outdoors near their residence is spent in the area in front of their own house, compared to 20 percent in their backyard. Be it a "front porch"

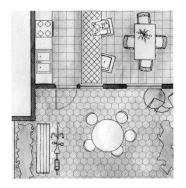

The easier it is to step outside, the more outdoor space will be used. Corridors, extra doors, and level changes should be avoided.

literally or figuratively, the area immediately in front of a house allows people to observe and take part in community life from their own perch as they choose. It's worth noting that cohousing's 80 percent front, 20 percent back design proportion is the exact opposite of the typical American single-family house.

With enclosed interior streets and courts, the transition area between dwellings and common space is reduced and less clearly defined, but it still plays an important role. Not having to worry about putting on shoes or warmer clothing in order to go outside their home, people can move more casually from private to common areas. Private entrances can be set back from a covered street to provide vestibules for storing shoes and other outdoor clothing. Casual sitting areas along the street are well used all day long.

A private outdoor space is usually provided in the rear of the house, although even here there has proved to be little need for barriers, such as fences or hedges. Usually, once residents get to know their neighbors, they find it unnecessary to define territory with fences. Visual privacy can be provided with plantings, and if at some point residents feel the need to

install fences, they will have a better idea of where and how high they should be after move-in.

Transitions within Common Areas

The common areas themselves should be designed to provide a variety of gathering spaces (architects call them gathering nodes), from sitting areas shared by five or six private dwellings to a "community plaza." Again, sensitive transitions from the most intimate to the most public gathering spaces encourage an active community life. For example, along the pedestrian streets, picnic tables can be placed where neighbors can gather over a pot of tea. And from these picnic tables, residents can have a view of the common house and patio, where people often gather on sunny afternoons. The Danes often place mailboxes and bicycle sheds near gathering nodes to create a nexus of activity.

Prior to move-in, some residents have expressed concern that local gathering places promote cliques, thus diminishing the quality of the overall community. In practice, such gathering places benefit the whole community because they bring residents out into the common areas, though it's natural for people to become better acquainted, at least initially, with their immediate neighbors. Stopping and resting places should be located where there is the greatest chance that they will be used. Besides benches and tables, low walls and steps make excellent perches.

Equally important is a community plaza for larger gatherings. When located just outside the common house, the plaza functions as the community's "front porch." Here residents gather before and after dinner, have summer barbecues, and hold other community celebrations. Ideally, people should be able to pass by the common plaza on their way out, or on their way home, to see whether others are there.

Living as Community

Spatial relationships among the individual dwellings and common spaces don't so much define a cohousing community as they express its possibilities. A good site plan fosters a lively neighborly community esprit that not only enhances an individual's quality of life, but also allows them to actively contribute more positively to the larger group.

Common House Design

If the single-family house is designed to spread people out across the landscape, then the common house is designed to bring them back together. You could say it bridges the gap between home and neighborhood. More, if a single-family house is designed to consume energy, time, and money, then the common house can be seen as a way of conserving all three. To create the right common house, you need a common house program.

In both Europe and the United States, clustered housing is preferred when attempting to create a social environment, as in this design for senior housing by the architectural firm of C.F. Møller.

Common House Program Defined

At The Cohousing Company, we dedicate two days to plan the common house with the resident group. This has proven to be quite adequate. We:

• Brainstorm, discuss, and decide common house goals. After all, none of the residents have a common house, and they cost $300,000 to $400,000 to build, so it had better serve some important functions. But which functions? Individual goals for a group's common house usually include things like supplementing the private houses, making life easier, more convenient, more practical, more economical, more fun, and many other goals. Each

The Beating Heart of the Community

More than just a nice place to have dinner with friends, the common house is the heart of every cohousing community. It is where you break bread together and, just as important, it is over dinner that you might decide to go bird watching together on Saturday, or to take a walk after eating. In other words, dinner is the number one place where relationships are built – not necessarily at the dinner table itself, but from all the activities that stem from dinner conversations. The common house is also the place where people drink coffee and play chess on a Sunday afternoon. It is inviting and friendly to the point where residents feel as if they are in their own space. Coziness, good lighting, good acoustics, good design, good company, and good food – now that's living!

group seems to find 20 to 30 community goals that their common house should strive to create or foster.

• Show images of common houses and amenities from around the world, which in turn helps everyone visualize and articulate the possibilities for achieving the aforementioned goals.

• Brainstorm, discuss, and decide the activities which directly serve those previously-stated goals – dining, laundry, playing cards, hosting guests, cooking, dancing, reading, and much more – activities that are better done together than at home. Usually groups list 40 to 50 activities that they would like to see accommodated in the common house. It's at this stage where groups begin to see exactly how, in practice, cohousing will enhance their quality of life. We all have a private realm (sleep, respite, reflective time) and a public realm (school, roads, hospitals, etc.), but a woodworking shop, for example, is hard to outfit adequately in the private realm, and rarely seems manageable in the public realm. In cohousing, a woodworking shop is a popular amenity to a common house because there are enough people to afford the space and tools, and – this is key – because people know and care enough about each other so they will not leave a mess or misplace tools. I have met a lot of folks (including myself) who tend toward leaving a mess in their own woodworking shop but wouldn't dream of leaving a mess in the common realm.

• Decide when these activities will be done (time of day, how often, with how many people)

• Determine which activities need their own space. Obviously dining does, but dancing can happen in the dining space at a different time, and meetings can happen at yet another time.

• Settle on a list of 15 to 20 places within or around the common house that are dedicated to a main activity and several ancillary activities. Each area must be

The common house faces a plaza, which the community shares with a surrounding housing development. Shown here is Nevada City Cohousing common house sketch.

Nevada City Cohousing common house side view.

Caregivers in the Common House

Common house suites are the cutting edge of senior cohousing in Denmark. Twenty years ago, in an effort to house professional caregivers on-site for an extended period of time, Danish senior cohousers installed one suite in the common house, then two suites, then three. They found that by having several suites, all of the under-utilized square footage in the common house was better used. And because the professional caregivers became more integrated into the community, residents (who needed professional care) received better quality care. These suites were designed with privacy in mind, and with the minimum space required for a comfortable extended stay.

designed for one primary activity. Multi-purpose means no purpose. As the Danes say, "If you try to do everything, you won't do anything."

• Prioritize the places. If a group can only build a dozen places (which is likely), then the group should build the dozen with the highest priority. If a group has this discussion now, these decisions can be finalized in 90 minutes. Groups that don't settle their common house priorities at this stage might never settle them and will spend hundreds of people hours not settling them.

• Program each space starting from the most important one. What other activities will happen in that space; i.e. how many dinners and on which days of the week? Groups who have this discussion now will only spend a few minutes on it. For those who wait, it will take forever.

• Define what details matter most (light and acoustics are paramount). These details will determine the size and shape of the common house. What is the character of the building (warm and cozy or antiseptic?). Groups will state the obvious. Where is the common house in relation to other spaces? We define these design criteria in as specific terms as possible. Unlike a more conventional design program, clearly defined functions to be accommodated are much more important than assigning square footage requirements. In other words, we recommend that a resident group figures out how many to seat in the dining room, or what activities the visitor's suites should accommodate, and let the architect determine how much square footage different design solutions require. The completed design program formulates these considerations in terms of desired physical characteristics and design requirements and objectives.

After these two planning days we take the resulting criteria, establish a schematic design, present it to the group (just before the private house workshop), and make changes as per the consensus of the group.

Spatial Relationships

As with the site plan, the relationships among the spaces in the common house – kitchen/dining area, lounge, workshop, visitor's suites – largely determine how well the whole works. Specific activities, such as attending common dinners, using the laundry facilities, or picking up something from the cooperative store, bring people to the common house, and the design should allow them to see if other people are there. The location and design of the kitchen can be a great asset in this

Muir Commons, Davis, California.

regard, since the cooks are usually working throughout the afternoon and evening. In a well-designed common house, one walks by, but not through the kitchen from any of the entrances. This allows the cooks to know who is coming and going. When the kitchen is closed off from the dining room and circulation, the cooks are isolated from other activities. When the cook can see and be seen, he or she is the hero of the day. When isolated, he or she feels like the slave of the day.

The relationship between the sitting and dining areas is also important. Although these spaces should be within hearing distance from each other, they need to be separate enough so that people can relax there before or after dinner. With this in mind, sometimes people use the common lounge to get away from people, and use it as a place to stretch or practice a musical instrument solo. The common house can be a place to go when someone needs to "get out of the house."

Making the Most of Available Space

Nearly every existing cohousing community contends that they need a larger common house, regardless of whether theirs is 3,000 or 8,000 square feet. Residents often cite the need for extra guest rooms, which can also be rented out to extended-stay visitors or be used by live-in professional caregivers. Building costs sometimes limit the space and amenities a community can afford. If so, it is critically important that the design provides maximum usability of what is available. If saving money while retaining community is a goal, then making the common house bigger and the private houses smaller is a wise decision.

In many cases, certain spaces in a common house are underutilized. The best example is that of a separate library. Why go to a common library when a cozy chair sits at home? Moreover, set off on its own, a library does not encourage interaction and, hence, becomes something of a white elephant.

A Question of Choice

I'm often asked, "How can you afford to spend all this time with the group?" It's a good question, but I think the real question is this: "How can we afford not to?"

By choosing to make a better life for themselves – one that fosters human-scale community while lessening their collective consumptive demands – each resident group actually accomplishes much more than their expressed goal of establishing a cohousing community. After all, if our second highest responsibility as a species (after replenishing the earth, which at 6.5 billion and counting we have obviously accomplished) is to create a viable society, then let us do that. How can we afford not to choose to spend our time building our communities?

During the planning process residents may envision using the common house like a neighborhood café, where they can read the newspaper, relax after chores, or meet with friends. By putting a casual sitting area at the edge of the dining area or near the main entrance, less space will be required and it will be used more frequently. Voila, an instant neighborhood café. People will gather there before and after dinner, and will also likely take advantage of whatever reading materials happen to be laying about.

Creating an Intimate Atmosphere

Designing for multiple use (not multi-use) is one way to take maximum advantage of available space. For example, the dining area can double as a meeting room. However, it is difficult to create an intimate atmosphere while, at the same time, providing for the needs of a large group. Which is to say that the dining area should be comfortable, not cafeteria-like, and that there must be places in the common house for both a few people to gather informally and for the whole community to meet. The kitchen should be efficient, with professional facilities adequate for efficiently preparing large meals, but it should not be institutional. Some communities have gone overboard to provide a professional kitchen and have consequently failed to create a "homey" atmosphere. Fundamentally, residents have to ask, "Do I like being there?" and "Is this a place where I will enjoy spending my time?" There is no reason to not make it warm and cozy.

Cooking and serving should be as convenient as possible, even fun. Visual access between the kitchen and dining areas helps create a residential feeling, as do the choices of interior finishes and light fixtures. For example, using natural wood finishes and warm lighting (rather than plastics, and ceiling-mounted fluorescent fixtures) helps to make the space cozier.

Acoustics

Because large groups of people will be gathering and conversing in the common house, good acoustics are necessary to create a pleasant atmosphere. If residents cannot talk in a normal conversational tone during dinner, they are likely to eat at home. Uncomfortably noisy areas are often the result of large, flat, hard-surfaced areas. Noise-absorbent surface materials can help reduce noise build up.

Guest or visitor suites are well used in senior cohousing communities.

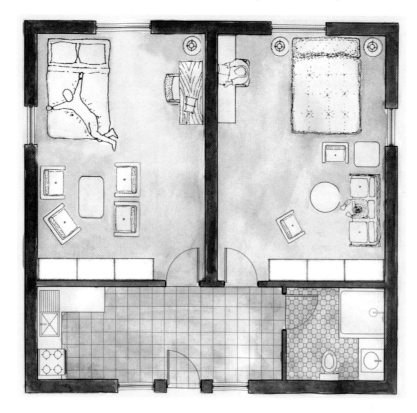

The bounce-back time of conversational noise should last about 0.5 to 1.0 second. Longer reverberation times will inevitably lead to the "cocktail party" effect where people must keep talking louder and louder in order to be understood. If the reverberation time is kept to less than one second, and the background sound level is moderately low (less than 60 dBA), it should be possiblle to carry on a normal conversation with someone at a distance of about 8-10 feet.

The design of the common house should avoid introducing loud noise sources such as televisions, dishwashers, window air conditioners, high speed supply or exhaust fans, or more likely, an oversized refrigerator, unless these sources can be managed so that they don't interfere with the ability to converse. Control of noise at the source is usually the most cost effective approach.

If problems do arise with reverberant noise, sound absorptive materials can usually be added to the walls and/or ceiling. There are many types of these materials, but a search on the internet for "sound absorptive materials" will get you started. Don't rely on your intuition for what materials provide good sound absorption; you may be wrong. In general, look for materials that have a NRC (Noise Reduction Coefficient) of 0.7 or greater.

Details

Even small details, such as the size of the dining tables, significantly affects the atmosphere of the common house. Two communities we know of felt it necessary to have extra-large tables. The result was that people sit farther apart, which

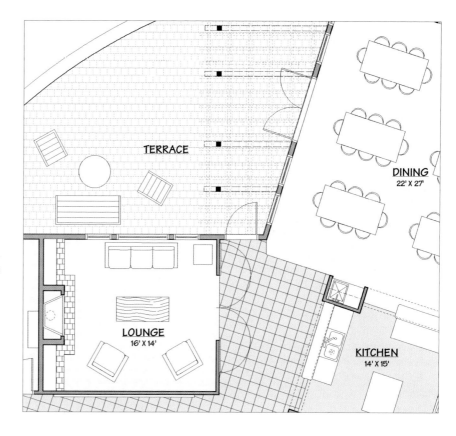

means they must talk louder to be heard from across the vastness of the table. This, in turn, raises the ambient noise level, which means that others must talk even louder ... horrible.

A 2-1/2 by 6-1/2 foot table, seating six to eight people, will permit comfortable conversation and promote a relaxed, enjoyable atmosphere. A smaller table or two might be provided for those individuals or couples who wish to be by themselves.

Laundry

When located primarily in the common house, laundry facilities generate the second highest number of people hours spent in that place (the only more utilized space is the dining/kitchen area). As a

When the lounge/sitting area is directly adjacent to the dining area, community members will use it as a gathering place. When the sitting area is located down a hall, isolated and away from the action in the dining area, it will likely be underutilized.

Highlights of Individual Residences

- Distribution of house types (number of studios, one-bedroom units, multiple-bedroom units, shared households, etc.)
- Functions to be accommodated (dining, sleeping, work, etc.)
- Desired characteristics (combined kitchen/dining/living room, open floor plan)
- Acoustic and light considerations (solar access, visual access to common house, neighbors, etc.)
- Indoor/outdoor relationship (access to terrace, etc.)
- Flexibility and future additions

Construction Phase Upgrades

- Individual upgrade options
- Post move-in options

A comfortable and relaxed common dining experience is literally designed down to the tables and chairs in senior cohousing.

result, this lonely chore instead becomes an opportunity to socialize, be it for a few minutes or an entire afternoon. You don't have much of a community unless you have things in common, and like the washing rock by the river, common laundry machines help achieve that sense of community. That said, many communities have made laundry facilities an optional feature for their private residences.

In terms of economics, it's more cost effective for a group to purchase a bank of machines than it is for each household to purchase its own set. Fewer machines purchased means less money spent, not to mention the per-household savings in construction costs. Common washers are also a cost-effective way to collect gray water for irrigation purposes that, in turn, amounts to water conservation. As well, the highest quality biodegradable detergents are affordable only when purchased in bulk (I've only seen this done when laundry facilities are located primarily in the common house). Laundry machines generate heat, and it's more difficult for each household to cut down on its air conditioner usage (or even eliminate it altogether) when washer-dryer heat is generated inside. Finally, the sound of a washer-dryer in your house is like a diesel truck idling in your living room.

All of this is not to say that individual households in a senior cohousing community can't have their own washer-dryer. It's just that with a truly usable common facility readily available, namely the common house, a common laundry is yet another way to maximize use of space while fostering community.

... And Finally

The primary purpose of the common house is to supplement the individual houses. But it accomplishes much more – it transforms a neighborhood into a community, and in so doing enhances the quality of life for everyone.

Private House Design

Just as each exterior space and common interior space (namely, the common house) in a cohousing community serves to foster livability on a human scale, so do the interior spaces of each individual residence. Architects need to work closely with residents so that each home reflects the residents' actual needs, desires, and priorities as stated during the private house workshop.

Private House Program Defined

At The Cohousing Company, we dedicate three days to accomplish the private house program and to finalize the schematic designs with the group.

We start by going back to the common house schematic design, because before we launch into the private houses we want the common house amenities to be fresh in the minds of group members. While the group provides design feedback and changes for their common house, they are reminded to the extent in which the common house supplements or potentially duplicates the features in their own house. For example, residents might decide that since their common house has two guest rooms, they might not need that extra guest room in their own home

With a soft edge design, semi-private front yards are used more than twice as often as private back yards in senior cohousing.

A "soft edge" in senior cohousing.

An enlarged balcony with a love seat, coffee table, and reading lamp provides a secondary private space in a scaled-down dwelling. Large front porches are the least costly part of the house, but can be one of the nicest areas in the house.

after all: The grandchild who visits from college can just as easily camp out in the common house guest room.

When we consider the goals of the private houses in context of the larger cohousing community, we address:

- The house matrix: How many studios, one-bedroom, two-bedroom units will the community contain; how many bathrooms each will have, and other plan options
- Slide images to help visualize and articulate possibilities
- House zoning issues
- Accessibility, adaptability, and visitability needs

- Kitchens – the size of everything, including refrigerators, sinks, range, etc.
- The number of stories for each unit type/structure
- Fireplaces
- Acoustics
- Heating and cooling
- Architecture and image

While house planning is the main issue for now, people can't always refrain from interjecting, "But I've got to have tile countertops like my daughter has." All well and good; those things will be accommodated, but in their due time. As such, all "accoutrements" are for the moment tossed into one big hopper and put aside. What's needed now is focus on the basic house plans. All extras (solar power, alternate building materials, attic access, built-in sound systems, bathtubs, and yes, those tile countertops) will be decided in the design development phases, during Study Group III.

In the evenings, we make an architectural tour of the neighborhood to look at good architecture – both historical and contemporary. We seek not only cultural architecture that is reminiscent of the architectural heritage and climatic reality of that particular location, but architecture that improves upon it, contributes to the built environment as a whole and our sense of place in it, and architecture that strives to make the bigger community feel remiss without it – not just put there.

After the first day, our office designs the four or five house plans that fit that program off-site. It takes about two to three weeks. On a Saturday we meet with each house group (one-bedroom, two-bedroom, etc.) for one and a half hours. The next day we meet with each house group a second time to go through plans that reflect their suggestions from the previous day. All the while we know what cost ramifications more square footage will have, and can explain the basic principle of how to maximize limited space.

Unlike most architecture, cohousing communities aren't just machines designed for making money (even though cohousing does seem to appreciate faster than other similar real estate). Danish architects often comment on how designing cohousing with the future residents is the only way to produce a meaningful

community. It's also the fastest way to do it. While this deliberately short (three day) and sharply focused private house program can lead to heated discussion, if done right it avoids any serious acrimony. We have done many projects without any arguments whatsoever, and created great houses in the process.

Special Design Considerations

Despite all of the concern for community and togetherness, people still spend the vast majority of their time in their own houses. As one woman puts it, "the beauty of cohousing is that you have a private life and a community life, but only as much of each as you want."

Dwellings in senior cohousing reflect special design considerations because of shared facilities, variety of residential needs, and the relationships among residents.

Cohousing communities often develop four or five house models to fit the different needs of residents.

> **Build Now, Customize Later**
> Cohousing communities can save money by limiting the number of floor plans to one for each house size and by keeping finish options (flooring, cabinets, bathroom tiles, etc.) to a manageable number. Residents may be able to accept such limitations if the units are initially designed so they can be easily expanded or customized later.

Hearthstone Cohousing private house interior.

With the common house as a proven asset that supplements the functions of the private houses, residents are less hesitant about reducing the size of their own residences. Space is no longer needed in the home for laundry facilities, guest rooms, or a workshop. Private kitchens should be fully equipped yet efficient in their use of space. A smaller kitchen is quite reasonable for residents who frequently eat their dinner in the common house, which, as it happens, can also be used for private parties or formal dinners. Additionally, the availability of common facilities makes it easier for people who have previously lived in larger houses to adjust to smaller spaces.

Adaptable Interior Design

One of the primary problems with conventional senior housing today is the feeling of impersonality. By contrast, new senior cohousing communities usually devise four to six different house plans for residents to choose from. The basic models are agreed on in the planning process, and those who prefer a specific model work with the architect to refine its design. Individual households often make additional changes (such as options and upgrades including flooring, appliances etc.), so that, in the end, every house is slightly different.

By being realistic about what the future may hold, senior cohousers can choose which features to include at construction and which may be added later. The design should be readily adaptable for sudden and unexpected needs of residents, including the possibility for residents to easily swap units. While it is not essential to make every unit conform to the highest accessibility standards from the beginning, it is important that there be contingency plans.

Adaptable design is probably the most challenging area for senior cohousing groups to work through during the private house program. Group members should prepare for some interesting

Dancing after dinner in the common house.

meetings as this territory is investigated, priced out, felt out, projected, analyzed, discussed, and finally decided upon. Historically, accessibility issues have always defaulted to code requirements, though seniors in cohousing usually manage to improve on these requirements considerably, as they should.

Resident stability is important in any neighborhood, and this is especially so in senior developments. If people must move from the community because their house no longer meets their needs, the long-range benefits of a stable community are jeopardized. Aging-in-place issues are something the group will have covered in Study Group I, though it is here where those issues and resolutions are made tangible.

A variety of dwelling sizes allow residents to move within the community as their needs dictate – the aforementioned unit swap. One resident commented just after swapping residences, "With the help of neighbors, we exchanged houses on a single Saturday afternoon. Of course, the paperwork took a little longer."

Standardizing Designs

Custom construction is typically twice as expensive as production construction; and the custom home experience is the opposite of the cohousing experience. All custom houses start with a standardized lot subdivided along with many others, by somebody else, and then a custom home is placed on it. In other words, what starts off as production housing (one of many), ends up as custom. Cohousing is just the opposite, in that it is unique in its inception, and ends up as one of many.

An open floor plan saves space by "overlapping" rooms or borrowing space from adjacent rooms, even if only psychologically. Local lighting, low walls, and/or flooring changes, rather than full-height walls, define areas in this house in senior cohousing.

Direct access from the entrance to the downstairs bedrooms allows for temporary boarders or live-in caregivers to have greater autonomy, or in this senior cohousing in Boulder, Colorado, the downstairs is a basement for storage.

A truly effective way to keep prices down is for residents to consciously limit the number of custom features incorporated into the design of their individual houses. The price of a custom house is substantially higher than that of a production housing, where a few floor plans are repeated over and over. As one contractor explains, "If the builders have to think about what they are doing, and if they have to keep track of what goes where and in which house, they charge more."

If not carefully planned for, "individualizing" can add considerably to the construction costs. Undisciplined design efforts have been known to increase unit costs beyond some people's reach. Unfortunately, some cohousing groups have only discovered this through costly experiences. Minor custom touches such as an extra wall or different bathroom fixtures, though relatively inexpensive when viewed one-by-one, have a cumulative effect that can increase the cost of construction exponentially for everyone, since they effect larger design considerations and construction time lines. Several communities have allowed residents to incorporate numerous additions and changes into the design. At the end, residents were shocked by a construction price of $5,000 to $10,000 higher than they had anticipated. Residents later calculated they would have been much better off if they had kept to standard designs, even if every household had gone back and customized with their own contractors, they would have ended up spending less when all was said and done.

Once the design has been finalized and construction begun, any subsequent changes, no matter how minor they appear, will increase the final price of the units. It takes a lot of self-discipline to impose limitations on what may be the residents' only chance to design their own homes. It proves difficult for architects, builders, and developers (as well as owners), to say "no" to future neighbors with whom they have been working for months or even years.

Doyle Street Cohousing private house interior. Mezzanines, high ceilings, and creative design make small dwellings seem larger.

Space efficiency can be achieved by having an open house plan such as this house in senior cohousing.

Setting a careful budget from the start and trying to stick to it can keep the conflict – and the prices – to a minimum. The reward to homeowners for such self-discipline can be lower mortgages, more money for later renovation, and even better houses, since complexity detracts attention from quality.

Designing Small Residences

The small dwelling sizes often necessitated by today's economy, the group's specific goals, and the needs of seniors to age in place as comfortably as possible for as long as possible, require residents to be more careful in establishing priorities and designers to be more creative in the use of space. It is easy to accommodate many different functions in a large house, but a small house must do more with less – small housing must fit like a glove instead of a grocery bag. In addition to avoiding

any overlap with the amenities provided in the common house, residents need to clarify for themselves (and the architect) what functions are the most important for their homes to fulfill. Besides establishing priorities for the allocation of space, residents can also establish priorities for construction quality. Speculative developers may choose to spend less money on sound insulation between units, in order to spend more on flashy kitchen cabinets that have more immediate selling impact. When residents are able to make these decisions themselves, they are more likely to consider long-term trade-offs, and therefore may choose inexpensive kitchen cabinets so they can afford better sound insulation. After move-in, it's a lot easier to upgrade kitchen cabinets than it is to rebuild walls and floors for better sound insulation.

Guest room in senior cohousing.

The use of mezzanines, high ceilings, light, and the juxtapositions of spaces can help make small areas feel larger. Ceiling height and window placement can have an enormous effect on how a room is perceived. The subtleties also add up: acoustics, storage, and even paint colors take on great importance in this regard. Making a small house work, requires attention to these types of details.

Breaking from the long tradition of locating the most formal rooms, typically the living room or parlor, toward the front of the house, cohousers have discovered many advantages to locating the kitchen on the public side of the house, toward the shared outdoor space. This layout creates a stronger link between indoors and outdoors and between private and community areas. Conversely, the private side of the house is usually toward the rear or upstairs, where there is as much peace and quiet as in a detached house. A small supplementary sitting/reading area can sometimes be provided in the corner of a balcony or hallway without taking up much space.

Multi-Story vs. Single-Story

Another important consideration in senior cohousing design is whether some or all of the units should be one-story flats. Most American seniors prefer single-level housing. While this is true, it isn't an absolute. Some residents may want to live in a townhouse style unit, and move to a flat later on only if the stairs really become a problem for them. For example, in a 16-unit senior cohousing project that we, The Cohousing Company, recently

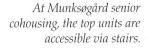

At Munksøgård senior cohousing, the top units are accessible via stairs.

designed, has all but six units had either loft or basement spaces. At the time of design, the residents of this community were looking to the future, but hadn't yet limited themselves. It's worth noting that these lofts and basements are non-essential spaces, spaces their visiting children will access when the residents themselves no longer can.

Because a senior cohousing group is involved in the design of its community from the start, personal preference can be built into the mix, and economically. In the case of Munksøgård, stairs were important to this group of 20 households. I was startled to find half of the houses in the development upstairs, and, as it turns out, the residents were weary of being quizzed about it. There is a long story behind the decision, but the short answer was succinctly provided by one resident: "It was the most economical way of getting this project built and we needed the most economical way." And as if to rationalize it a little, he added, "Besides, walking up and down the stairs keeps us younger." The Munksøgård seniors found that if all the houses in their community were single story, the building costs would increase along with the building footprints. Indeed, if single-story houses had been built, the square footage of each unit would have been smaller than usual and each would have cost 25 percent more.

Munksøgård's residents, of course, recognize that they are aging. Therefore when they made the decision to build two-story housing they also modified their community co-care agreements. In Munksøgård today, when a mobility limitation becomes a reality for someone in the community, the affected person will be the first on a waiting list to get a downstairs unit. And if that were not possible, an oversized guest room is to be made available for them in the common house. And if that isn't possible, they will take turns caring for the disabled person in an upstairs home until a downstairs unit becomes available. Although most Danish senior cohousing features easily-accessible ground-floor units, thus sidestepping these specific co-care issues altogether, Munksøgård shows what sort of exceptions can be made when affordability is an issue. In senior cohousing, community trumps design constraints, every time.

Bathrooms

While the houses in senior cohousing typically run on the small side (averaging 800 or 900 square feet), the bathrooms within the units are quite large, often 6 ft by 9 ft (54 sf). In contrast, a standard bathroom size for other housing types is 5 ft by 7 ft (35 sf). In addition to increased size, bathrooms in senior cohousing units are designed to be exceptionally flexible, functional, and easy to clean.

Although it is rare for an individual to move into a senior cohousing community while in a wheelchair, a good design plans for that possibility. A flexible design provides living spaces that meet a resident's needs at move-in and will accommodate their needs in the long-term. In practical terms, a bathroom can keep its "desired feel" and still be able to provide optimal utility. If optimal utility is not incorporated initially, the design can be made to be adaptable, such that the necessary utility can be added when it is actually required.

Note the roll-in shower and the sink that can accomodate a wheelchair. Wait to put in grab bars later, only if and when they are needed.

Utilitarian bathrooms do not have to be without charm.

A new cohousing community grand opening.

A Word About Architecture

One of the things I like most about designing cohousing is that it takes architecture to the people (something that is historically reserved for the rich). Indeed, the private houses in a cohousing community can be more beautiful and more functional than any home the residents have ever lived in.

A bad design program guarantees bad architecture, but a good program doesn't guarantee good architecture. A good architect needs to be skilled in provoking and inspiring the group to new architectural heights from a social and aesthetic point of view. Which is to say that good architecture comes from the heart and a heartfelt appreciation for what a resident

group is trying to accomplish. Find a good architect. One who truly appreciates the cohousing concept. One who understands the needs of today's seniors. The end result is worth the search.

Finally, good architecture doesn't come from a particular process. But if the senior cohousing design program is efficiently accomplished, the architect will have the time, energy, and motivation to make beautiful buildings. Too often, a bad and inefficient programming process doesn't allow the architect to focus on the design that the residents will love. Experiential spaces and meaningful places are missing from most institutional settings, and most private settings for that matter. Beauty takes time.

Front porch view of the Pleasant Hill Cohousing private houses, Pleasant Hill, California.

Final Thoughts on Design

The discussions here about design should be used to broaden and guide the dialogue between designer and residents, and should not replace it. When residents and designers consciously consider the activities they want to occur subconsciously later, only then will a community emerge that's designed to emphasize a community approach to living while protecting the privacy of individuals and families within the community.

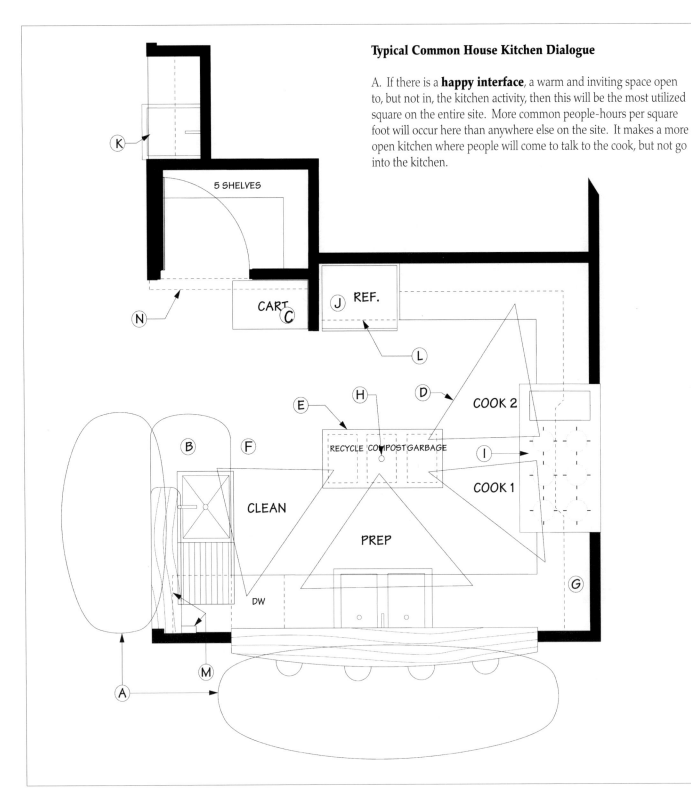

Typical Common House Kitchen Dialogue

A. If there is a **happy interface**, a warm and inviting space open to, but not in, the kitchen activity, then this will be the most utilized square on the entire site. More common people-hours per square foot will occur here than anywhere else on the site. It makes a more open kitchen where people will come to talk to the cook, but not go into the kitchen.

5 SHELVES

K

N

CART C

J REF.

L

E H D

COOK 2

B F

RECYCLE COMPOST GARBAGE

I

COOK 1

CLEAN

PREP

G

DW

M

A

B. The **countertop** is open and unencumbered, making room for dishes ready to go out to dining and dirty dishes coming back to the kitchen. This eliminates unnecessary walking around the bar, especially when two people are working together (one person puts stuff on the bar, and another puts it on the table).

C. The **cart** takes things to the table and brings them back efficiently. Clean dishes go from the dishwasher to the cart , ready to go directly to the table the next day. There is no extra motion of putting the dishes unto the shelves, only to take them out again. No shelves, no wasted motion.

D. The theoretical **four activity triangles** (prep, cook 1, cook 2, clean) should not overlap in order to facilitate safety and efficiency.

E. The **central island** brings people and activities together – it facilitates community. You'll find folks there drinking coffee 'til the wee hours if the kitchen is otherwise warm and cozy and attracts people. You'll find the lights on there when they are out everywhere else (except maybe the sitting room). Common kitchens are designed to be centripetal, that is to bring people together, to make cooking social and fun.

F. Probably most important is a **cozy feel**. people will want to be in an extraordinary space – and that is essential to the success of the kitchen – people will fundamentally want to be there. To accommodate this, the kitchen should be:

1. **Open**: to see and be seen. The pleasant distraction of saying hello to a passer-by. To be appreciated: "It sure smells good." The cooks need to see folks and folks need to see them. Seeing them will attract other non-related activities. Not seeing them facilitates an otherwise empty common house.

2. **Warm**: lots of natural wood; rounded wood edging at the countertop; wood cabinets (upper and lower). Besides the custom upper cabinets, I recommend a shaker lower, of which there are many reasonable manufacturers on the market, a deep, rich linoleum color at the floor; natural finish at the door to the pantry; natural wood baseboard; and other aesthetic touches.

3. **Light**: Lighting needs to be at the task (100 foot candles) without too much general lighting (50 foot candles). No ceiling-mounted fluorescents.

4. The **feel** should be gourmet: "Wow, what a great kitchen,"– like you would find in a nice house – but never commercial. Commercial kitchens are designed to keep everyone separated and task focused.

Cohousing kitchens are designed to bring people together, to make cooking fun – like a French country kitchen – yet very efficient.

G. **Finding everything is faster**: if there are no doors on the upper cabinets and if most utensils can be seen. We have stayed in the guest rooms of many common houses. In half of them, you could always tell when it was 4 p.m., because you could hear the noise as people went through the cabinets, trying to prepare themselves since they last cooked a month ago. Having things open and accessible, such as the French utensil bar, the pot rack over the island, and the pull-out shelves facilitates a j.i.t. kitchen (j.i.t. means just-in-time in manufacturing parlance).

H. The **floor drain** saves the cook or assistant 15 minutes at the end of the evening – just when you need it most. The last thing done is mopping the floor. The floor drain makes that a lot easier, and therefore helps to keep the kitchen sanitary, too.

I. **Industrial kitchen** equipment is important. When it's a quarter to six, you're expecting 50 people for dinner, and the pasta water is not boiling, that "wooff" of the 15,000 btu/hr burner is music to your ears. The dishwasher needs to take less than 3 minutes, etc. But this in no way implies that the kitchen needs to feel cafeteria-like or institutional in any way.

J. The **refrigerator** should be easily accessible from outside and inside – that is, closest to dining. Accessing the refrigerator will be the number one reason a non-cook/assistant will enter the kitchen. Non-cooks/assistants walking around the kitchen can be dangerous (sharp knives, hot pots, etc). Making that circulation minimal is beneficial. It also keeps people out of the cooks' way, especially because people often want to access the refrigerator (to see if that orange drink they left there last week is still there, for example) just before dinner when the cooks are the most frantic.

K. A **wet bar** keeps the thirsty out of the kitchen. Grabbing a glass is the second most common reason someone will wander through the kitchen. Placing glasses and drinking water just outside the kitchen, but close to the refrigerator and the dishwasher, is the most efficient solution.

L. **Storage** above for salad and punch bowls.

M. Accessible phone and cook books.

N. A plate rack over the door displays large decorative platters.

Residents preparing common dinner
in Bellingham Cohousing.

CHAPTER NINE

Study Group III
Policy

The core resident group is strong, has had its say during the design of the project, and the final architectural plans are being drawn up. It's time for the architects to go to work, develop the design, do the construction documents, get it permitted to build, and bid out the project. It's also time for the community to finish up the specifics for this particular community – its process of creating the social community if you will. How will we maintain the place, what are the final agreements, regarding who will take care of who? How will we run our meetings?

Forward Progress Via the Participatory Process

It should be obvious by now that the participatory development process is an established, step-by-step procedure for creating cohousing. And it is only through this process that senior cohousing communities have optimally been built.

At this stage, because real money and real people's lives are on the line, everyone involved must have clear roles to play. For example, if the group clearly stated how many bicycles they wanted to be accommodated on the site during Study Group II, and if they have retained a good architect, the group never has to think of where the bicycle sheds will go, and what they will look like. Everyone plays their role for a given issue and moves on. (I recommend that anything subjective and design-oriented be handled by the professionals later. Group involvement on subjective, hence irreconcilable, matters at this stage will simply cost too much and take too long.) Bottom line, the goal here is to get the community built, with quality, on time, and on budget.

Moreover, a successful group sets and sticks to realistic timelines that outline the phases and timing of key decisions. Where to locate the site; what professionals to hire; what to put on the site and where; the types of financing; and so forth. If the decisions required of residents are made as scheduled, the project will keep moving forward (and there will also be less resident turnover during the development process).

One successful way to work with a developer is to agree that if decisions are not made within a certain time, then the

During the six months or so it takes to compile construction documents; take bids; and negotiate with contractors; get permits; the group needs to address key issues that affect both the economic and social health of the community.

Economic Policies

From the outside looking in, the number and variety of economic issues confronting a resident group may seem considerable. However, when broken into component parts (which may not be obvious), these issues are straightforward and easy to solve with basic policy choices.

developer will make a default decision. At this stage, however, when a developer is too flexible, they are not doing any favors for the resident group. Flexibility at this juncture means changes and delays – and changes and delays mean increased costs. More on this important issue in a bit.

Keeping to a timeline also means avoiding backtracking. Once decisions have been made at each phase, the group must move on to the next phase. If everyone understands the issues and the agreed-upon solutions at the time, old issues are less likely to resurface. But most importantly, if the group backtracks, they will inadvertently chase away the can-do people who they need to get the project done. It is discouraging (and disrespectful) for members of a group to make a decision one Saturday, only to have it raised again five Saturdays later. If 12 people sat through a discussion for 20 minutes, that's four people-hours that went into that discussion. A marginal improvement might be made by raising the issue again, but one that's probably not worth the discouragement. Of course, no one wants to close the door on good ideas, and some groups re-raise an issue if two thirds of the people there originally agree. It doesn't happen very often – it's usually more important to keep moving. And in the context of trying to get others to re-raise a question, usually it becomes clear why the current decision was reached.

How new members are recruited and oriented also affects a group's ability to stay on track. To retain continuity, it is best not to bring in new members in the middle of a phase, such as the preparation of the design program. Ideally, groups

---

Financial Estimates (professionals)

Since the site, common house, and private residence design workshops are complete, and the program has been compiled, the project's cost can be updated. Reasonable estimates can now be updated for projected:

- site improvement costs
- construction costs per square foot for houses
- costs for common areas
- development timeline

This updated information is critical for individual households to secure their necessary financing; and for when the group takes bids on the project and negotiates with a builder.

Pre-construction the professionals will:
- Complete working drawings and building specifications
- Obtain building permits
- Solicit and negotiate construction bids
- Select contractor
- Finalize construction contract, loan, and schedule
- Secure construction financing

Pre-construction the residents will:
- Complete recruiting efforts, if necessary
- Finalize community participation ownership agreements
- Do financial estimates. The group needs to ascertain what their monthly association fees are (maintenance, tools, insurance, hired help, if any, birthday cakes, etc.) The entire replacement costs of roofs, water heaters, etc., are done separately)

During construction the professionals will:
- Monitor contracted work
- Help secure mortgage loans

Post-construction the residents will:
- Complete any resident-built work
- And phase III will go into post-occupancy

---

should only bring in new members at the beginning of a new phase of the development process. In actual practice, once the initial program has been set, unless there is an overflow of participants, new members are usually accepted at any time until all units are filled. Recruitment campaigns should be organized at key points, such as before site purchase and before taking a construction loan. New members should be oriented as to the history and status of the group, which decisions have already been made, and which are still open for discussion. Empirically for most people that means sitting down one-on-one and going through the previous materials.

Turnover of participants is inescapable. Someone might land their dream job on the other side of the country. Family matters may intervene. Regardless, the number of residents who participate in the entire process does not seem to affect the success of a project once it is completed. The backbone of the project is the organizing group and the participatory culture it creates. The momentum of the people committed to it, because they intend to live there, carries the day.

Resident Committees

Committees come and go as necessary. As work needs to be done, interested individuals set up and join a committee; then disband once the particular project has been seen through to completion.

Committees at Work

Whatever the problem, a committee first brainstorms with the whole group. For instance:

- A 10 minute brainstorm on recruitment - how many open household spots need to be filled, income threshold, ideal commitment timelines for new prospects; who to contact for publicity and when; what angle to take per outlet; location of the meeting, the agenda, etc.
- Then the committee goes away, does some research, creates a proposal, comes back, and presents it. Brief and to the point is best.
- The whole group discusses the relative merits of the proposal.
- A vote is taken, consensus is reached, and then the committee takes over and soon has something to hand to the local newspaper's lifestyles editor for the Sunday paper and the ball is rolling.

Finally, when people are in the group they contribute to it while they are there (even if they move on), and in turn help to build the community – a community responsive to real people's needs because real people were involved to solve real life issues.

Respectful Dissent

What do you do with the problematic person who's never learned the art of discussion issues with other people or how to find the best solution for everyone, not just for themselves. This concern has come up at every single cohousing seminar I have ever given – and I've given hundreds. So. What to do? Respectfully say your piece. Hold your ground. Listen attentively. Be willing to compromise. Remind yourself it isn't about "who wins" and "who loses." Be willing to accept a solution or approach you don't necessarily agree with. Call the vote. Make the decision. Then move on.

Obviously, people are much more dynamic than simply being "cooperative" or "non-cooperative" in a group setting. If an individual has a tendency to storm out of the room every time he doesn't get his own way, they probably won't last long. While people aren't born with an inate ability to cooperate (but you'd think we would be since it appears to be the best way to survive), it can be learned. And while people may have less than perfect manners when they join the group, if they are willing, motivated and work hard they might become the most giving, thoughtful and considerate neighbors you've ever had. Or they will soon figure out that this is not for them and move on. Group members might also drop a hint: "Look

The first public presentation for the Nevada City Cohousing community

if you don't want to cooperate with your neighbor then there are other options out there waiting for you. And there is probably someone else waiting to live here who would like to."

It doesn't mean this individual won't turn out to be the best community member and neighbor that anyone has ever met. It just takes a few months to figure out who's who, and under what circumstances.

In studying cohousing for over two decades, after living in it for over 14 years, and by helping plan about 40 cohousing communities, I've attended (I hate to admit this) almost 750 cohousing meetings. As in a small town, community and belonging coexist with accountability.

Recruitment: Before Move-In
At this stage if a core group has not filled out its ranks with a full roster of households, now is the time to do so. Make no mistake, since the resident group itself

is ultimately responsible for ensuring the success of their project, if there are not enough households to fill out the group (even while the architect is working on the drawings), then the group needs to put their recruitment efforts into overdrive. Potential residents may (and do) drop out during the Study Group II process for any number of reasons and the group needs to maintain its numbers in order to retain its social and economic viability – the architect will be spending a lot of money on the group's behalf with civil, structural, mechanical, soils, and sometimes acoustic engineers, landscape architects, and even interior designers.

There are many ways to go about filling in the open spaces, tactics the group is probably quite familiar with by this point: placing local newspaper ads, getting the ear of a sympathetic local journalists, and any other number of schemes. Get creative. And don't forget to tap the already-friendly local officials and

Nevada City Cohousing under construction

senior organizations for a helping hand. The good plans already in place will make the project a compelling opportunity for all involved.

The recruitment goal at this stage is to inform as many prospective households as possible about the senior cohousing community under development – what it is, what it isn't, what it can be. Since the group already has as sense of the sort of community it desires – low income, high income, mixed; ideal number of households; co-care responsibilities; and so on – the purpose now is to find others who might share these same views. You can't please everyone, and that's precisely the point. This informational meeting is designed to attract others who might be interested in the basic sort of community that the core group has already envisioned. This in and of itself is a self-selecting process. Those people who like the concept of senior cohousing but don't share the core group's vision can, of course, start their own group.

New Residents: After Move-In

All well and good but people often ask, what about people waiting to move in after the group is all together and has been living there. Although turnover in cohousing is much less than in regular neighborhoods (if you've spent two years putting a custom-made neighborhood together that supposedly fits like a glove, you're not motivated to readily move. But things happen and people do move.)

As for people joining the group after move-in, the community itself and a strong participation agreement go a long way toward attracting potential residents. After a couple of common dinners, a couple of workdays, a couple of common management meetings, and a guided tour through the participation agreement, potential new residents will know exactly what they are buying into. Moreover, showing prospective new residents early design plans and decisions will help them to know where the community is coming from, and where it is likely headed.

Lest one thinks it is difficult to attract cooperative-minded people to a group, know that most existing cohousing communities in the United States today have waiting lists of potential residents. In this regard, demand far and away exceeds supply.

Changes During Construction

Groundbreaking is an exciting time for all cohousing groups. All the months of planning and long meetings finally begin to take tangible form. This doesn't necessarily mean the group can relax. Typically, a "building committee" is delegated responsibility for bi-weekly contact with the architect – the project manager earns his or her keep here – and for making many decisions.

A common mistake at this stage is allowing changes during construction. Allowing virtually no changes (except for the bare minimum necessary to accommodate local code updates) is the only way to not complicate the building process and complications always add unanticipated costs.

The terms of the construction contract should be carefully worked out beforehand with no changes allowed during construction, except for a defined set of options that were determined by the entire group earlier. Usually there are about 20 options in total: countertops, flooring, appliances, and so on. Residents may swear at the contractor and the committee for not allowing "just this one little change," but in the long run, a firm "no-changes" policy will save the community a lot of grief and money.

As for the order of what should get built when, we offer this mantra: "Finish the common house first." It is a great asset to have a place to meet, eat, and do the laundry while the houses are just being occupied and people are still moving in. Also, having a functioning common house from the very beginning establishes a pattern of daily use, helps to break the old habits of people used to having one of everything, and who have never had such facilities before. The common house works like a dream if it is designed effectively and the timing is right.

Work days are usually one Saturday a month. There are often two or three coaches – that is, those who organize the project and buy the materials.

Finance Essentials

In the United States, banks typically require purchase commitments for at least 70 percent of the units before they will approve a construction. Those who put up the initial investment for consulting fees and uncommitted shares are reimbursed later from the construction loan. This is a critical stage, in that members are now taking a real risk. Should the partnership decide to dissolve, a portion of the individual investment will have already been spent and could be lost. I should point out that, to the best of our knowledge, every cohousing community that has started construction has been successfully completed and occupied.

Fannie Mae and Personal Mortgages

A bank can handle personal mortgage loans in two ways. With a portfolio loan, the bank keeps the loan in-house, holding on to the 30-year note and absorbing the risk itself. However, many banks prefer to sell the loan to a federal mortgage company that buys loans from banks on a scale large enough to minimize its own risk. The loans available through this secondary loan market often (though not always) deliver the best rates and certainly broaden the choices of an individual shopping for a loan.

There is a catch: A new development must be approved by the Federal National Mortgage Association (nicknamed Fannie Mae) before any bank can offer a secondary market loan on it. Many banks, and even portfolio lenders, will not loan on projects that have not been approved. They fear losing money if they should have to foreclose on the unit and fail to find a buyer. Single-family houses are a safe bet because there is a confirmed market for this type of housing. Even conventional condominiums occasionally have difficulty in getting Fannie Mae approval. Few banks are willing to be adventurous with their loans. They look to Fannie Mae to weed out the bad risks.

Banks typically want to see 20 to 30 percent of the project's cost already invested in equity before it will loan the remaining 70 to 80 percent. This equity is amassed from a number of sources: money already spent on land purchase and project approvals; cash from investors both resident and non-resident; and any amount the current landowner is willing to carry until the completion of the project. The commitment of the future residents is essential. Their money invested in the project shows that they are serious and able buyers.

Sources of financing outside the large banks can be found. Small local banks

River City Cohousing, Sacramento, California

might step to finance local projects when larger banks take a more conservative stance. Innovative energy-saving measures might provide a group access to low-rate, government-sponsored mortgages. Where there is a will, there is a way.

Consultants

Enlisting the assistance of facilitators, architects, lawyers and financial consultants who are supportive of the group's goals significantly expedites the development process and its ability to meet a budget. The more experience they have had with cohousing, the better.

Consultants who are familiar with land and development costs, financing possibilities, and ownership options can assist in defining the realistic financial expectations early in the process. Consultants who are themselves committed to the cohousing concept are more likely to provide the nontraditional services required in participatory process, such as extra meetings, field trips, explanations of options, or facilitation of group decisions. At the same time, consultants must not dictate decisions for the group, and just because their hearts are in the right place does not mean that they can get the job done.

Sometimes professionals within the resident group can provide some consultant services. While this may apparently reduce costs, it can also create conflicts between the personal and professional interests of the resident consultant, and should be given careful thought beforehand. Traditionally, if a consultant is not performing to the standard a group requires, the first impulse is to get rid of that consultant as soon as possible (after

a couple of gentle warnings, perhaps). But when that consultant is also a group member, this impulse can short circuit – it is painful to fire a group member. Whether or not a group member should act as a consultant depends, of course, on who that person is.

Chris Miller, mechanical engineer and resident of the Nevada City cohousing community, never had any difficulties in combining these two roles for two reasons: First, there was never any question that he was always looking out for the interests of the group – though not to say that he couldn't be firm with his professional opinion; and second, Chris did not try to control every aspect of every thing that came to his attention. For this group, he was the right man for the jobs he did.

Site plan of Frog Song Cohousing, Cotati, California

Living room in Otium senior cohousing.

As the saying goes, "by the time you know the tricks of the trade, you have the attitude of the trade." Which is to say that too many consultants get flustered when novices question their expertise. A truly professional consultant is able to listen very carefully to what people are trying to say, stays patient, is never patronizing, and never feels threatened with this in mind. A group member who is considering a turn as a professional consultant (for his or her own group) needs to do a gut check before starting and ask him or herself if they are ready for what may come. But more likely, in our experience of working with many cohousing groups, a group-member/consultant will work extra diligently to achieve the desired outcome. I'm certain that the term "conflict of interest" was cooked up by a legal system interested in creating acrimony. In a village, by contrast, conflict of interest works to everyone's advantage because it enhances accountability.

In considering how best to use consultants, residents must decide how involved they want to be in various aspects of the process. Whereas issues of ultimate livability need to be decided by the resident group, countless technical decisions can be delegated to the developer and to outside consultants. Everyone plays a role. Communities developed in recent years have felt it less important to be involved in every aspect of development, and often gave more responsibility to the architect and other consultants than did their predecessors, partly due to increasing economic pressures to keep to a strict timeline, and because it has been demonstrated that

State Supported Care, Danish Style

In Denmark, there is government support for individuals to stay in their private house as they age. The government delivers medicine (but doesn't pay for it all anymore), some food, and provides personal care and basic housecleaning services. So when people move into a senior cohousing community they are in effect complementing their government services with those that will be provided by their neighbors.

These Danes know that government officials and workers won't sit and play cards with them, or even share a pot of tea and chat. And these official caregivers certainly won't pull the weeds from their garden, come by for a birthday surprise, or invite them over for a snack and a movie.

The Danish healthcare system, as good as it is, doesn't provide emotional support, and, obviously, can't do everything. This is why, even in Denmark, people are choosing to live in senior cohousing versus staying in a single-family house. In-house care is on the wane in Denmark, yet another reason why senior cohousing is becoming more and more popular there.

cohousing groups that establish a clear criteria and then get out of the way control costs best. In addition, many European and increasingly American architects today have a firm understanding of how to design toward the needs of prospective senior cohousing residents. Typically, residents play a very active role during the initial planning stages then delegate greater control to the architect and other consultants as the process proceeds.

I've noticed that since Danish architects are held in such high regard in their society (for good reason – they really do actively and visibly contribute to the viability of their society) residents tend not to second-guess them as much. However, not all architects are treated equally: In Denmark, architects who have designed 15 or more senior cohousing communities do not seem to get second-guessed at all. Those who have designed only one or two should have been second-guessed – they just don't know what they are doing yet.

Social Policies

The plans are approved by the municipality. Consultants are hired, and a developer has been contracted. Permits are in the works and a groundbreaking date is penciled in. All well and good. This group of people will soon do more than just hold meetings; they will actually move out of their existing homes and move in together as a neighborhood community. That's a big change, right? What happens if someone gets ill? What if someone no longer wants to or is able to participate in the community? What sort of policies should

Flexibility in Tasks

Since seniors have more free time (they're either retired, or about to retire) their relaxed schedules provide plenty of time for getting things done. As such, seniors usually need few rules for many ordinary tasks in senior cohousing. If the lawn needs mowing and you're able-bodied, you'll probably just mow the lawn, unless you hate mowing the lawn. In that case, someone who likes to mow will do it, and you'll tend to the planter boxes and flower gardens instead. Senior cohousers typically recruit help from their fellow neighbors for these tasks, not because they need to, but because it's more fun.

The Danes in senior cohousing have curbed the use of lengthy formal agreements and rely more on organic methods for most chores. These less formal methods have worked. However, working this way requires an act of faith. People who haven't lived in cohousing before, would probably be nervous about leaving it all to chance. It seems overly optimistic. But as one Danish senior cohouser told me: "Our approach is that whenever we have a specific need, we put it on the agenda, brainstorm, discuss and decide. Usually very quickly."

The result is a custom solution for a given task, at the moment it's needed, forged by the group. The point is that it is not always necessary to absolutely fix the level of cooperation ahead of time, provided all members of the community can agree on a plan for working out issues in an ad hoc fashion, whenever problems arise. A smart list (an agreed-on plan) covers basic issues like: How many dinners in the common house a week; who cooks; who maintains what and when; who belongs to which committees (finance, social, kitchen, etc.)?

Who Does What?

As retirees, seniors have time to pace themselves for getting tasks done. Senior cohousing communities often assign tasks in an informal fashion, and may even leave many tasks open to whoever is motivated at any given time, according to age and energy.

The more able-bodied, say those 55-65, would probably assign themselves the more physically-demanding tasks; the healthy 65-75 year olds might do mid-range chores like tidying the workshop or cleaning the shelves in the common house; and those 75 or older might mend the curtains.

the group put into place that will ensure as healthy a community as possible, for as long as possible?

While a group's social policies will be specific to that group (the social policies of two senior cohousing communities are at the end of this chapter), there are a few issues that every senior cohousing group will take up at some point during the planning and development process. The most far-reaching and personal of them have to do with co-care. What can and should residents expect in terms of co-care? Conversely, what should be the limits?

Agreements About Co-Care

Since aging gracefully includes the possibility of aging suddenly, certain basic co-care issues have to be resolved far in advance of move-in. Residents need some common ground for what will be expected of them in this regard. In addition, these contingencies should be codified in the bylaws of a senior cohousing community. In writing, these contingencies are usually extremely brief. For example: "If you haven't raised your blinds by 10 am someone will knock on your door."

Codified co-care issues should address who does what and when, and what each member commits to doing, or not doing. A group will undoubtedly want agreed-upon understandings for tasks that are seen as unpleasant, such as changing soiled pants, bathing, or spoon-feeding someone. It's about boundaries. Most residents just want to be neighbors, after all, not health aides.

Separating neighborly care from professional care is not a colossal task in senior cohousing, for two reasons. First, people who live in cohousing readily learn to say no. Second, the size of the community means that co-care burdens are easily distributed as a natural, normal part of everyday life. Picking up someone's medicine while you're picking up your own is just not that big of a deal.

Meeting in Doyle Street Cohousing

The bottom line is that residents need to be able to give themselves the permission to say, "No, I can't do that." Of course, some gray areas might slip through the formal-discussion cracks, like:

- The "is anyone home?" checks
- Assisting an ill person to and from common dinners
- Picking up medicine or groceries
- Taking an ill person out on a day trip

In this Study Group I phase, a group should simply put gray co-care issues on the table and address them. Better now than after move-in. However, after living in a senior cohousing community for a while, residents will likely find that their agreed upon codified co-care tasks are not an undue burden. Rather, they will be naturally easy-to-do and immensely rewarding. Said one resident:

> *"I love the support I get from this small group of people – but it also works because I don't depend on it. I could live without it, but then again why would I?"*

Co-care basically comes in three categories:

1. That which you have agreed to do. For example, bring dinner to people when they can't make it to common dinner.

2. That which you have agreed that you would not do, for example change pants.

3. That which you never imagined you would do before you cared about this person, but it turned out to be easy, and he's

---

Co-care Issues

Some of the issues about eventual co-care that might be addressed are:

- What are the extents and limits to care that residents should be expected to provide to other residents? At what point can an individual say, "No, I can't do that."?
- How are the costs of outside caregivers shared?
- When residents become seriously ill, under what circumstances should they move out?
- What sorts of accessibility standards should be incorporated in all units vs. those that are optional? (This will be addressed at length during Study Group II, but will inevitably come up here.)
- What amount of work (chores, etc.) should be required of each resident, depending on age, or length of residence in the community?
- How much privacy can ill residents expect vis-à-vis security: people checking in on them?
- What are the rules for new residents entering senior cohousing? Age limits? Health?
- How do the economics work: rental units, coop store, and the like?

These are a few examples of the kinds of issues that could be addressed. Residents should consider enough scenarios to feel comfortable. That said, I often argue that people who are new to the cohousing concept should just take a deep breath and relax. After they experience the upside of living in a cohousing community, they often discover that, in retrospect, they worried too much about these issues.

---

just next door so it's convenient enough. I've noticed cohousing to be readily available karma – you do stuff for others and before you know it someone's doing something for you.

Typical Co-Care Tasks

The American Association of Retired Persons (AARP) divides assistance for everyday senior activities into two categories:

1. ADL's, or "Activities for Daily Living." Bathing, dressing, toileting, eating, and getting around the house.

2. IADL's are "Instrumental Activities of Daily Living." This includes preparing meals, shopping, managing money, using the telephone, doing housework, and taking medication.

Munksøgård's Rules & Regulations

The senior cohousing group at Munksøgård devised a set of rules with regards to:

A. Community relations

B. Residents' payments to a common fund paying expenses for equipment, plants, etc.

C. Rules for administering the waiting list for people who would like to live here.

D. An annual general meeting and a board of three members who handle current issues.

E. Cohousing group meetings held according to need – initially once each week, later once every other week, and then once a month.

F. Ad hoc working groups which are formed when needed, for both theoretical and practical tasks such as house maintenance, lawn and garden maintenance, snow removal, common house matters, etc.

Special rules that have proven particularly useful include:

1. Decisions of special importance must be presented at one cohousing group meeting, but not decided on until the following meeting.

2. New group members must be between 50 and 65 years of age and cannot have children living with them.

3. At the moment, the community consists of 17 women and 6 men, so we aim to have at least one third male members.

4. When an apartment becomes vacant, it is first offered to the other cohousers. If none of them wants the apartment, it is offered to those on the waiting list, which usually has between 40 and 80 people on it. Usually between five and ten people show an interest, so the first five are invited to an interview with all of the current members of the group. Everyone tells them a little about living in a senior cohousing community and the candidates are given the opportunity to explain how they think they can contribute.

- Olaf Dejgaard, resident of Munksøgård

The interesting thing about these communities is that while each community's rules are different – each one fits themselves.

In 2002, 14.2 percent of people over 65 needed help with ADL's and 21.6 percent needed help with IADL's. The second category, IADL's, include the sort of tasks that neighborly senior cohousers might do for each other. In order to get a better fix on the issue, however, it's okay to consider a hypothetical case based on the plausible fourth quarter scenarios.

Joe Smith, a previously healthy 60-year-old in a senior cohousing community, has a sudden stroke. With his right side paralyzed he can't dress himself. He may not be able to talk coherently for a while. He cannot do anything that requires the coordination of both hands and all maintenance tasks are out for him, perhaps permanently. How do the routine tasks that he was happily performing get shifted around to other seniors? Must Joe hire an outsider to mow the lawn?

Of course these are minor issues compared to Joe's healthcare needs. When Joe gets out of the hospital and wishes to return home, does co-care in senior cohousing include assigning another man or two to help him to dress in the morning and undress in the evening? Can Joe make it to the common house for dinner? Can he cook for himself? Who might bring him three meals a day, or stock his fridge with microwaveable frozen dinners as a fallback? Who will take charge of installing the extra safety bars for the shower? Does he need a wheelchair? Who is going to take him to physical therapy sessions at the medical clinic two or three times per week, maybe for months? Maybe it will be someone from the group or maybe not. They key is to avoid overburdening the individuals within the group.

While the questions are many, the answer is straightforward: cohousing residents can be counted on to do these sort of tasks long enough to organize a permanent solution. This community approach is tantamount to carry-over care, and will give Joe's family enough time to find more permanent assistance for him (a HMO provider, for example), and can play a huge role in keeping Joe out of institutional care. Senior cohousing's built-in intermediate co-care feature is perhaps the most important, and certainly the most tangible, method for successfully aging in place.

Planning for Acute Disability

Joe's story brings up the obvious question: What sort of agreements should a resident group make about allowing a disabled senior into the community early on and when someone is too sick to remain? Where does a group draw the line?

Entry into the community would not be a problem for a person like Joe, since he was already living in cohousing before his stroke. But should someone with Parkinson's disease, or multiple sclerosis (or other long-term diseases that are increasingly debilitating), be admitted? How

Single women find particular harbor in cohousing.

does the community make sure that there are enough caregivers? Answers to these questions all depend on the group and their individual and collective sensibilities and when they get addressed it has to be done openly and honestly. If people feel that they are getting saddled inappropriately the whole thing falls apart.

Dinner Policy

Dinner is important; we have to eat. But in the context of senior cohousing it is not only where residents get physiological sustenance, it is where they get emotional sustenance as well. So many seniors say that, especially after 70, they have to make a very conscious choice, a choice that is not that easy, every day. That is, the choice

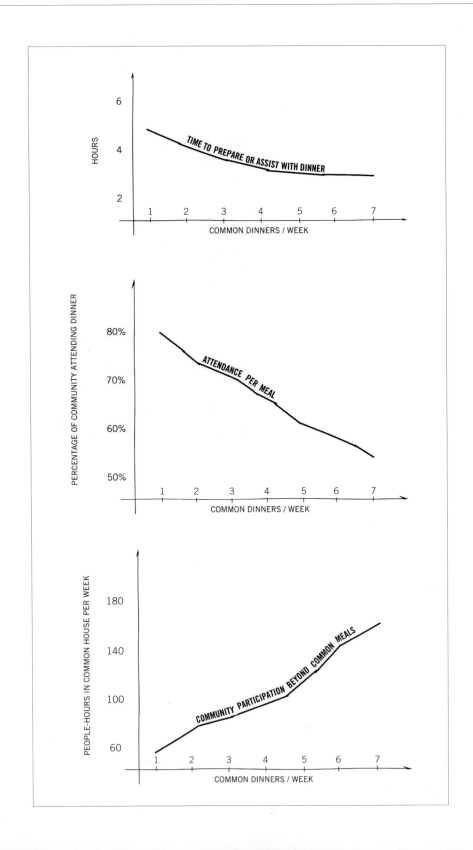

A little dance after dinner.

to get up and be active, or to think "maybe I will just lounge around today. I don't have that much energy."

In senior cohousing residents have to get up – someone might come visit, there might be something really good to eat in the common house; someone might want to do something fun, and, oh yeah, there is someone else to do it with.

Senior cohousing is for people who don't like to be alone, or at least, not all the time. Residents could have had dinner at home – that choice is always available – but Munksøgård residents say that they eat in the common house more than they thought they would. As proof, common dinners at Munksøgård are available five times a week.

Follow Munksøgård's lead. Live the good life, every day. With purpose. With conviction. With family, neighbors, and friends.

Andedammen Rules

Karen, Tua, and Kirsten (three elderly women – all over 70) have written down the following rules of their cohousing community, Andedammen in Birkerød, Denmark.

Decisions about the committees are made at the common meetings, which are held on a monthly basis. Membership of the committees is not fixed; members can move from one committee to another.

The Basic Committees:

- **The Outside Committee**
  Responsible for:
  - Maintaining the outdoor areas: lawn mowing, hedge cutting, pruning and planting
  - Upkeep of the driveway and parking lot
  - Sweeping the flagstones on the footpath and the square
  - Buying sand for the sandboxes and gravel for the road
  - Cleaning the duck pond and the hedge around it
  - Clearing snow
  - Buying and maintaining the garden tools

- **The Garbage Room Committee**
  Responsible for:
  - Cleaning the garbage room: removing old newspapers, cardboard boxes, sweeping the floor
  - Ensuring that the garbage truck has clear access each week

- **The Vegetable Garden Committee**
  Responsible for:
  - Sowing, planting, weeding, harvesting of vegetables and flowers
  - Bee keeping

- **The Shopping Committee**
  Responsible for:
  - Pricing and ordering of supplies, including beer and soda
  - Keeping supplies in order, maintaining accounts
  - Cleaning and maintaining the common refrigerator and freezer

- **The Kitchen Committee**
  Responsible for:
  - Buying and maintaining the service machines, and cleaning supplies for kitchen and basement

- **The Common Living Room Committee**
  Responsible for:
  - Maintaining the hall and common rooms
  - Washing sofa covers
  - Decorations and flowers in the common rooms
  - Maintaining the furniture, lamps, and plants

- **The Laundry Committee**
  Responsible for:
  - Maintaining the machines and clothes-lines
  - Purchasing detergent
  - Keeping the laundry and drying rooms clean

- **The Social Committee**
  Responsible for:
  - Organizing common parties and get-togethers, Christmas parties, etc.

- **The Workshop Committee**
  Responsible for:
  - Creating and maintaining a workshop for the residents of the cohousing community
  - Maintenance of the common tools

- **Cleaning Rules**
  A resident has been appointed who is responsible for overseeing the cleaning.
  - All common rooms, on the ground floor and basement must be cleaned every Sunday morning.
  - The cleaning team makes sure that everywhere has been cleaned thoroughly, including the kitchen, tables, floors, and window sills in the common living room, the staircase, and the bathroom in the hall.

- **Kitchen Rules**
  The cooks:
  - Decide the menu and post it on the kitchen message board as early as possible. The cooks shop for, cook, and serve the meal, and keep receipts for reimbursement.
  - Set the tables.
  - Clean and do the dishes; put crockery and cutlery back into place.
  - Ensure that the dining room is cleaned up, floor swept, and tables wiped clean. The cooks put buckets of soapy water out on the tables, and the residents clean their own tables. The chairs are put back after the floor has been swept. Empty beer and soda bottles are put in boxes under the kitchen table, and wine bottles are put in the bottle containers.
  - Toss out the leftovers, if none of the residents want them. Feed for the chicken must be put in their respective bowls and taken out to them.
  - Clean the kitchen floor, and the big trash bag must always be taken to the trash room.

PART FOUR

CHAPTER TEN

Pioneering Senior Cohousing in America

The Beginnings of an American Movement

Senior cohousing development in the United States is still in its nascent stages. Yet we have learned lessons that will make it easer for communities to be built. We take a look at two emerging communities, ElderSpirit in Virginia and Silver Sage in Colorado. Two very different communities with two very similar mandates. Finally, we explore some final thoughts on what cohousing is. And what it isn't. And what it can be.

*Resident group of ElderSpirit
Senior Cohousing.*

ElderSpirit

Abingdon, Virginia
29 Units
Architects: The Highland Group P.C.
Tenure: 16 condominiums, 13 rental units
To be completed: 2005

Spirituality can be an incredible source of strength for seniors and a great common focus for a community. Many seniors use spirituality to reach greater insight and self-awareness either through established religions or just through activities like yoga or tai-chi. ElderSpirit is a senior cohousing community that is based on the desire to explore the potentials of late-life spirituality and mutual support.

The idea behind the community came from a committee of the non-profit Federation of Communities in Service (FOCIS). FOCIS was started in 1967 by a group of women working with community service and development organizations.

When some group members reached retirement age they decided to explore the possibilities of creating a senior community, and in 1995 they formed a committee named FOCUS FUTURES. Inspired by the growing cohousing movement they decided to create a cohousing community specifically for people above the age of 55. They wanted to attract seniors who regarded their senior years as a phase brimming with possibilities, not a boring and depressing end to a long life. The result is ElderSpirit, a senior cohousing community designed to enable them to explore all the opportunities the senior years afford. While late-life spirituality and mutual assistance are the keywords that express the sensibilities of this group of people, in order to better realize their vision they defined these terms and, in turn, formed the social framework of their community (see the accompanying sidebar).

After extensive research in the Appalachian area the group decided to place their community in Abingdon, and with the help of Dene Peterson they found a 3.7 acre site along the Virginia Creeper Trail. A corporation (Trailview Development Corp.) was formed to purchase the property and FOCUS received a three-year grant from The Retirement Research Foundation of Chicago for predevelopment expenses. A board was established, a part time staff hired, and an architect engaged. Project manager Dene Peterson contacted government housing agencies to find ways to make affordable housing a part of the project. A community coordinator, Jean Marie Luce, worked on getting the word out about the project and gather prospective residents. This was primarily done by teaching classes at the local College for Older Adults.

During the programming process, the architect collected input and ideas for the design from a building committee and future residents. The result is a community consisting of 29 homes: 13 privately owned one and two-bedroom attached homes, 16 income-restricted rental homes, a common house, and a spiritual center. The private houses are laid out along a pedestrian path with the common house and a plaza in the center. Parking is behind the houses on the edges of the site. Construction began in 2004 and the move-in is anticipated to be in June 2005. ElderSpirit is one of the first senior cohousing communities to be built in the United States.

ElderSpirit Community is now an organization for seniors that works on the formation of senior communities and spiritual programs. The untraditional values of the ElderSpirit Community in Abingdon has created a lot of interest in the project and it has inspired people to start creating similar spiritual communities all over the U.S. and Canada.

ElderSpirit Senior Cohousing under construction.

ElderSpirit Community Values

Spirituality:

Members believe that spiritual growth is the primary work of those in the later stages of life. Members encourage one another in the search for meaning in life and commitment to a spiritual path. Freedom of religion is fundamental.

Mutual Support:

Members develop face-to-face relationships through which they offer and receive support. They express their needs and convictions, listen to each other and strive to act responsibly, considering their good and the good of the other.

Simple Lifestyle and Respect for the Earth:

Conscious that over-consumption by persons in wealthy countries threatens the earth's living systems, members seek a simplified lifestyle that reflects a respectful relationship with the environment.

Arts and Recreation:

Leisure, recreational activities, and travel contribute uniquely toward refreshing the mind, body and spirit. The arts form an integral part of the community. Members share and develop their gifts and talents through such activities as music, dance, theater, storytelling, gardening, crafts, weaving, etc.

Health:

The word "health" comes from the same root as "heal," "whole," and "holy". Recognizing this, members pay attention to nutrition, rest, exercise and social interaction.

Resident members also commit to the following values:

Care During Illness and Dying:

The common goal of the ElderSpirit cohousing community is to offer care to one another in the later years. It affirms home care and dying at home. However, when institutional care occurs, a member of the community stays in touch with the person and closely follows her/his condition. Members recognize that the process of living involves one's desire for tolerable health and a capacity to be generative. Within the community, the process of dying raises one's awareness that all surrender physical life, not in isolation, but as a sister or brother of the human community.

Mutual Assistance:

Sharing of goods and services is the norm in the ElderSpirit cohousing community. When members have needs beyond the individual and family group, they are encouraged to make their needs known. Community meetings and common meals provide opportunities for open discussion, sharing, and mutual assistance.

Silver Sage

Boulder, Colorado
16 units
Architects: The Cohousing Company
To be completed: 2006
Tenure: 10 condominiums, 6 rental units

More and more cohousing communities are faced with the question about how to accommodate their senior residents as they grow older and their needs and physical abilities change. Some of the first cohousers to actively address the issue were the residents of Nyland Cohousing in Boulder, Colorado, 10 years after their own community had been built. Their first idea was to extend their community with more units especially designed for the needs and preferences of their senior residents. They also considered subdividing their 42-acre site to create a second cohousing community for seniors, but unfortunately that didn't work out.

In order to find out more about the possibilities of making senior cohousing, they hosted two public presentations

mission statement

At Silver Sage Cohousing Community, our purp

*"Spiritual Eldering : nurturing and end
ing of people's desire to keep learning
ing, and participating."*

The term Spiritual Eldering is defined this way
November 2003 *Spiritual Eldering Newsletter*

*"As the baby boomers approach their elder ye
need a psycho-spiritual model of development
enables them to complete their life journey, ha
wisdom of their years, and transmit a legacy to
generations... Sages draw growth techniques f
modern psychology and contemplative technic
the world's spiritual traditions to expand their c
ness and develop wisdom... This ongoing proc
spiritual eldering, helps us consciously transfo
downward arc of aging into the upward arc of
consciousness that crowns an elder's life with*

used in referen
and the terms
reference to the

SILVER SAGE
SITE PROGRAM

the project

The Silver Sage Community will be a small, 16 home community to be built on a one acre site located directly south and across the street from the Wild Sage Cohousing Community in the Holiday Neighborhood in North Boulder. The community will be created to appeal to the desires, needs, and inspirations of a community consisting primarily of adults over the age of 50.

zoning summary

Zone	: MXR-D
Lot	: Lot 6, Buena Vista Subdivision Section 7, TWP 1N
Lot Size	: ± 133' x 273' ; 36,401 sf. ; 0.83 acres
Current Zoning	: Mixed Density Residential - Developing
Allowable Units	: 16 (6 must be affordable)
Actual Units	: 16 (6 affordable units)
Required Parking	: 16 parking spaces
Max. Height	: 35' for <u>Principal</u> Uses
	: 18' for <u>Accessory</u> Uses
Max. Stories	: 3 stories

SILVER SAGE
SITE PROGRAM

Perspective sketch of Silver Sage Senior Cohousing

about Danish senior cohousing that I did during two winter holidays.

The Nyland residents found more interested seniors, and in 2003 they had gathered a group. Their vision was a small-scale participatory cohousing community where everybody knows each other and amenities are close at hand.

The developer who had built Nyland, Wonderland Hill Development, then proposed a one-acre site in the new-urban Holiday Neighborhood two miles north of downtown Boulder. Holiday, a new residential neighborhood, includes community gardens, a one-acre park, bike trails, artists' studios, pedestrian walkways, and a projected Boulder Public Library Branch. The prospective site was located just across the street from Wild Sage – an existing intergenerational cohousing

common courtyard

ACTIVITY	CHARACTER	RELATIONSHIP	DETAILS
• Gardening	• Pedestrian oriented	• Porches, decks, and patios open onto court	• Community garden
• Performances	• Beautifully landscaped	• Links via pedestrian paths to all houses, to 16th street and 17th street sidewalks and to rear alley	• Bocce ball court
• Bocce ball	• Shaded areas		• Casual amphitheatre and platform
• Playing instruments	• Sunny areas		• Gathering nodes
• Concerts	• Colorful		• Paved exterior extension of workshop/ arts/crafts building
• Meditation	• Fragrant	• Bocce ball court to be near Common House patio	• Raised beds for accessible gardening
• Reading	• Accessible	• Retention pond and swales to act as landscape elements	• Planters
• Outdoor gathering		• Stairs to podium level to act as landscape elements (trellised entry, bridge or gate) if possible	• Trellises
• Casual meetings			
• Conversations			
• Strolling			
• Arts, crafts, and woodwork			

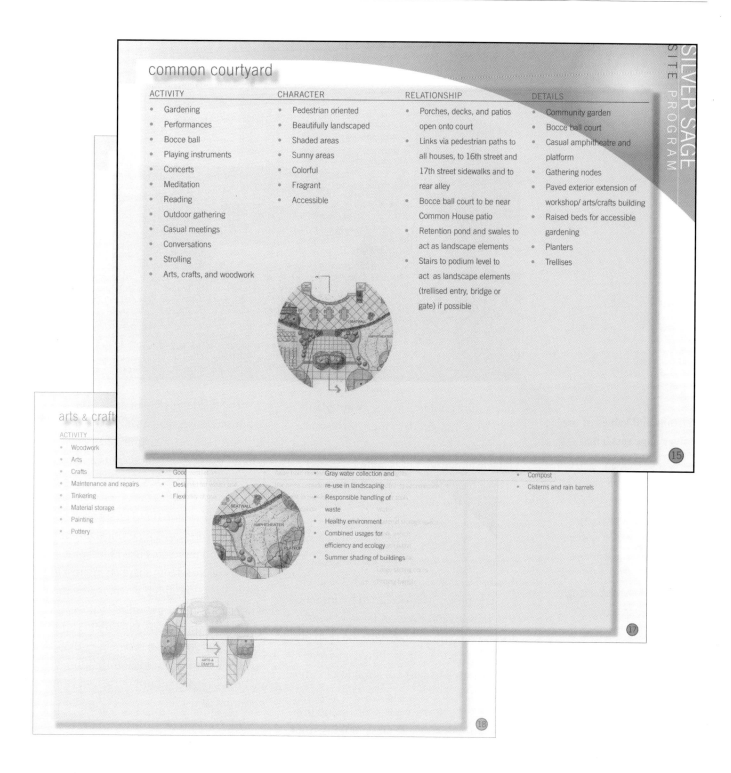

15

arts & craft

ACTIVITY		
• Woodwork		
• Arts		• Good
• Crafts		• Desi
• Maintenance and repairs		• Flex
• Tinkering		
• Material storage		
• Painting		
• Pottery		

• Gray water collection and re-use in landscaping	• Compost
• Responsible handling of waste	• Cisterns and rain barrels
• Healthy environment	
• Combined usages for efficiency and ecology	
• Summer shading of buildings	

17

18

Developer of Silver Sage Senior Cohousing, Jim Leach from Wonderland Hill Development with associates.

Visions and Values of the Silver Sage residents:

- Nourish body and soul with good food, good health, and good company.
- Live mindfully in community, encouraging wisdom, compassion, and interpersonal growth.
- Experience stylish, thoughtfully-designed interior living.
- Share inviting outdoor spaces such as gardens, courtyards, decks, patios, and views of the Flatirons.
- Enjoy North Boulder's urban options, including hiking, biking, cafes, and public transportation.

community built in 2004 by Wonderland Hill Development. Working with a local non-profit housing advocate, Wonderland Hill Development put together a varied income project and worked through all but one of the steps for creating senior cohousing: feasibility, and Study Groups I and III. Our firm, The Cohousing Company, was hired to work the group through the participatory Study Group II.

The project was designed in our office in Berkeley, California, and subsequently documented the design with the help of Boulder architect, Bryan Bowen. Silver Sage is slated to start construction in the fall of 2005.

Silver Sage will consist of 16 duplexes and attached homes in sizes ranging from 800 sf to 1600 sf, a community-owned common house and a common green with internal sidewalks and rich landscaping.

The residents helped design the common house, which will have a large kitchen, a dining area, intimate sitting parlors, guest rooms, and crafts and performance areas. They envision a variety of common activities taking place there, including common dinners, speakers, films, house concerts, reading groups, fitness classes, and more. Just like ElderSpirit, Silver Sage residents share an interest in spirituality, although this will not be the emphasis of the community's values.

In order to inform the public and themselves about the progress of the project, the group holds information meetings once a month in the Wild Sage common house.

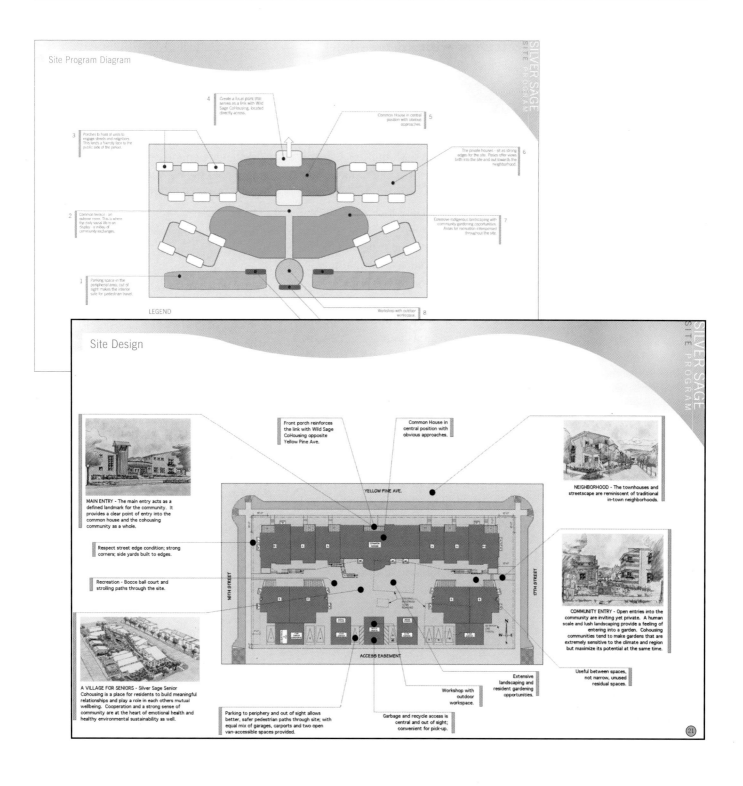

Interview with Arthur Okner
March 22, 2005

Arthur Okner MSW is a 62-year-old single gentleman. After a successful career in business which included five years with the U.S. General Accounting Office (a Congressional Auditing Arm), four years, two months, six days and 15 hours in the U.S. Air Force and 25 years as a self-employed small business consultant and expediter, he turned his attentions to community building. In 1999 he relocated to Boulder from Greenwich Village, New York, where he became very active in affordable housing issues going so far as to man (or person) a booth at the Boulder Farmer's Market for two years extolling the virtues of affordable housing to low income passers-by. The next year he discovered cohousing and has been hooked since then. Arthur moved into Nomad Cohousing in North Boulder where he now resides. Prior to moving into Nomad, he was a founding member of Wild Sage Cohousing in Boulder. If you plan to visit on Wednesday or Sunday evening you can even share dinner with the community and get to meet his gaggle of adopted grandkids. And get beaten in pool.

Kurt McCulloch is an architect working for the Cohousing Company.

Kurt: Tell me a little bit about how you live – are you retired? How do you spend your time?

Art: I retired when I was 50 and began to really search for a community, an ecosystem to live in. This eventually moved me

to go to graduate school in the early 90's when I got a Masters degree in Community Organization at Yashiva University in New York City. After living in Greenwich Village in New York from 1975 to 1999, I moved to Boulder, Colorado. I was very lonely here, and to overcome this I began doing volunteer work for the City of Boulder's Dept. of Affordable Housing.

Kurt: Okay, so how exactly did you get involved in cohousing?

Art: When I met Jim Leach and Chuck Durrett in April of 2000, I was asked by the Director of the Dept. of Housing to attend what she thought was an informational seminar on cohousing – it was actually a kick-off meeting for what became Wild Sage Cohousing. After this experience, I thought there was no better place on earth to live than cohousing. Since then I've been working on developing cohousing communities. I try to have as much leisure time as possible – but it's a mix because I spent a hell of a lot of time on cohousing (more elder then multi-generational). I'm interested in cohousing because cohousing makes sense in so many ways and is a movement as well as a wonderful place to live.

Kurt: You live in cohousing at the moment, right?

Art: Partway through the Wild Sage development process a unit became vacant at Nomad Cohousing and I thought I would live there temporarily until Wild Sage was completed. However, two little girls at the time 2 ½ and 3 ½ – my neighbors at Nomad – started coming over to my house every day. I couldn't leave them. However, since then, Silver Sage and the Elder Cohousing movement has taken my interest and I've been involved in this community's development. Senior cohousing suits me even better than cohousing and those girls will be near enough that I'll still be able to see them. They will be 8 ½ and 9 ½ when I move.

Kurt: What are your goals and expectations for Silver Sage Cohousing? How are they different from Nomad, the cohousing community where you live now?

Art: My goals? Well, even though I love being with children, I'm not involved in raising children full-time or in the capital formation period of my life as working parents are. There is a certain period of people's lives when it's important to earn money, focus on a career and children who are in school. Work and children. That's not where I am right now, and so it's better for me to live with people where these things aren't central. I'm comfortable financially, and retired. In a senior-targeted community where people are finished raising children, they're around for a drink at 4:00 p.m. It's easier for people to reach out to each other when they're in the same place in their lives. In other words, I need more people to "play" with.

Kurt: What about the fact that you'll only be living with older people?

Art: Consider the alternatives. The location of most senior living facilities is determined by the affordability of land. Silver Sage, however, is intentionally located in order to allow for interaction. And much energy will be spent in reaching out to all generations through mentoring programs and a coffee shop, amongst other ways.

Kurt: Tell me more about the alternatives for seniors?

Art: I just got back from the National Conference on Aging. There are many institutions ready to take on the emerging senior demographic – but they are institutions where a resident follows the rules and is managed. At the Conference there was much talk on the Dell-Webb model of elder life. This is an illusion-based advertising campaign that paints a picture of a white haired couple playing golf and tennis and sitting around the pool. In this model there is nothing to support life. There are only things. Things are bullshit. I'm not interested in paying to live at a place where I'm asking, "where's the management?" – I want to be the management. Besides, it's only a very small percentage of the population that can financially support this way of life – for most people this illusion is something that they'll never have the money to buy. Community is about getting closer and closer to each other. The Dell-Webb model tells us that our lives as contributing members of society are already finished. In cohousing there's something more than just things, there's a shared sense of values and purpose. Institutions kill people. They make people sick, and eventually kill them off before their time. I believe that.

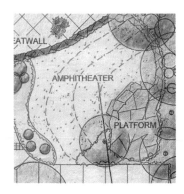

Kurt: How does cohousing operate when someone's health begins to fail? How does cohousing address this?

Art: The design of senior cohousing provides people with the ability to age in place for as long as they possibly can. For example, there may be an extra room in your home where a professional care provider could live, and walking distances to the common house have been designed to be minimal. There's a suite in the common house for caretakers to work and live. And cost-efficient cluster care will be encouraged. As a community we've agreed to make such arrangements before we're faced with these realities. Aging sneaks up on people and then slams them into reality. However, we're thinking ahead. We're not in denial of our own mortality.

Kurt: Do you have any concerns or fears about living in cohousing?

Art: I'll miss the youth. I'll miss having people in their 30's and 40's in close proximity. But everything's a trade-off in life. The place I live currently isn't specifically engineered for seniors. And as I stated previously, the vast majority are very busy raising their children or earning money?

Kurt: What sorts of people live in senior cohousing?

Art: People who aren't in denial. People who are proactive, intelligent and caring. People who want to laugh at the world and themselves. All of the institutions for seniors are talking about "aging in place". These days families are geographically spread out, making it difficult for children to care for their aging parents. So many people have bought into the "subdivide and conquer" housing-tract lifestyle. Erik Utne of the Utne Reader has said: *"give up your dream home, place, for your dream community"*. We've coined a phrase here in Colorado that means something more than "aging in place". It's "aging in community".

--

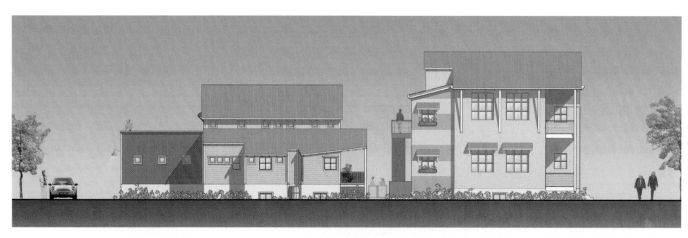

Interview with Silvine Farnell
March 22, 2005

Silvine Farnell, 62, currently lives with her husband Stewart, a financial planner, in a townhouse in Boulder, Colorado. Both are retired college professors, and they have no children. She is currently working as a freelance copy editor and has been very involved in the growth of the Silver Sage Cohousing group for about ten months.

--

Kurt: How did you hear about cohousing, how did you become interested in joining a group?

Silvine: I have known a little about cohousing for a while and chose not to become involved until recently because I was put off by the idea of long meetings, the fact that most groups consist mostly of younger people, and my own shyness. What really caught my attention was seeing an ad in the Spiritual Eldering Newsletter, put out by Rabbi Zalman Schachter-Shalomi's organization, about Silver Sage, an elder cohousing project with a spiritual angle. The thing that appeals most to me about Silver Sage is the awareness of the spiritual dimension. The spiritual dimension is so practical, and so important.

Kurt: What is it about the spiritual dimension that's so important to cohousing?

Silvine: One thing I've learned about cohousing is that it isn't about living with people who are all your best friends. In fact, you want diversity – but then it's crucial that you build community effectively. We can learn about the practice of spirituality as an effective community-building tool from the work of Rachael Kessler, who has developed a way to bring spirituality into the public schools that is well received by everyone from fundamentalist Christians to atheists, partly because she makes obvious how spirituality speaks to basic human needs. Just take a look at the title of her book – The Soul of Education: Helping Students Find Connection, Compassion, and Character at School. We just have to discover the deep connection we have, simply because our deepest nature is to give attention and space to each other – which is another way of saying, to give love to each other. If we are given the right kind of activity to encourage the giving of attention and space, to ourselves and to others, love will happen, and we will find it deeply satisfying. We will become a community.

Kurt: Compassion and attention to others sounds important for all cohousing groups – is it especially relevant for elder cohousing?

Silvine: The best way I know to answer that is with a few lines from a poem by Yeats.

An aged man is but a paltry thing
A tattered coat upon a stick, unless
Soul claps its hand and sing, and louder sing,
For every tatter in its mortal dress.

Kurt: Is this poem about how the man's tattered clothes visually express the trials he

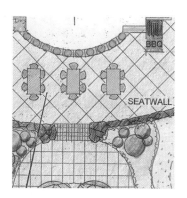

has gone through and the inner wisdom he has gained from that, and his enduring joyful spirit even as his body fails?

Silvine: The joyful spirit part, yes, absolutely, but Yeats did have a tough time with getting old. I think this poem is mainly about how getting old and deteriorating physically is pretty rough, unless your soul is growing at the same time, unless aging becomes saging. Your soul can't help growing when you're willing to engage at a deep level in a community and work through whatever comes up.

Society is much more prescriptive for those people with developing careers and growing families. The world isn't so clear in telling older people what to do. So what do we do as seniors? Go off to Tucson and play golf for the rest of our lives? For some people being retired, with the children gone, is depressing, they're at a loss, it feels like society has told them their life is over. Rabbi Zalman Schachter-Shalomi, who's the spiritual leader of the

Jewish Renewal Movement, found himself in deep depression after he turned 60, and he realized it was because our society didn't have any kind of positive view of aging to offer him. Out of his exploration of the wisdom of other societies and his own spiritual work came a different way of looking at the whole process, and that's the heart of his book, From Ageing to Sage-ing: A Profound New Vision of Growing Older. Do your inner work, harvest the wisdom of your life, and you'll become a true elder and people will want to listen to you – you'll have something to give. And much less to fear. Did you know it was Rabbi Zalman's book that inspired Jim Leach of Wonderland Hill Development to start Silver Sage?

Kurt: No, I didn't know. So, I can see how senior cohousing with a spiritual angle can be a path to individual development. But how can it be more than a bunch of old people sitting around doing organ recitals? You've started to address what senior cohousing may have to offer those outside the immediate community; to the neighborhood, Boulder, and beyond. What will this look like?

Silvine: Well, the answer to this question starts small and works outward to the greater communities. We have Wild Sage Cohousing right next door. There are many of us yearning to be surrogate grandparents for some of the children there. I plan to host a reading-out-loud time that kids can come to. Most of all, I believe that people can get deeper into poetry by performing it, and that poetry has real gifts for anyone who does go deeper into it, and so teaching people to perform poetry is my main way of giving back. Silver Sage provides a platform for me to do this; the common house is a perfect place to host poetry performing workshops. And in the same way it will be a focal point for all kinds of activities. Our members have so many gifts.

Kurt: Knowing what you do about the architecture of Silver Sage, how do you think living in cohousing will change your daily patterns?

Silvine: For one, the common house will really be an extension of our individual home. Our actual home will be smaller than the one we will be leaving, but having a common house will provide us with a chance to expand. We won't have to spend money going to movies because of the home theater that's planned – and we'll be watching those movies with people we know and care about. I'm looking forward to coming down to the common house to do laundry, and there will be a cool deck that I want to do my stretching exercises on. Then there'll just be much more bumping into people and chatting than we experience in our current neighborhood. There are people who you

want to chat with for a little while, or to eat dinner with, but not necessarily have over for the whole evening – but our current situation doesn't allow for this at all. We have older neighbors right now who need more attention than they get, people I'd really like to spend some time with, but I'm just not the kind of person who can make things like that happen. You know the majority of people in cohousing are introverts, and I certainly am, so I love the idea of interactions being made easy. In cohousing, everyone expects you to behave like old-fashioned neighbors. The design of Silver Sage supports community as opposed to working against it. I'm also looking forward to common meals. I don't think we can have them too often.

Kurt: Don't you have some concerns and fears about moving into cohousing?

Silvine: Sometimes I get cold feet. Life now is very comfortable. I live in a secluded place that's very comfortable indeed. Everything is under control. To live in cohousing you have to let go of a lot of control, there's a surrendering. I'm drawn to the growth that comes out of this surrender, and still, sometimes I ask myself, "What am I getting into?"

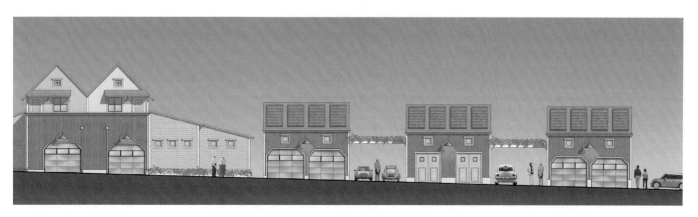

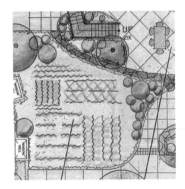

Kurt: Isn't getting old and dying depressing? How do you feel about living with people who will be aging and, like all of us, eventually dying? How will you take care of each other? Is that something you want to do?

Silvine: We need to do a lot more talking about that. This is a strong concern for many people. At a very personal level, if I want people to support me as I get older, I need to be ready to support them. We'll also have a relationship of mutual support with our neighbors at Wild Sage. I can think of babysitting for the kids of the young parents at Wild Sage as a long-term investment – some day they may do some babysitting for me. Any way you look at it, aging is going to happen. Senior cohousing is for people who are not in denial about aging and dying. Living in a nursing home would be a hell of a lot more depressing than living in senior cohousing, and we're expecting to be able to stay in our own

home much longer this way. It's also true that we want a broad age range at Silver Sage. Currently we're mostly in our early 60s. It is easier for older people to take care of other older people because we're moving at the same pace, and it's even better if there's a diversity of ages within the category of "senior," so that not everyone is experiencing exactly the same stage at the same time. A lot of us don't want to be a burden to our children, and are happy to help others if that means we get help when we need it.

Kurt: How do you feel about the roles the community group, architect, and developer played in the design and development process for Silver Sage? Was the process successful in creating a community? Why?

Silvine: This process is so much more trouble than simply buying a typical townhouse. It's also so much more worth it. It's fantastic to have an impact on the

design of the community. It's fantastic to form a community of people before moving in. I have been on the board of my HOA in my current neighborhood, in fact, I've even been the president of the HOA, and still I don't get to see very much of my neighbors. There's really zero community here. There may be some tough meetings during the development of the design for a cohousing community, but there's a payoff. People end up feeling good about themselves and about each other in the end. I think we felt rushed at times; as you get older your decision-making process slows down. The developer's leadership and early involvement in this project created some tensions as we worked out our common house design, but having experienced professionals on board also made it possible to get this complex project finished, with everyone feeling good because the professionals listened to us members.

Kurt: What sort of a role do you play as an individual in the community-building process? Are you a leader, a facilitator, an active participant, or more of an observer?

Silvine: I'm definitely a big mouth in meetings, and recently facilitated a meeting. I've pretty much taken on a leadership role. I have a lot of ideas and really enjoy expressing them. My husband has also taken a leadership role, in perhaps a quieter way, as he's great at sending out eloquent emails when the need arises. One thing that's great about cohousing is that it can accommodate all sorts of personalities. Jim Leach is always talking about synergy.

Kurt: It sounds like you have people with a variety of skills in your group, and there's a strength in diversity. We can be greater than the sum of our parts.

Silvine: Yes, and things really work when we get rid of the garbage that prevents our love from coming to the fore and being expressed. We're going on a retreat in May, and this will give us some concentrated time for really listening to each other and for strengthening the compassion, connection, and inner growth that Rachael Kessler talks about. We've already had some great experiences of deeper connection, and I love that we're focusing on strengthening that.

--

Living room in Senior Cohousing.

Where Do We Go From Here?

The legacy of multi-generational cohousing in America will be much more than cohousing itself. The same is true in Denmark. In Denmark, 30-plus years after the first cohousing community was built, less than one-percent of the population lives in cohousing. However, all aspects of the housing market have been affected by its influence: residents on streets with single-family houses might vote to park all of the cars at the end of the block and have folks walk to their houses. It's even got a formal name, a Chapter 40 Street (named after the law), and you can imagine what this alone does to facilitate community and relationships on a street. Moreover, almost no Danish multi-family housing project is designed without at least a focus group involved, which always has a positive influence on the project.

Cohousing is as much a process for developing housing as it is a new housing type. The innovation is in the concept that ordinary people actually build neighborhoods that truly address their people-friendly, child-friendly, senior-friendly, and earth-friendly needs.

The effects of cohousing can already be seen in U.S. housing. Our architectural firm, McCamant & Durrett, has worked on many developments modeled after, but not identical to, cohousing (so by the way, we don't call it cohousing). For example, we designed an entire new neighborhood for single parent households (all moms) on government assistance. The moms had to be in school. Childcare, shared cooking, and other shared facilities were on site. The point was that the moms would take turns cooking so that the others could do their homework. We insisted on working with the future residents because neither Katie nor I are single moms: We didn't want to decide what the moms would share and what they wouldn't.

Since then we have designed many multi-family housing projects with input from the future residents. We have also worked on many developments modeled after senior cohousing. One example is Casa de la Flores, a 20 unit senior housing project, that added a common house (onto its roof) to better facilitate community. Change comes in unexpected ways.

The senior cohousing movement had a turbulent start in Denmark. Determined seniors were desperate for more humane housing options, and despite adversity and setbacks they kept on trying, never gave up, and finally realized their dream. Their lack of a deliberate method meant a lot of agonizing, frustrating and sometimes dead-end experiences. No one believed them in the beginning, nor took them seriously. However, the senior cohousing movement fundamentally changed the general perception of seniors in Denmark. The fact that the seniors took responsibility for their own future led to this change. And the somewhat condescending and patronizing way that seniors were treated before has since been replaced by a new kind of respect and attention. The energy and the drive of the first Danish senior cohousers also helped create the picture in Denmark of the active senior – one who faces the challenges and opportunities of his or her retirement life openly and consciously.

Perhaps even more importantly, the Danish government has stopped building traditional assisted care homes and has started building senior housing as assisted care senior communities, where the seniors have their own moderate units and carefully designed common facilities. While this is not senior cohousing per se, it is strongly inspired by key features from it.

Similar inclinations stylized on senior cohousing have been seen in the U.S., but senior housing here still rarely meets the Danish standards. For cultural, psychological, and even physiological reasons, we simply have not found how to care for older people. (Physiological perhaps because there is something in us that wants to look past the aged to gaze with infatuation on the infant baby.) Ironically the problem with assisted living here is not necessarily economic – we spend plenty of money taking care of our elders. But as John Lennon and Paul McCartney said, "money can't buy me love." Since with rare exceptions we Americans can't, as a nation, seem to care for our aged with honor and decorum, people have to figure it out for themselves.

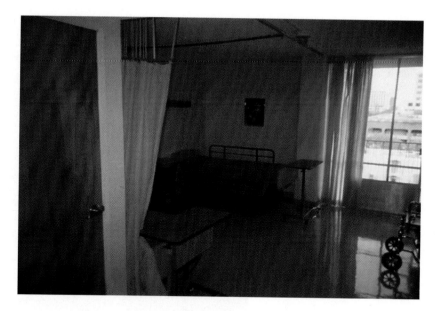

Typical assisted living in America.

Creating senior cohousing in the U.S. does not have to be a go-it-alone experience. The difficult preparation work is done. The path is open. All groups have to do is take that proverbial first step.

After participating in the design of 38 projects and the development of many of them we learned a few things about making it better, much better, less costly, and faster. Our collective job has become making cohousing available to more and more folks. Katie and I have figured out how to complete the necessary site planning with a resident group in four days, the common house in two days, and the houses done in three days (the group will make hundreds of decisions each day). This seems to be a perfect tempo, and gives the group all of the input they want. By contrast, I went to one senior housing discussion in Florida where the facilitator said that because senior housing preferences are so local, she spends two days minimum with focus groups discussing private houses for seniors in that area. In

Physical architecture like front porches. The social desire to cooporate begins to stick us back together as a society.

other words, a custom-designed senior cohousing takes just one extra day of work versus speculative senior housing. I mention this because people often think that building cohousing has to be exhausting for the professional. In fact, if you're well organized, the opposite is true. Building cohousing can be much faster than a traditional, speculative housing project because the guessing and second guessing aspects of the process are omitted. The residents know what they want and need, it's up to the professional to realize those desires and realities. As a result, building cohousing can be extremely gratifying and can also really galvanize the larger community. Building cohousing takes energy, but it gives back more in return.

There are so many professionals in the U.S who are not comfortable and not organized enough to build cohousing. As a result, they want to rush the project and get it out of the way. And of course there

are others who would just like to build a cohousing-looking development but willfully ignore the social-building aspects of the process. These developers also tend to include design elements that compromise community, like a too-small common house. These developers, well meaning as they may be, essentially want to Americanize it to make "fast cohousing."

However...

Cohousing is more than just boxes on the landscape. You have to have things in common if you're going to build and sustain a community (you need more than a philosophical and political common ground). There have to be physical excuses to get together. And if your home has a full kitchen (which they always do in cohousing), and is big enough to have a guest room (or there are too few guest rooms in the common house, or they are not designed comfortably enough that you feel good enough about putting guests and family there), and you have your own laundry facilities, all of a sudden community members don't have anything real in common. "There is an empty box over there … does that make us cohousing?" And the developer hedges his bets and puts the cars closer to the houses which, in turn, short circuits any possibility of sustaining community over time.

We have a single request. Just so that there is no confusion. If it isn't cohousing, if the resident group does not participate in a meaningfully way to build the community; if the common house is poorly designed such that it thwarts community, if cars creep into the spaces that should be reserved for people, if residents don't have anything real in common, then do not call it cohousing. Because it isn't. It is something else. As we all know, there's a big difference between fast food and a meaningful meal. Likewise, there is no such thing as "fast cohousing."

On a positive note, developments created to look like cohousing provide much greater community than continuous regular sprawl. As stated earlier, the greatest legacy of cohousing is not that everyone is living in cohousing (still less than 1 percent), but that it has had and can have such a deep impact on every other type of housing development. When you walk by a cohousing community, you see a profound way to live, and many people involved in housing would like to emulate it as much as possible – you can't blame them.

With this book, and with this book being so thorough, the goal is to help folks move beyond the prejudices, beyond

Hanging out at the common terrace at Doyle Street Cohousing.

the superficial "oh, that's just not me," and find out if senior cohousing is a viable option for them. As Steve Covey says: "One of the worst and most self-limiting habits is to limit yourself by definition."

Next Step: New Industries

I'm hoping for the beginning of an entire new industry in the U.S. - Study Group I facilitation. Advisors and facilitators with experience and knowledge about senior issues; people who will sit with 20 others and figure out how to age in place, gracefully and with dignity. The only way to do that is with preparation. And Study Group I is all about getting ready.

I expect these advisors to come from the ranks of the many people who have been assisting seniors for years. These advisors have to be prepared to patiently walk people through the issues of aging in place. It is not a weekend endeavor. It takes a couple of nights a week for a couple of months to successfully raise the consciousness of participants to "A: This is for me," or "B: This isn't for me," in the context of really knowing and grappling with the issues.

What to Do?

If you are interested in moving into senior cohousing – or starting a new community – the best thing to do is to contact The Cohousing Association of the United States (www.cohousing.org). It has information about cohousing groups starting up and existing cohousing units for sale and for rent. You can also post a classified on their website that describes what you're looking for (especially handy for people who want to start a senior cohousing group). We are currently working on establishing a national list of seniors interested in senior cohousing. Call, send, or email your contact information to The Cohousing Company and we will put you on the list. Our contact information can be found on the back pages of this book.

It may seem overwhelming if you don't know anyone in your area who shares the interest, but don't give up. Spread the word! Try to find people who could be interested in starting a cohousing group. Contact your local senior center, church, AARP branch, College of Older Adults, and more. It is a lot easier to get something off the ground if you have a few folks working together. Senior cohousing groups are currently forming all over the U.S. and there might be one in your area that you don't know of. There are also conferences about senior cohousing which are now being held on a regular basis. Contact The Cohousing Company if you are interested.

Be realistic, and try to imagine how you want your life to be in two, five, ten, and 20 years. What are the senior housing options in your area? How would you ideally like to age? Discuss it with your family and ask them how much they will be able to assist you. Maybe senior cohousing is just the right solution for you, maybe not. It can be uncomfortable to try to predict how your life could look if one day you no longer want to drive as much as you do now, and want to have fun (but self directed) activities nearby. It doesn't matter how old you are – there is nothing like having a place to go to hang out and talk to others whenever you want.

Someday you'll probably be grateful that you deliberately faced these issues before they grew into unmanageable problems.

The Deliberate Choice

One day many years ago, my sister called to tell me our mother had caused a little fender-bender; and though no one was

Nevada City Cohousing under construction.

hurt, she would lose her driver's license. Of course, since mom could no longer drive, it would be all but impossible for her to care for herself in her modest house in the "burbs". The solution was to sell her house and move her into a small apartment that was within walking distance to a shopping center. It was her version of moving into a so-called retirement community.

Meanwhile back in my own cohousing community, one of our founding members, Margaret, a dear friend and neighbor – a woman 73 years young – was diagnosed with an especially aggressive form of cancer.

As for my mother, over the ensuing years I repeatedly offered, demanded, and pleaded for her to move into a cohousing community. But she wouldn't hear of it. Despite the obvious, she was determined to live out her days on her "own terms," telling herself that she was in complete control. Nobody was going to tell her what to do and how to live. Besides, her health couldn't get any worse. Could it?

Ten years later, we have the answer: While at times we can still catch glimpses of her former self, her body, increasingly frail, demands full-time institutional nursing home care. And since her mind has become a confused house of fading memories, she has no choice but to live according to the whims and timetables set by the staff of her nursing home. With the exception of the visits of family members, she lives alone among strangers, her chance to make a deliberate and realistic choice as to how and where she would live out her last years long since past.

Margaret Hall in her kitchen in Doyle Street Cohousing.

My mother made the typical American choice to ignore the elephant in the living room, and, much to her dismay, found herself in institutionalized nursing care. And if neither I nor my family were able to help her avoid a life of unhappy institutional dependence, who could have? The answer is as straightforward as it is simple: She could have made the conscious choice to take control of the inevitable, in an effort to live as independently as possible, for as long as possible, within a community she could have relied on for support.

As for Margaret, who lived in my cohousing community, she died of cancer in 1996. She was 73. She chose to live, and to die, in her cohousing community. In Margaret's last six months, she received a considerable amount of care from the members of our cohousing group. As is too often the case, her children lived out of

The Danish Experience

Twenty of the last twenty-five recently-built Danish cohousing communities have been senior cohousing communities. The reasons are basic to economic and social well-being: Seniors living in Danish senior cohousing communities require much less government and other institutional care, and are happier and more independent; a fringe benefits are cost savings for the residents, for the government, and for supportive non-profits.

Senior cohousing, as a housing type in Denmark, has received support not only from the residents, but also from social institutions, the financial sector, and government agencies. In order to address the housing needs of the elderly and scale down their reliance on formal care programs, the Danes have solidly included cohousing communities into their spectrum of housing for the elderly. And lots of institutions do what they can to help.

town and their busy lives precluded them from devoting themselves wholly to her care. Where and when her children were unable to assist, our cohousing community stepped in. Probably seventy percent of the people-hours she spent with others were with her cohousing neighbors. Someone brought her the must-have latte from the cafe across the street every morning. Someone read to her. Someone helped with food, picked up the medicine, took her to the doctor, and handled the confusing and relentless streams of paperwork. As her health declined, her cohousing neighbors increasingly helped her in any way they could, eventually taking on her otherwise-normal cohousing duties as their own. It wasn't about taking away her independence and valued contributions, it was about helping her to live to the best of her abilities.

Perhaps it's easier to take care of someone else's parent than your own. Perhaps it's easier to care for your neighbor than your own sibling. I can't explain it other than to say though Margaret and I had no common past, except that we helped create and lived in the same cohousing community, I found it a great honor to do whatever I could to assist her. My assistance was more than appreciated – and it was easy, she lived just downstairs. I can only assume that this sort of mutual respect, this sort of life quality only comes with 'village' life, no matter how manufactured.

The Future

Is senior cohousing in our future? You bet it is. The 21st century will be an entirely new era in respecting the possibilities for

quality of life in the fourth quarter. In the 21st century people will be getting older on their own terms. Not in denial but with the clarity of consciousness. If the 20th century made education almost universal in this country, the 21st century will bring a renaissance to ageing gracefully and respectfully in place. There's a lot of work to do but the potential for enhanced lives is enormous. Never before have there been opportunities for seniors like this in America. The era of creating housing for seniors has to end and the era of creating housing with seniors has to emerge and flourish. We have demonstrated that we can't do very well for them. This is not about experts; this is about facilitators. People who listen, not dictate. People who want to see seniors make a place that they will use and love. Senior cohousing is where people live – "housing with goods in it," as the Danes would say – not warehousing. Remember our second highest responsibility as a species is to create a viable society (the first is to replenish the earth – we've apparently accomplished that.) Our elders are a critical part of our society. Highly unconsidered to date. The time to start is now. And while this book can be information overload – the key thing is to get going and get organized.

Sure it will take two years but as the resident of Danish senior cohousing Korvetten said, "I think now that I have moved into senior cohousing I will live 10 years longer." Not because it's a magic medicine but because it's fun to be alive.

One might ask if we really need yet another book about cohousing in the U.S.? Perhaps not. As a culture we are

AFTERWORD

The American senior cohousing movement is off to a good start. When our first book came out in 1988 there was a welcome reception. Although all publishers we talked to said that it would only sell 1,500 to 2,000 copies – it sold 3,000 copies the first six months, and it has sold over 34,000 copies to date. We were on the Today Show three times, and there was a lot of press including two half page articles in the New York Times.

Today there are about 80 intergenerational cohousing projects built in the U.S., 100 more being planned, including about 20 under construction. Since my first slide show about senior cohousing in Boulder, Colorado in 2000, there has been an inordinate amount of interest in senior cohousing and now several are being planned. Because American seniors are so active, the interest in new housing and community possibilities would have happened anyway. I'm just glad I have a chance to play my part.

This handbook is a working document. If you think I've omitted some compelling information, please send me a letter (yes, a letter, and hand-written is fine) as soon as possible. If that missing information is truly compelling, I'll make sure it is included in the next edition. I'm looking forward to your letters. I'd also appreciate hearing what you thought was really important for you – I don't want to edit out the baby with the bathwater. Even more importantly, if you see information that you do not consider essential, let me know. I really want to boil this handbook down to its essence. Not a word more than necessary.

Finally, if you are ready to start a project let us know.

Thanks for reading,
Charles Durrett
Charles.durrett@cohousingco.com

To order more books send $30 to:

McCamant & Durrett Architects,
241B Commercial Street,
Nevada City CA 95959, USA
(shipping is included within
the U.S.)
1-530-265-9980

You can also call Ten Speed Press at 1-800-841-BOOK or go to www.tenspeedpress.com to order a book with a credit card.

Or shop online at
http://ben.davies.net/books.htm

THE SENIOR DILEMMA

Compassionate adults worry about their older loved ones, especially those who live in isolated fashion, alone or with spouses, (84% of the senior population in the U.S.). It begs the question: How is it that our elderly population has become so hard pressed? One problem is lack of available caregivers. Children today are not trained to regard the care of elderly parents as a primary responsibility; moreover, aging parents do not want to reverse this trend, but wish to maintain their own independence, and strongly resist the idea of becoming a burden to their children. (Only 13% of seniors in the U.S. live with relatives.) However, this comes at a price, monetarily or otherwise.

Most seniors in America spend an inordinate amount of their diminished income as retirees on medical care. Only half of necessary medical expenses are covered by Medicare or by HMOs. There are simply fewer children than before to care for parents, more women than ever before work outside of the home and are less available than they used to be (and they used to do most of the care).

Why is it this way? Theories abound. And as usual, no matter how well found-ed, theories take more words than facts. So let's see some facts. In the world of el-der care these statistics mean something. In the world of senior cohousing they are interesting - but not that interesting. We included them not only because some people think that a book about seniors requires dire statistics, but more impor-tantly, they are relevant fodder for Study Group I discussions.

Remembering of course that your responsibility is to go forth, have fun, and build relevant relationships, these facts are of minority interest until they become relevant to your own life. Even then, when the day comes that you require assistance to dress, you find the assistance. It doesn't really matter what percentage of the planet needs such assistance.

The American Association of Retired Persons (AARP) divides assistance for everyday senior activities into two categories:

1. ADLs, or 'Activities for Daily Living'. Bathing, dressing, toileting, eating, and getting around the house.
2. IADLs are 'Instrumental Activities of Daily Living'. Preparing meals, shopping, managing money, using the telephone, doing housework, and taking medication.

From the 'Sources of Payment' diagram we can see that most seniors must rely on limited Social Security payments or their savings to pay for needed assistance, and they are hard pressed to pay other living expenses.

Cohousing has always been based on cooperation and mutual respect. Just as in mixed-age cohousing, senior cohous-ers plan on knowing their neighbors well; they agree to share tasks, based on their abilities, so that each person contributes to the well-being of the whole, feeling val-ued in the process and less helpless, less dependent. The interdependence of all in a cohousing community eases the worries of elders, and their children, and assures the independence of senior members into advanced age.

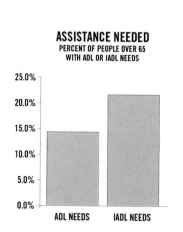

ASSISTANCE NEEDED
PERCENT OF PEOPLE OVER 65
WITH ADL OR IADL NEEDS

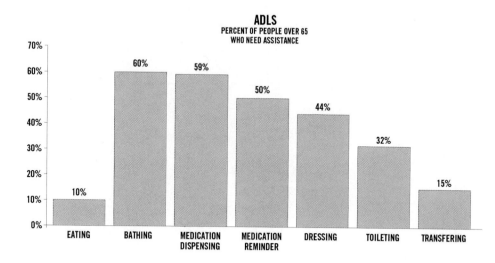

ADLS
PERCENT OF PEOPLE OVER 65
WHO NEED ASSISTANCE

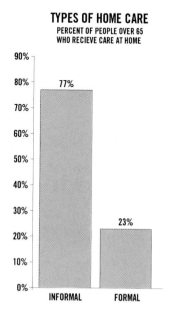

TYPES OF HOME CARE
PERCENT OF PEOPLE OVER 65
WHO RECIEVE CARE AT HOME

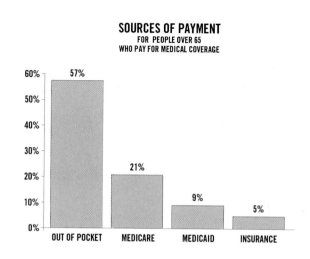

SOURCES OF PAYMENT
FOR PEOPLE OVER 65
WHO PAY FOR MEDICAL COVERAGE

Summer Solstice Party in Munksøgård.

UNIVERSAL DESIGN

Definition: Access Friendly Design is a holistic approach to providing the maximum amount of affordable accessibility in every facet of the built and social environment, whether or not it is required by code.

The applicable building code in many localities will require that a small percentage of housing units are fully accessible and, in some situations, will also require that other units are of moderate accessibility with adaptable features. These code requirements ignore the majority of the units in typical multi-unit dwellings. These code requirements can also ignore some common areas with potential for increased accessibility.

In senior cohousing communities, the code requirements should, of course, always be met. It is also important that senior cohousing go above and beyond the code requirements in every aspect of the built environment along with many aspects of the social environment. Community interaction and the ability of one neighbor to visit another's home are key elements in any cohousing community. The successful facilitation of community interaction and "visitability" in senior cohousing is contingent upon a completely Access Friendly environment and results in greater independence for seniors.

Examining Code Requirements

In a typical senior cohousing community with 25 units, many state, local or municipal codes would require that one unit is fully accessible and at least 20% of the ground floor units are adaptable (they could be changed into accessible units

with moderate expense).

Common spaces and areas that serve accessible units are generally required to be accessible. At least one of each type of recreational facility, on site, is generally required to be accessible and at least one accessible parking space is required. Accessible walks are required between accessible units, accessible parking and accessible common facilities.

As you can see, the code leaves the majority of units free of any accessibility requirements. Some areas of the site may also be free of any accessibility requirements.

Access Friendly Design

We always recommend that all elements of a cohousing community follow the Principles of Universal Design, if possible. The Center for Universal Design at NC State University has compiled a comprehensive list of guidelines for Universal Design Features in Housing. The Center acknowledges that not all (features) are expected to be included in any given home. While many Universal Design Features in Housing can be accommodated by a conscientious and experienced architect without adversely affecting the budget, other features may increase the cost of the project.

It is important that an open dialogue occurs, between the future residents of a Senior Cohousing Community and their

Architect, regarding Universal Design Principles. One of the key advantages to the self-development process that we recommend for cohousing is that the future residents themselves (not some outside developer) will be able to weigh the Principles of Universal Design against their budget. The future residents are most capable of making informed decisions regarding the potential compromise between complete accessibility and affordability.

Nonetheless, many future residents may underestimate their future needs. Although cohousing residents may have the advantage of being able to switch units when necessary to accommodate their changing needs, this should not be depended upon. We make the following recommendations for minimum standards of accessibility throughout the community in order to assure an Access Friendly Environment:

Minimum Standards for a Disability Friendly Community (in addition to code requirements) are:

1. An accessible path of travel should connect the parking and primary pedestrian entrance of the community to all common facilities, and to all residential units. All paths should be well lighted. Benches should be located regularly along the paths.

2. All common facilities should be completely accessible (i.e., a single story common house or an elevator, an accessible common kitchen, garden areas where plants are easily reached for pruning/maintenance, etc.)

3. Entrances to all units and common facilities should be devoid of steps and have low thresholds, lever or other effortless hardware, and space beside the door. All entrances should have 36-inch wide full-light doors and be well lighted. House numbers should be a minimum of 3 inches tall with high contrast between the numbers and their background. All doorbells should be lighted and doorbell signals should be both audible and visual.

4. If site density requires second floor units, the entrances preferably should be off of a common balcony that is in turn accessed by an elevator. If this is not financially feasible, the stairs to the second floor units should be wide enough and have a large enough area at the top and bottom to accommodate a platform lift. They should also preferably be completely indoors.

5. Every unit should have an open plan (kitchen, dining and living all in one great room).

6. If possible, all units should be one story. If not, the stairs to the second floor should be wide enough and have a large enough area at the top and bottom to accommodate a platform lift. An alternative is to include, toward the middle of the unit, a set of closets, one above the other, that is the shell for a residential elevator. The cab could be added when needed at a fraction of the cost if done as a retrofit later.

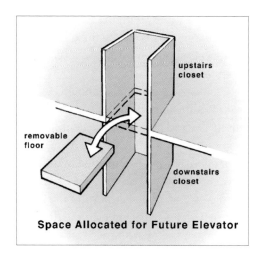

Space Allocated for Future Elevator

7. Interior unit doors should have at least a 32-inch clearance and lever handles or push plate hardware.

8. A 42-inch wide circulation route should exist throughout all units. If possible, every room should include a 60-inch diameter turning space once furniture is in place. If space is limited, the furnished room should at least be laid out in a way that allows a wheelchair to make a three-point turn

9. Every unit should have at least one first floor bedroom.

10. Preferably the first floor bathroom of every unit should be completely accessible minus the grab bars (but with blocking around the toilet and bathing fixture for installation of bars in the future). Toilets should be at an accessible height (17 - 19 inches above the floor) and should be centered 18 inches from any side wall. Lavatories should be at an accessible height with space underneath and pipes should be insulated to prevent contact with hot or sharp surfaces. Vanities should have removable doors and bases to provide accessible under-sink space. Bathtub sides should be a maximum of 15 inches above the floor. Bathtubs

should have grab bars, an interior rim that will support a removable seat, and a floor that does not slope abruptly so that a shower bench is stable. In addition, other important features to include are a hand-held showerhead and controls offset toward the outside of the tub with a pressure balancing mixing valve. Some units may include curb-less showers. All faucets should have single-lever water controls. Mirrors should start 36 inches above the floor and continue up to 72 inches above the floor so both standing and seated people can see themselves. There should be a 30-inch by 48-inch clear floor space at each fixture. The first floor bathroom should preferably have a 60-inch diameter turning space. If space is limited and a 60-inch diameter turn cannot be accommodated, the room should at least be laid out in a way that allows a wheelchair to make a three-point turn.

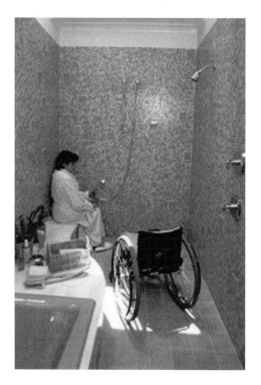

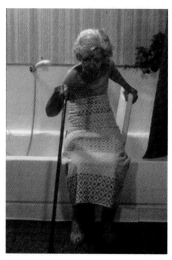

11. Kitchens should have a minimum 30 x 48-inch clear space in front of cabinets and appliances. Sinks should be at an accessible height with space underneath and pipes should be insulated to prevent contact with hot or sharp surfaces. Cabinets under sinks should have removable doors and bases. All countertops should be at an accessible height and large stretches of continuous countertop should be provided immediately adjacent to appliances and sinks. Raised dishwashers are a real advantage and minimize unnecessary stooping and bending. Care must be taken when locating the dishwasher so it does not interrupt the necessary workspace. Wall-hung cabinets should have adjustable height shelves. All appliances should have front mounted controls. Refrigerator/freezers should be of the side-by-side variety or may be the over under variety with the freezer space in a pull out drawer below the refrigerator. All faucets should have single-lever water controls.

12. Washers and dryers should be front loading with front controls, and raised 12 to 15 inches off the floor to make loading and unloading easier. A 36-inch clear space should be provided in front of washers and dryers. The clear space should extend 18 inches beyond the left and right sides of the washer and dryer. Laundry sinks should be accessible.

13. Half of all storage should be less than 54 inches high.

14. Garage doors should be power operated, remote control. All parking should be at grade level and should be connected to the rest of the community by an accessible path. Van accessible parking should always be provided.

15. A deck should be at the same level as the floor of the rest of the house or common house.

16. All cabinet doors and drawers should have loop handles.

17. Window sills should be a maximum of 36 inches above the floor for seated viewing. All operable windows should be crank operated.

18. Lighting should be adjustable. Bright, focused lighting should be provided at all work surfaces. Switches, along with thermostats, should be 48 inches above the floor. Switches should be easy-touch rockers. Electrical outlets should be a minimum of 18 inches from the floor.

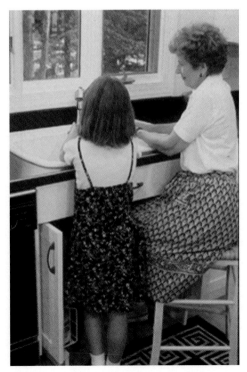

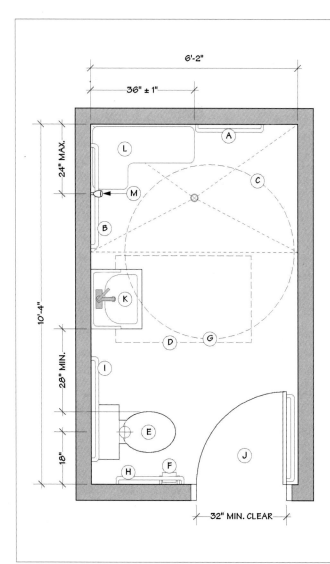

A   24" MIN. LENGTH GRAB BAR MOUNTED SO THAT ITS CENTER LINE IS 33"-36" ABOVE THE FLOOR.

B   36" MIN. LENGTH GRAB BAR MOUNTED SO THAT ITS CENTER LINE IS 33"-36" ABOVE THE FLOOR.

C   FIVE FOOT DIAMETER WHEELCHAIR TURNAROUND (MAY EXTEND UNDER SINK WHERE THERE IS CLEARANCE FOR KNEES).

D   ADA WHEELCHAIR MENEUVERING SPACE FOR TOILET. THE DOOR MAY NOT SWING INTO THIS SPACE.

E   TOILET WITH 17" TO 19" ABOVE FLOOR.

F   TOILET PAPER HOLDER MOUNTED SO THAT ITS CENTER LINE IS 19" ABOVE THE FLOOR.

G   MANEUVERING SPACES MAY OVERLAP.

H   36" LONG GRAB BAR MOUNTED SO THAT ITS CENTER LINE IS 33" ABOVE FLOOR.

I   42" LONG GRAB BAR MOUNTED SO THAT ITS CENTER LINE IS 33" ABOVE FLOOR.

J   DOOR MANEUVERING SPACE.

K   SINK WITH 29" MINIMUM CLEARANCE ABOVE FLOOR.

L   ADA FOLDING SEAT MOUNTED AT 18" ABOVE FLOOR.

M   ADJUSTABLE HEIGHT, MOVABLE HAND SHOWER HEAD OR 60"-72" FLEXIBLE HOSE.

OTHER COHOUSING PROJECTS & FIRM PROFILE

McCamant & Durrett Architects is an architecture and development consulting firm founded by husband-and-wife team Kathryn McCamant and Charles Durrett in 1987. With an experienced staff, that includes several licensed architects, the firm provides complete architectural services for a wide range of clients. It is particularly well known for its design of cohousing communities, multi-family housing and childcare facilities, and for its ability to facilitate participatory design processes that involve client groups in the design of their buildings. McCamant & Durrett Architects includes two branch businesses tied to the firm's two specialties, **The Cohousing Company** and **Spaces for Children.** With an eye to aesthetics, we believe that a building should have a strong sense of place and contribute to its surrounding environment. The firm has considerable expertise in energy efficiency, environmentally sound building materials, and sustainability in the context of budget.

Internationally, McCamant & Durrett Architects is best known for its work with cohousing communities, an innovative approach to housing that combines community facilities with private dwellings. Kathryn and Charles are authors of the book *Cohousing: A Contemporary Approach to Housing Ourselves* (Ten Speed Press, 1988, 1994, with reprints and updates through 2005) that introduced this housing approach to the United States. (As noted in the Oxford English Dictionary, Charles and Kathryn coined the word "cohousing".) The firm often works with resident groups on housing projects throughout the development process so that the community responds directly to the residents' needs. In addition, M&D provides development consulting services to cohousing groups in the areas of group formation and facilitation, site search and acquisition, land development, project management, and financing, giving the firm a thorough knowledge of the entire development process and its repercussions on design. Since 1987, M&D has designed and consulted on almost forty communities nationwide, in Canada, New Zealand and on projects in Japan and Denmark. Two communities won awards from HUD for *"Building Innovation for Home Ownership,"* The National Homebuilder's Association awarded the *"Best In American Living Award - Best Smart Growth Community "* and in 2001 the United Nations awarded the *"World Habitat Award."* McCamant and Durrett's work with cohousing communities has received national recognition including coverage on *ABC's World News Tonight, CBS's Nightly News,* and *NBC's Today Show,* and articles in *U.S. News and World Report, Architecture, Utne Reader, The New York Times, The Los Angeles Times,* and *The Wall Street Journal.*

McCamant & Durrett Architects has adapted its cohousing design experience to affordable housing developments such as two communities for low-income single-parent households with on-site childcare facilities, and a five-story residential hotel in San Francisco and many more affordable housing neighborhoods, including several senior neighborhoods. The firm has worked on a variety of other project types, including custom straw bale single-family homes and commercial projects. They have found their participatory design methods useful when working with groups on many types of projects, as well as with couples on the design of their home. Our office has also been involved in and continues to be involved in mixed-use and town planning projects.

McCamant & Durrett Architects under the name Spaces for Children, also designs childcare facilities. The firm's expertise in this field ranges from the overall programming and design of childcare buildings to furniture and play structure design to the specifics of appropriate materials, fastenings and finishes that will assure optimum function, play value, child safety, durability, maintenance and economy. Working in conjunction with Louis Torelli, who is known nationwide as a premier child development environmental designer, the firm has designed childcare facilities for a diverse group of clients including universities, corporations, non-profit agencies, and school districts.

COHOUSING COMMUNITIES PROJECTS

SILVER SAGE VILLAGE, BOULDER, CO

One of the first senior cohousing communities to be built in the United States. Part of the new Holiday Neighborhood in North Boulder, this 16-unit community is situated around a garden court and features a 5,000 sf common house, a workshop, a common deck and community gardens. Providing design services and some construction documents. Currently in design development.

NEVADA CITY COHOUSING, NEVADA CITY, CA

A 34-unit community on 11 acres within walking distance of the small town "Main Street" of Nevada City in the Sierra Foothills. Site plan also includes seven single-family lots with seven carriage units for a total of 48 units. Providing full architectural, project management and development services. Under construction.

COTATI COHOUSING, COTATI, CA

A mixed-use project located at the edge of a small downtown. This 30-unit community shares a common house, garden and workshop and includes 7,500 sf of commercial storefronts. Provided full architectural and project management and development services. Construction completed October 2003.

TEMESCAL CREEK COHOUSING, OAKLAND, CA

Buying several buildings in an existing neighborhood, this 8-unit "retrofit" cohousing community added a new common house and will grow as neighboring houses become available. Provided design and development services.

PLEASANT HILL COHOUSING, PLEASANT HILL, CA

A suburban in-fill site of 2.2 acres; the 32-unit community shares a 4,000 square foot common house, a pool, garden and workshop. Provided full architectural, project management and development services. Construction completed November 2001.

TEMESCAL COMMONS COHOUSING, OAKLAND, CA

A resident group combined two urban lots to develop an infill cohousing community. One lot contains an old residence divided into two flats, four new homes and a common house. Opening a fence to an adjacent property creates a 9-unit community. The community incorporates many sustainable building techniques. Provided full architectural services and development consulting. Construction completed June 2000.

TOUCHSTONE COHOUSING, ANN ARBOR, MI

The third adjacent community in Ann Arbor's cohousing neighborhood. 46 homes on a 6-acre parcel next to the Great Oak and Sunward communities. Providing design services for modular construction process. Currrently in the design phase.

GREAT OAK COHOUSING, ANN ARBOR, MI

A 37-unit community next to Sunward Cohousing. Provided design services. Construction completed 2003.

HEARTHSTONE COHOUSING, NORTH DENVER, CO

This 33-unit cohousing community is the first built as part of a "new urbanist" planned unit development. The townhouse courtyard layout fits comfortably within the new mixed-use neighborhood while maintaining a strong sense of community within the cohousing site. Construction completed September 2001.

BELLINGHAM COHOUSING, BELLINGHAM, WA

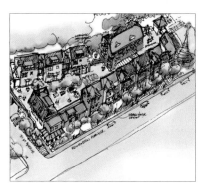

32 townhouses cluster on a 5.8 acre site that includes over 2 acres of wetlands and a stream. The original farmhouse was remodeled and incorporated into the common house. Provided full architectural and project management services. Construction completed June 2000.

PRAIRIE SKY COHOUSING, ALBERTA, CANADA

Located in the inner city community of Winston Heights near downtown Calgary. 18 units and a 3200 sf common house, with underground parking, on 0.75 acres. Provided programming and schematic design. Construction completed June 2003.

METRO COHOUSING AT CULVER WAY, ST. LOUIS, MO

40 condominiums and a common house in historic factory buildings in St. Louis. Includes live/work options and underground parking. Provided programming and schematic design as well as the common house kitchen. Currently in design phase.

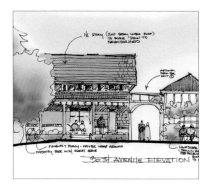

CASA VERDE COMMONS, COLORADO SPRINGS, CO

34 units and a 3000 sf common house on a 3 acre in-fill site, located near downtown. Provided site programming. Winner of 2003 E* EPA/New Millennium Award for energy-efficiency.

MIDTOWN COHOUSING, DENVER, CO

Community of 18 courtyard condominiums and a common house on one-half acre in an old, centrally-located neighborhood. Developed by a non-profit developer in conjunction with the residents, the community accommodates low, moderate, and market-rate home buyers.

SONORA COHOUSING, TUCSON, AZ

36 courtyard homes on a 4.8 acre infill site in a low-income neighborhood share a straw bale common house. The common house consists of three separate buildings, tied together with porches, which create a comfortable courtyard for gathering. Passive cooling was major consideration in the design. Completed 2001.

SWAN'S MARKET COHOUSING, OAKLAND, CA

Design and development consulting services for a 20-unit community adjacent to 18 units of affordable housing as part of a downtown, mixed-use project in the historic Swan's Market building. The development is an important anchoring point for new infill development in downtown Oakland. Construction completed June 2000.

BERKELEY COHOUSING, BERKELEY, CA

Development project management and complete architectural services to resident group to create a 14-unit community on a .75 acre site with several existing buildings. Project included adding four new units, substantial renovation to four units, and subdividing property as condominiums. Construction completed 1997.

THE DOYLE STREET COHOUSING COMMUNITY, EMERYVILLE, CA

A 12-unit cohousing community that reuses an existing brick industrial building with a new second story. Provided complete architectural and project management services. Construction completed 1992.

RIVER ROCK COMMONS – COHOUSING ON THE POUDRE, FT. COLLINS, CO

Provided participatory programming and design services for 34-unit community with 2500 sf common house on 4 acres, 5 blocks from Historic Downtown district. Construction completed 2000.

WINDSONG, VANCOUVER, BC

Provided participatory programming, schematic design and design consultation services to resident group and local architect for this 34-unit cohousing community. First cohousing community with a glass-covered street in North America. Construction completed July 1996.

HIGHLINE CROSSING, DENVER, CO

Provided programming, schematic design and design development drawings for 4000 sf common house as well as consulting on the site plan and unit design of this 36-unit cohousing community. Construction completed 1995.

CARDIFF PLACE, VICTORIA, BC, CANADA

Worked with group and developer's architect to program and redesign plans for turning a 17-unit condominium into a cohousing community. Extensive remodel of an existing structure and new construction of a 4-story, 120-unit building. Construction completed Fall 1994.

SUNWARD COHOUSING, ANN ARBOR, MI

Provided programming and design services for site plan and common house for a 40-unit community on a 5-acre south-facing sloped site. Construction completed 1998.

SOUTHSIDE PARK COHOUSING, SACRAMENTO, CA

A cohousing community of 25 townhouses and 2500 sf common house in downtown Sacramento. The project worked closely with the City to provide affordable units. Provided participatory programming, schematic design services, and development consultation. Construction completed 1993.

MUIR COMMONS, DAVIS, CA

A cohousing community of 26 townhouses and 3600 sf common house. Provided participatory programming and schematic design services. Construction completed 1991.

SAN JUAN COHOUSING, DURANGO, CO
Providing programming and design services for the site plan. The community is clustered on a small portion of a 300-acre site.

WASATCH COHOUSING, SALT LAKE CITY, UT
Provided programming and design for site plan and common house for a 26-unit community on a 4.2-acre site.
Construction completed 1998.

LIBERTY VILLAGE COHOUSING, FREDERICK, MD
Located on a 23-acre site at the edge of Libertytown with 15 acres of undeveloped land. Provided programming and design services for a 3,900 sf common house. Currently under construction.

EAST LAKE ECOVILLAGE, ATLANTA, GA
Provided programming and design services for site plan and community facilities of a 67-unit community on a 20-acre site near historic East Lake District of Atlanta. Construction completed 2001. (Two adjacent communities)

GREYROCK COHOUSING, FORT COLLINS, CO
Provided programming and design for a 4,200 sf common house for a 30-unit community. Construction completed 1996.

A variety of design and development services have also been provided to numerous other cohousing communities, including the following:

- Faraway Ranch, Telluride, CO
- Deschutes Cohousing, Tumwater, WA
- Milagro Cohousing, Tucson, AZ
- Benicia Waterfront Commons, Benicia, CA
- Mission Bay Cohousing, Auckland, New Zealand
- Synergy Cohousing, Delray Beach, FL
- Acacia Cohousing, Santa Rosa, CA
- Winslow Cohousing, Bainbridge Island, WA
- Commons on the Alameda, Santa Fe, AZ
- Eno Commons, Durham, NC
- Westwood Cohousing, Asheville, NC
- Burlington Cohousing, Burlington, VT
- Nyland Cohousing, Lafayette, CO
- Cambridge Cohousing, Cambridge, MA
- Dallas Cohousing, Dallas, TX
- Lake Claire Cohousing, Atlanta, GA
- EcoVillage at Ithaca, Ithaca, NY
- Lyons Cohousing, Lyons, CO
- Fresno Cohousing, Fresno, CA
- Harmony Village Cohousing, Golden, CO

ECO - FRIENDLY
NEVADA CITY COHOUSING

COMMUNITY = SECRET INGREDIENT IN SUSTAINABILITY

In the design of a cohousing community, there is a great deal of opportunity to live in a considerably greener architecture. This example (Nevada City Cohousing) is just one of many. Preliminary data shows at least a $100 a month decrease in energy usage per house. That is just one of a couple dozen ways the project treads lighter on the earth.

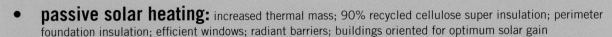

- **passive solar heating:** increased thermal mass; 90% recycled cellulose super insulation; perimeter foundation insulation; efficient windows; radiant barriers; buildings oriented for optimum solar gain

- **passive cooling:** no air conditioners in homes; increased thermal mass; whole house fans; radiant barriers; ceiling fans. cross ventilation

- **active solar heating:** water for radiant floor heat and domestic hot water is preheated by solar panels and fed to a single boiler that serves 3 to 6 units

- **low electricity use:** almost all lights are fluorescent; energy-efficient refrigerators; photo-voltaic solar panels (36 kw); projected $30/mo. winter energy bill per household vs. typical household in the area of about $150/mo.

- **reduced asphalt:** 900 S.F. per house vs. the typical 3,000 S.F. per house. (these values include street area needed to access home, driveway and garage area)

- **low toxicity materials:** bamboo flooring; cellulose insulation, low-toxicity paint; low formaldehyde materials; recycled and wool carpeting; marmoleum flooring

- **responsible water use:** low water use per house fixture (such as: savings of 4,000 gallons per toilet per year alone) 100,000 gallons of water used per household per year for the first five years projected, 75,000 gallons per year per household after that. City average is about 164,000 gallons per year per household

- **responsible forestry:** almost no clear cut lumber (FSC certified); advanced framing; 25% to 40% less lumber used to build the same square footage; less than half the lumber used than for a typical new house

- **responsible waste stream management:** no vinyl flooring; refinishable marmoleum floors, (marmoleum is made primarily of cellulose & linseed oil and composts into landfills)

- **responsible resource use:** recycled paint; low construction waste; recycled cellulose; sustainable ceiling tiles; average house size = 1,250 S.F. compared to the average of new American houses of 2,300 S.F.

- **air quality:** there are no wood stoves in any of these 34 homes; and no auto garage attached to houses, a common cause of indoor air polution

- **walkable to downtown:** goods and services (dentist, store, church, bus stop, work places) are available without getting into a car; pedestrian/child friendly site design

- **minimum impact:** minimum grading and tree removal; 60% of site has been preserved as open space

- **responsible landscaping:** planting more than 100 new trees; indigenous grasses & wildflowers; minimum water use and other key permaculture attributes; minimum grading and tree removal; on-site drain water management at densely planted bio-swale; water retention on site

- **workforce housing:** allows for more affordable housing than other new houses built in the area; creates housing for a diversity of incomes

- **reduced driving:** studies show that folks who live in cohousing drive 25% less and own fewer autos

- **urban ecology:** replaces Nevada City housing stock that has been lost to recent commercial development

- **preserves rural Nevada City community feel:** by building where services exist (sewer and water) county wide sprawl is reduced

- **handicap accessibility:** exceeds state and national requirements

- **appropriate architecture:** architecture that fits with the cultural heritage of the area

- **community:** this intergenerational community allows for sharing resources, such as autos, camping stuff; education regarding using less water; less resources; less energy; and just less. Community facilitates environmental stewardship

AWARDS

"Best In American Living Award – Best Smart Growth Community" from the National Association of Home Builders, for Cotati (Frog Song) Cohousing, Cotati, CA, 2004. Best smart growth project in the United States for a project under 151 units.

"Design Award Citation" by the American Institute of Architects, Redwood Empire Chapter, for Cotati Cohousing, Cotati, CA, 2004.

"Mixed-Use/Mixed Income Development Award" by The American Institute of Architects for East Lake Commons, a cohousing project, Atlanta, GA, 2001.

World Habitat Award" presented at the United Nations World Habitat Day in Fukuoka, Japan, for East Lake Commons Conservation Community, Atlanta, GA, October 1, 2001.

"Best of Sonoma County" by the Land Use & Transportation Coalition, Fall 2003.

"Award of Excellence" from Berkeley Design Advocates in Berkeley, CA, for Berkeley Cohousing, 1997

"Certificate of Recognition" in the 1997 Best In American Living Award Competition from the National Association of Home Builders Professional Builder Magazine for duplex design at Berkeley Cohousing, Berkeley, CA.

"Outstanding Commercial Rehabilitation Award" from the Berkeley Architectural Heritage Association for the Adeline Street Office Building, 1996.

"Building Innovation for Home Ownership Award" by the U.S. Department of Housing and Urban Development (HUD), 1996 for the Berkeley Cohousing Community in Berkeley, CA

"Building Innovation for Home Ownership Award" by the U.S. Department of Housing and Urban Development (HUD), 1996 for the Synergy Cohousing in Fort Lauderdale, FL.

"Best Social Innovation in Housing Award" from the Institute of Social Innovations in London, 1989.

FREQUENTLY ASKED QUESTIONS

What follows are some of the frequently asked questions and answers about cohousing. Until people have experienced life in a cohousing community, they often have questions and concerns about the details of daily living. But once they have moved in, they find their concerns mitigated by the trust, respect, and commitment neighbors feel for one another. In this atmosphere, long discussions of policy give way to human interactions.

I'm a healthy, able-bodied 55 year old. Why would I want to live in senior cohousing now?

Moving into a senior cohousing community when you're a healthy, able-bodied 55 year old is a bit like putting a bit of money aside from each paycheck into a 401k plan. You're saving surplus money while you're young because you plan to use it later – when you're older and will need it most. Seniors who move into a senior chousing community when they're younger are essentially doing the same thing. Over time (day-by-day, project-by-project, year-by-year), they cement the personal relationships, community routines, and expectations from a group of peers that allows everyone involved to live longer, healthier lives. They know their community will be there for them when they are needed most (it's like tapping that 401k account). But you can't tap that account if you don't have it.

Yeah, but who takes care of who?

In senior cohousing, you only help someone if you want to. It's an individual choice. Nobody has to take care of anyone. This individual choice in terms of co-care is a fundamental aspect of a senior cohousing community that works. But you will want to. Believe it or not, after building and living in a senior cohousing community you probably will want to help someone who needs it – it'll just be what you do. No big deal. This question also cuts the other way: If you are the person who is sick, who would you prefer to take care of you? A visiting nurse just making the rounds, or your close friend who also happens to be your next-door neighbor?

Why live in cohousing?

Most people searched for words like "family" and "village-living". Many elderly people I interviewed in Denmark cited the word "hyggelig" – cozy, pleasant, homelike, in terms of quality of life, but in the end returned to quality of life – "hyggelig." In Holland they use the word "gezellig," which has the same approximate meaning.

What is senior cohousing?

Senior cohousing (sometimes called elder cohousing) is a lifestyle choice for folks 55 years or older, where people get together and make a neighborhood that suits their particular needs, from an economic, physical, social, practical, and emotional point of view.

How is senior cohousing different from a condominium or a cooperative?

Condominiums are a type of ownership where everyone owns their own house and any common facilities together. Cooperatives are a type of ownership where everyone owns an interest in what amounts to a corporation. Cohousing is about cooperation rather than type of ownership. And, as it turns out, this cooperation transcends ownership type.

How do prices compare to other kinds of housing?

Cohousing can initially cost as much as, or sometimes even more, than other kinds of new-build housing (though often it is less). Cohousing may cost more when the project is not well planned and organized, and not made to fit optimally into production construction (versus custom construction). Cohousing can cost less even when the group asks for more accessibility and more ecological design features (custom construction), but in order to keep costs down these "custom" features must fit into a standard design process – which they can be made to. Where the real savings are to be made is after move-in. The increase in disposable income can be well over a $1000 a month for each house in senior cohousing because of the things that people do for each other as a natural part of a normal day, rather than having to pay a stranger for.

What are some of the unique design elements in senior cohousing?

First and foremost, unlike traditional senior housing, a great deal of attention truly paid to the success of the social aspects of the community. Kitchens are placed to the front of the house so you can wave to a neighbor passing by. Houses are placed in close physical proximity to each other. Individual houses are smaller, but have more attention paid to good design detail. More attention is paid to present and future mobility challenges. Sustainable design and low-toxic materials are given more consideration. Finally, the entire community is designed with conscious consideration paid to the life between the buildings and every other nuance that affects social success.

If I live in cohousing, will I have my own kitchen?

You won't believe how many times I've been asked this question by reporters standing in my kitchen!

How does cohousing differ from other kinds of living arrangements?

In cohousing you have as much privacy as you want and as much community as you want. In your private house, you get as much privacy as you want and as much privacy as you want. Or later, in assisted living, you get as much institutionalized cajoling as you want or as much isolation as you want. In cohousing you realize the benefit of sharing with your neighbors – the advantages of cooperating as a means of enhancing quality of life.

Why cohousing just for seniors?

I've visited close to 300 cohousing communities now, a couple dozen of them senior cohousing. Consistently the residents living in senior cohousing were having the most fun of any group of people I have ever met. Fun-o-meter readings aside, since relationships are paramount in a cohousing community, residents live next door to their friends. Seniors in their own cohousing community live among people with whom they share a common bond of age, experience, and community – a community they themselves built to specifically meet their own needs. These relationships provide purpose and direction in their lives and are as meaningful as any they have ever had. Seniors will probably end up living with mostly seniors anyway. The only question is when and how. Will it be on their own terms or on the terms of others? Additionally they should be able to decide for themselves and without judgment – do what you want and allow for others to do the same. And finally they are not by themselves. Somebody's grandchildren visit just about every day – lots of people visit. And because everybody has a relationship with everyone you end up visiting everyone.

Is there a screening process? Who decides who lives there?

Some groups do have vetting and interview procedures for new members. But these are often less than successful because people may be good talkers, able to say just the right things at the right time, while not being truly committed to the concepts embodied by cohousing. (The basic one: Giving cooperation with the neighbors the benefit of the doubt)

Most established groups now agree that nothing works better than self selection. They invite prospective new residents to a common dinner or two, to

a workday, and to a common meeting. Spending some time this way gives people the chance to see if they think cohousing is right for them, if this particular group is right for them, if they really think cooperating with their neighbors is the way to go, and whether they can handle the responsibilities expected of them. People recognize that if they are not into the whole cohousing concept, then other, more conventional options may be better for them, and for the group they were considering joining.

How often do people eat in the common house?

It varies. After interviewing hundreds of cohousing residents, the vast majority said that they ate in the common house about twice as often as they thought they would before moving in. That is unless the common house is designed poorly, which does happen. (See the Study Group II chapter for design best practices.)

How does resale work?

Theoretically your house is for sale on the open market and again there is very little vetting by the community at-large. Usually folks who buy into a project that has already been built are quite familiar with it. Still most groups ask prospective members to come to a couple of common dinners, to participate in a common workday, and attend to a common meeting. The key thing is to help people make sure that cohousing is for them. Since supply is far short of demand, even in Europe, it's best that the folks who can really appreciate the benefits of cohousing, and who are best able to contribute, be the ones to move in. Empirically it has been proven to work best if prospective residents are fully apprised of the development of the community to-date. The best and clearest data to go through might be the site plan program (every community will have this on file), which explains why the buildings were placed where they stand, what common facilities there are, and even why the houses were designed the way they were. As well, all of the agreements the group has to date and details of the active committees will be available for review. And the "buddy" who's showing a prospective resident around will probably also describe some of the nuances of the subculture – who appreciates it when you come to dinner on time, who's a good organizer, and who it's best to talk to about whatever you might be interested in, like landscaping or such.

What has been the response of planners and city officials?

Most all city officials recognize that new positive housing options are necessary. Most city officials don't really get to put forward positive solutions – they just edit mediocre possibilities. When cohousing comes along, those officials who have the best interests of the community in mind, and see their job as to serve that community, really come forward to support it. Unfortunately, as we all know, some city officials are there just to further their own needs. If so, there's nothing that cohousing groups can do about that other than to put forward a more informed solution that the public-at-large can support. Large-scale support ultimately

prevails at city hall. After 38 projects, we've only had one project declined by the city or county officials.

What is the ideal size of a senior cohousing community?

There are lots of theories, but after interviewing hundreds of residents of cohousing, the answers always seem to be somewhere in the range of 15 to 25 houses. Too big, and the discussion always seems to be too much like politics than consensus building. By their own admission seniors want and need more time to discuss issues of mutual concern. The advantage of larger sized communities however, is that it increases the chances that each person will have something in common with several people, and will make more close friends – a very satisfying experience. A larger group also helps amortize the cost of a larger common house. The smaller the community is, the more community/ social and financial responsibilities each household will bear. Just like Goldilocks, not too big, not too small – better to be just right.

What about pets?

Pets mean a lot to people, and to seniors in particular. Invariably people worry about others having too many unruly pets much more than actually happens. I'll never forget (while planning the twelve unit Doyle Street Cohousing) one woman exclaiming, "Yes, but what if everyone has two cats? We'll have 24 cats!" That's about as likely as being hit by a meteorite. The residents moved in with 12 cats, and interestingly, 10 years later they had none.

When the cats died they weren't replaced. It turns out that having real people to talk to made the cats less essential. Since then a cat or two has been replaced, but I think you get the point. Ultimately it is up to the group to formulate their own pet policies during the Study Group III phase of the project.

How does the community deal with differences in food tastes and requirements?

Sometimes there are formalities around food – you have to make a vegetarian entrée if you make a meat entrée. But usually, the residents of a community care about one another enough that they will accommodate each other. "Oh, Joe is coming to dinner and he can't have lactose. We'll just whip up a cheese-free pizza to go with the other home made pizzas we're having tonight."

How is a community managed?

By the residents, by consensus. Therefore people cooperate if it makes sense but consensus has back up super majority voting for time-critical issues.

What is the price of a house in cohousing?

It depends on a lot of factors. Some say that you can expect to pay the same amount per square foot as other multi-family projects. But we have found that through very careful, deliberate work, you can make cohousing houses less costly.

Do I need big bucks to move into cohousing?

Not really. But you do need a little bit of entrepreneurial spirit. An advisor (a key participant in the development of a senior cohousing community) will help the resident group to find the resources available in order to make a senior cohousing dream a reality. There is another way to look this question: Getting older gradually is expensive. Hired help, home remodels, or (most expensive of all), assisted care facilities, all cost big bucks. So if you can get your senior cohousing project built, and design it such that you can easily live there for the rest of your life, then you will save considerable amounts of money and effort over the long haul.

How much participation is required?

While building a community, that is to say the social and developmental side of the equation, most groups meet twice a month for about a year.

What about rentals?

When non-profits develop cohousing in Europe, they tend to be rentals. In regular cohousing it is up to the group to decide how many units can be rented. Not that renters harm the social dynamic necessarily, but it's the absentee owners who hesitate to make timely investments that make having rentals in cohousing a little more complicated. However, there were two to three rentals in the 12-unit cohousing community we lived in with no problems, and the renters were great contributors to the community.

Do I have to be an extrovert to live in cohousing?

When I lived in a single-family house it was hard to get away from the neighbor once a conversation got started. It happened so rarely I didn't want to seem rude. Cohousing is different. People know you, and when you say "Can't talk - gotta go", they assume you mean you can't talk – gotta go. You can be honest. However, introverts thrive in cohousing, possibly because they don't have to be an extravert just to have somewhat normal relationships. And if it happens that you're married to an extrovert, s/he always has someone to chat with and you don't have to drive somewhere to be with others, and then subtly nag them that it's time to go home.

Yeah, but what if there's one, you know, jerk that lives there?

There might be, but at least you'll know who it is, and the interesting thing about cohousing is, if you know you are grating on others you will probably move out.

How do I get started?

Email The Cohousing Company at coho@cohousingco.com. Let us know where you live. The Cohousing Company, and others in the U.S., have worked hard to figure out how to make developing cohousing as easy, economical, and successful as possible.

Are people in senior cohousing isolated from children?

While some may assume that senior cohousing is taking the elder away from inter-generational contact. It doesn't seem to be true. People who live in senior cohousing do have exposure to mixed ages. Rarely is there a meal in the common house that does not include children and younger adults. I don't think there was a single dinner that I went to where there weren't grandkids visiting, playing and interacting with the senior residents. The children have room to run around in the common house and can go outside to play, often with other visiting kids. This is in contrast to what occurs in the usual neighborhood, where a 17-year-old would rarely interact with a senior neighbor. Senior cohousing, with its separate guest quarters, encourages visits of parents with toddlers who might otherwise cringe at the idea of staying under the same small roof with grandma.

SELECTED BIBLIOGRAPHY

Ambrose, Iver. "Looking Towards the Future: Danish Cohousing Focuses on Seniors." *CoHousing Journal* Fall 1993: 4+

American Association of Retired Persons. *Changes in Home-care Use by Older People With Disabilities: 1982-1994.*

Bofællesskaber for Ældre: Rapport fra seminar 16-18 september 1994. Conference Proceedings. Gilleleje, Denmark; Foreningen af 1994

Brenton, Maria. *We're in Charge: Cohousing Communities of Older People in The Netherlands: Lessons for Britain?* Bristol, England: Policy Press, 1998

Christensen, Karen, and Levinson, David. *Encyclopedia of Community: From the Village to the Virtual World.* Berkshire Publishing Group, 2003.

Co-Housing for Senior Citizen in Europe. EU Conference *Growing Grey – in a Happier Way,* September 1993. Conference Proceedings. Copenhagen, Denmark: Boligtrivsel i Centrum, 1993

Dejgaard, Olaf. *Registrant over 42 seniorbofællesskaber. Foreningen Bofællesskaber for Ældre.* September 1997

Duke University Center for Demographic Studies. *National Long Term Care Survey,* 1982-1999. New York.

Durrett, Charles. '*Cohousing - A Neighborhood That Works*', *Seniors' Housing News.* NAHB, Fall 2002

Franck, Karen A., and Ahrentzen, Sherry. *New households, New Housing.* Van Nostrand Reinhold, 1989

Gerontologisk Institut Publikationer. *Bofællesskaber i bestående byggeri.* Første delbetænkning.

Hyman, Anne Kopp. *Architects of the Sunset Years: Creating Tomorrow's Sunrise.* Central Coast Press, 2005.

Krull, Kim Plummer. *Alternative Living Choices for Older Adults: New Housing Options Offer Companionship and Support.* General American Solutions, Spring/Summer 1998: 10+

MacMillan, Jeffrey. *Feathering a Shared Nest: How Three Groups of Seniors Created Their Own Alternative Lifestyles.* US News & World Report 12 June 1995: 86+

Marcus, Clare Cooper, and Wendy Sarkissian. *Housing as if People Mattered.* Berkeley: University of California Press, 1986.

McCamant, Kathryn, and Durrett, Charles. *Cohousing: a Contemporary Approach to Housing Ourselves.* Berkeley: Ten Speed Press, 2004.

Ornish, Dean. *Love and Survival: The Scientific Basis of the Healing Power of Intimacy.* Perennial Currents, 1999

Pedersen, Max. *Nybyggere - i den tredje alder.* København: Boligtrivsel i Centrum, 2000.

Pedersen, Max. *Seniorbofællesskaber: Hvorfor og hvordan: Evaluering af BiCs model til etablering af seniorbofællesskaber.* Boligtrivsel i Centrum, 1999

Stock, Robert W. *Seniors Living Independently, but Not Alone.* The Press-Enterprise, 15 January 1998.

U.S. Department of Health and Human Services. *A Descriptive Analysis of Patterns of Informal and Formal Caregiving Among Privately Insured and Non-privately Insured Disabled Elders Living in the Community.* April, 1999.

U.S. Department of Health and Human Services, Administration on Aging. *A Profile of Older Americans: 2002.*

VanVliet, Willem. *Co-Housing the Elderly in the Netherlands.* CoHousing Journal, Spring 1993:4

Winters, Ben. *Cohousing: Restoring the Traditional Sense of Community.* Senior Beacon, September 1996: 1+

Links

The Cohousing Association of the United States:
www.cohousing.org

The Cohousing Company:
www.cohousingco.com

ElderSpirit Senior Cohousing:
www.elderspirit.net

Elder Cohousing Consulting:
www.abrahampaiss.com

SilverSage Senior Cohousing:
www.silversagevillage.com

Wonderland Hill Development:
www.whdc.com

The Canadian Cohousing Network:
www.cohousing.ca

BiC, Boligtrivsel i Centrum (Quality of Living in Focus):
www.boligtrivsel.dk (in Danish only)

DaneAge (ÆldreSagen):
www.aeldresagen.dk

Senior Cohousing
www.seniorcohousing.net

INDEX

Charles Durrett and his daughter Jessie interviewing Grethe and Ib Mittet at Trudeslund Cohousing.

ABOUT THE AUTHOR

Charles Durrett has designed over thirty cohousing communities in North America and has consulted on many more around the world. His work has been featured in Time Magazine, the New York Times, the LA Times, the San Francisco Chronicle, Architecture, and a wide variety of other publications. He and his wife, Kathryn McCamant, have received numerous awards for their work including, the most recent World Habitat Award, presented by the United Nations; and the Mixed Use, Mixed Income Development Award, presented jointly by the American Institute of Architects and the United States Department of Housing and Urban Development. Charles has given many public presentations for groups from the U.S. Congress, the Commonwealth Club, scores of Universities, and most importantly, new cohousing groups just getting started.

He has developed group process and design approaches to meet the tight constraints posed by balancing a budget, providing a high standard of value, developing successful community, and achieving the sustainable design goals and aspirations of cohousing groups. These techniques include architecture with maximum potential for sustainability; architecture that best assures the long-term success of the community through facilitation and group process and incorporates highly valued lifestyle goals, such as natural light, beauty and delight and architecture that brings together the needs, wants, and desires within budget and balances community and privacy.

Charles Durrett has also co-authored *Cohousing: A Contemporary Approach to Housing Ourselves*, the book that introduced the concept of cohousing to the United States. He currently lives in Nevada City, CA, while his new cohousing community is being constructed (Nevada City Cohousing, which includes 17 seniors). He lived in Doyle Street Cohousing with his family for 12 years. As credited in the Oxford English Dictionary, Charles with his wife coined the word 'cohousing'.